W9-ARA-495

NO HIGHER COURT

CONTEMPORARY FEMINISM AND THE RIGHT TO ABORTION

NO HIGHER COURT

CONTEMPORARY FEMINISM AND THE RIGHT TO ABORTION

Germain Kopaczynski, OFMConv.

SCRANTON: UNIVERSITY OF SCRANTON PRESS

© 1995 by University of Scranton Press

Library of Congress Cataloging-in-Publication Data

Kopaczynski, Germain.
   No higher court: contemporary feminism and the right
   to abortion / Germain Kopaczynski.
       p.   cm.
   Includes bibliographical references and index.
   ISBN 0–940866–50–1 (hc). — ISBN 0–940866–51–X (pbk.)
   1. Abortion—Moral and ethical aspects. 2. Abortion—
Religious aspects—Catholic Church. 3. Pro-choice move-
ment. 4. Feminism.
I. Title
HQ767. 15.K66   1995
363.4'6–dc20   95–40854
                                                                        CIP

Marketing and Distribution
Fordham University Press
University Box L
Bronx NY 10458

PRINTED IN THE UNITED STATES OF AMERICA

To My Mother
Who gave me birth and
Showed me faith.

CONTENTS

ACKNOWLEDGEMENTS   xiii

PERMISSIONS   xv

PREFACE   xvii

    The Power of Words
    Abortion and "The Problem That Has No Name"
    A Word About the Title

INTRODUCTION: "A FIGHT AGAINST THE WORK OF GOD" 1

    Setting the Stage
    Preliminary Considerations
    Abortion and the Different Waves of Feminism
    Abortion and Religion
    Abortion and Catholicism
    Abortion, Technology, and Nature
    Abortion and the Sexual Revolution
    Abortion and the Worldviews
    Abortion and the Four Feminists
    An Overview
    Transition to Simone de Beauvoir

CHAPTER ONE: SIMONE DE BEAUVOIR, 1908–1986   19

    THE EPISTEMOLOGY OF ABORTION
    The Mother of a Movement
    "La Grande Sartreuse"
    Beauvoir and Ethics
    Beauvoir, Atheism, and Religion
    The Writings of Simone de Beauvoir on Abortion
            Two Early Fictional Accounts
                    When Things of the Spirit Come First, ca. 1937
                    The Blood of Others
            Abortion in *The Second Sex*

The Body as Problematic
The Lack of Maternal Instinct
The Passivity of Mothering
Beauvoir's Case for Abortion in *The Second Sex*
    The Total Package of Reproductive Freedom
    The Religious-Moral Argument Against
        Abortion
    Abortion and the Question of Patriarchal
        Control
    Abortion and Killing as the Key to the
        Whole Mystery
    Summary of Abortion Arguments in *The
        Second Sex*
Abortion in the Autobiographical Volumes
    Memoirs of a Dutiful Daughter
    Force of Circumstance
The Shorter Pieces on Abortion
Commentary on Simone de Beauvoir
Transition to Mary Daly

CHAPTER TWO: MARY DALY, 1928–   **61**

THE METAPHYSICS OF ABORTION
Some Signposts for the Journey
Early Efforts
A Creature of the Sixties
Daly's Debt to Simone de Beauvoir
Daly and Abortion
Abortion in *The Church and the Second Sex*
Beyond God the Father
    Abortion in *Beyond God the Father*
    The Anti-Abortion Devices of Patriarchy
    Abortion as an Issue of Power
    Some Conclusions from *Beyond God the
        Father*
Abortion in *Gyn/Ecology*
    Daly's Separatist Metaphysics
Abortion in *Pure Lust*
    Daly Beyond Beauvoir

Commentary on Mary Daly
    Some Positive Points
    Some Criticisms
Beauvoir and Daly
    The Universal Patriarchy
    The Hypocritical Ethic
    Male Sadism
    Is Nature Misogynist?
    The Surprises of Christian Ethics
    The Sex That Kills
Transition to Carol Gilligan

CHAPTER THREE: CAROL GILLIGAN, 1936–

CHAPTER THREE: CAROL GILLIGAN, 1936–   101

THE PSYCHOLOGY OF ABORTION

Abortion in a Different Voice
The Importance of Psychology
Gilligan's Critique of Kohlberg
In a Different Voice
    The Shadow of Simone de Beauvoir
    Gilligan's Moral Theory: Contextual
        Relativism
    The Return of Complementarity
    The Danger in *Difference*
    Gilligan on Abortion
    Religion in Gilligan's *In a Different Voice*
    Two Catholic Women Tell Their Stories
    The Violence in Abortion
Commentary on Carol Gilligan
    Gilligan's Two Moral Ideologies
    Summary and Conclusions
Transition to Beverly Wildung Harrison

CHAPTER FOUR: BEVERLY WILDUNG HARRISON, 1932–

CHAPTER FOUR: BEVERLY WILDUNG HARRISON, 1932–   137

THE THEOLOGY OF ABORTION

Harrison and the Catholic Ethical Tradition
Misogyny in the Christian Tradition
A Search for the High Moral Ground

The Influence of Beauvoir
 The Control Over Nature
 The Well-Chosen Title: *Our Right to*
  Choose
The Influence of Daly and Gilligan
Harrison's Case for Abortion in *Our Right to*
 Choose
 The Power to Control the Species
 Reproductive Rights: A Matter of Justice
 Four Masculinist Theologies
 Relationality
 A Feminist Reading of Christian Moral
  Teaching
 A Feminist Perspective on Abortion
 The Status of the Fetus
 The Politics of Abortion, American-Style
 Harrison's Personal Postscript
Commentary on Beverly Harrison
 Some Positive Elements
 Some Criticisms
Transition to the Final Chapters

CHAPTER FIVE: PRO-CHOICE FEMINISM   **181**

Abortion and Autonomy
Simone de Beauvoir: Epistemology and Killing
Mary Daly: Metaphysics and Power
Carol Gilligan: Psychology and Choice
Beverly Harrison: Theology and Right
 Abortion and Christian Feminism
Abortion as the Linchpin of Contemporary Feminism
Transition to the Final Chapter

CHAPTER SIX: PRO-LIFE FEMINISM   **203**

Ideas Have Consequences
Beauvoir and Guardini on Abortion
"The Question That Will Not Go Away"
The Haunting Violence

The Pro-life Worldview
A Question of Anthropology
A Pro-life Feminism
Some Elements of a Pro-life Feminism
        Challenges Facing a Christian Pro-life Feminism
Abortion and the Male as Model
The Two Worldviews and the Moral Imagination

BIBLIOGRAPHY   **227**

INDEX   **239**

ACKNOWLEDGEMENTS

Abortion and feminism—these are highly-charged issues. And a male religious Franciscan no less, writing on them! I am who I am. How dare I write on such an issue? What can I know of women's experience? In the course of our study we shall come across much talk of women's experiences, to be sure. The authors we shall discuss make it an important part of their approach to the abortion question. We shall try to learn what we can from them. Yet *experience* is a notoriously protean concept: *whose* experience is to count in evaluating the morality of abortion? Simone de Beauvoir's or Sidney Callahan's? Mary Daly's or Mother Teresa's? Radical feminism's or the Catholic Church's?

Perhaps a comment made by Beverly Harrison will have to do as my best defense regarding the *experience* that allows me to write about such a topic. She is answering the question: would she have wanted abortion legal when she herself was born?

> "The question, when it has been pressed on me, has always caused me to smile; for I almost was a medically dictated abortion, and I have lived much of my life with that knowledge. But I also know, as anyone who comprehends the development of self-awareness will understand, that if I *had* been aborted, there would have been no 'I' to experience it" (*Our Right to Choose*, p. 257).

Abortion is neither a man's nor a woman's issue exclusively, neither a feminist nor a Catholic issue exclusively. It is rather a human issue of the first magnitude, one involving men and women, feminists and Catholics, to be sure, but all human beings as well. The very definition of who we are is at stake. In the abortion controversy, at stake is *not* so much the humanity of the fetus; at stake is *ours*. Should some feminist ask: How dare I write on such an issue? My only rejoinder is: How dare I not?

Some may consider this work to be a part of the current culture war; if so, its author has no wish to wage it by vitriol or name-calling. Saint Francis of Assisi was known especially for his *cortesia*, the great respect he showed to all things living. My translation of that virtue will be to allow the feminists to present their case for abortion in their own words. Disagreements with their ideas regarding the meaning of human abortion and its effect on women are meant to be taken neither as arguments *ad hominem* nor *ad feminam* but rather as arguments *ad errores*.

I owe a debt of gratitude to my religious brothers in the Franciscan community. The great love that St. Francis had for all of creation is mirrored in many ways in their lives as well, especially in their respect for women and in their regard for life. The help of two Redemptorist moralists, Brian Johnstone and Sean O'Riordan, proved extremely beneficial in keeping me on a Franciscan path.

Special love and gratitude go to the gentle, strong Christian women who have taught me about life by their own lives of faith, hope, love, and sacrifice: my mother and my aunts, relatives, the Religious Sisters who helped educate me, as well as the devoted women who are the heart and soul of the pro-life movement. Without their example of courage in the defense of life, this work would never have been conceived, never have seen the light of day.

I am appreciative also of two Christian gentlemen: Mr. Thomas Hurley for his considerable editorial expertise, and Dr. Donald DeMarco for his suggestions and encouragement. To Rita Hurley and Mary DeMarco: thank you both for letting me borrow your husbands to help in this work.

I am especially indebted to my students, men and women, religious and lay. Their questions served as a spur to this present work.

I also owe a debt to those feminists who read and took the time to comment upon the various stages of this work. They and I did not always agree, but we did take the time to listen to what each other had to say. I hope my readers will do the same.

I am grateful to the librarians at Mount Holyoke College and Amherst College for allowing me to use their resources. No library has been more useful than the one at St. Hyacinth College and Seminary in

Granby, Massachusetts, staffed by Brother Christian Katusz and Bev Wilson, Donna Carpenter and Pat Bombardier.

Permissions

I am pleased to also acknowledge the following for permission to reprint previously published material:

From *The Second Sex* by Simone De Beauvoir, trans., H. M. Parshley, Copyright 1952 and renewed 1980 by Alfred A. Knopf, Inc. Reprinted by permission of the publisher.

From *Our Right to Choose* by Beverly Wildung Harrison. Copyright © 1983 by Beverly Wildung Harrison. Beacon Press, Boston, Mass. Reprinted by permission of the publisher.

From *Beyond God the Father* by Mary Daly. Copyright © 1973 by Mary Daly. Beacon Press, Boston, Mass. Reprinted by permission of the publisher.

From *Public Affairs Quarterly*: excerpts from the article "Abortion and the 'Feminine Voice,'" by Celia Wolf-Devine; Volume 3, Number 3, (1989), pages 81-97. *Public Affairs Quarterly*, University of Pittsburgh, Pittsburgh, Pennsylvania. Reprinted by permission of the publisher.

From *Abortion: The Clash of Absolutes* by Laurence Tribe. Published in 1990. W. W. Norton & Co., Inc., New York, New York. Reprinted by permission of the publisher.

From *In a Different Voice: Psychological Theory and Women's Development* by Carol Gilligan. Copyright © 1982, 1993 by Carol Gilligan. Harvard University Press, Cambridge, Mass. Reprinted by permission of the publisher.

4 Lines to Be Used as an Epigraph from *Dialogue Between Ghost and Priest* from the Collected Poems of Sylvia Plath by Sylvia Plath.

PREFACE

How did the practice of human abortion go from its atheistic roots in the existentialist philosophy of Jean-Paul Sartre and Simone de Beauvoir to the classrooms of Christians? To explain how pro-choice feminism came about is one of the two major aims of this work. The second is to argue for a pro-life feminism, a feminism without abortion as its mooring and mainstay. Our study will lead to two conclusions regarding abortion and contemporary feminism: 1) Atheism, not feminism, is the real root of the abortion rights mentality; 2) there are many feminisms.

The right to abortion begins to take shape when Simone de Beauvoir articulates the feminist culturalist credo: "One is not born, but rather becomes, a woman." All of contemporary feminism is a commentary on this single sentence.

The Power of Words

The octogenarian priest and I approached the little group of approximately twenty-five college students. They were sitting on the ground in a semicircle and chanting the refrain: "Our bodies, our lives, our right to decide."

We walked by the group without incident and entered the auditorium at Smith College to hear Alice von Hildebrand lecture on feminism, abortion, and motherhood.[1] On the ride back home, I

---

[1]Smith College in Northampton, Massachusetts is the alma mater of American feminists Betty Friedan and Gloria Steinem and plays an important role in the former's *Feminine Mystique* (New York: Dell, 1963) and the latter's *Revolution from Within: A Book of Self-Esteem* (Boston: Little, Brown and Company, 1992).

pondered the power of the two messages we had heard that night, pro-choice outside the hall, pro-life within.[2] It occurred to me that the chant outside the hall and the lecture within were also part of that long-running commentary upon one sentence from Simone de Beauvoir: "One is not born, but rather becomes, a woman."[3] So is this present study.

Am I attaching too much weight to the words of a single sentence? I do not think so. Simone de Beauvoir once observed:

> By trade, by vocation, I attach an enormous importance to words. Simone Weil used to demand that anyone who used writing to tell lies to men should be put on trial, and I understand what she means. *There are words as murderous as gas chambers.*[4]

Beauvoir, of course, is right: "Abortion is what really frees women."[5]

In the course of our investigation I hope to demonstrate that such a sentiment—that the right to abortion and the advancement of social justice for women go together—enshrines at the heart of much of contemporary feminist thought the victory of what I call "The Male as

---

[2]Finding the right terminology for the abortion discussion is never easy. As a general rule, I will use the terms "pro-choice" and "pro-life" as the terms the adherents of each view would prefer their own position be called; on occasion, the terms "pro-abortion" and "anti-abortion" shall be utilized.

[3]Simone de Beauvoir, *The Second Sex* (translated and edited by H. M. Parshley) (New York: Bantam Books, 1962), p. 249. This is a one-volume English abridgement of Beauvoir's two-volume *Le deuxième sexe* (Collection Folio/Essais) (Paris: Gallimard, 1949; renouvelé en 1976). Beauvoir's culturalist thesis is continued by many, including Sherry B. Ortner, "Is Female to Male as Nature is to Culture?" in Michelle Zimbalist Rosaldo and Louise Lamphere (eds.), *Woman, Culture, and Society* (Stanford: Stanford University Press, 1974), pp. 67–87.

[4]Simone de Beauvoir, *Force of Circumstance* (translated by Richard Howard) (London: André Deutsch and Weidenfeld and Nicolson, 1965), pp. 21–22; my emphasis.

[5]The words are those of Mary Gordon, "The Irish Catholic Church," in Peter Occhiogrosso (ed.), *Once a Catholic: Prominent Catholics and Ex-Catholics Discuss the Influence of the Church on Their Lives and Work* (Boston: Houghton Mifflin Company, 1987), pp. 65-78. The quote is on p. 76.

Model" theory. It too is a part of the commentary on Beauvoir's sentence. It too will be a confirmation of Sylvia Plath's insight: "There sits no higher court/ Than man's red heart."

An illustration may help. Several years ago I remember reading of an Italian court decision which adjudicated that international soccer star Diego Maradona is indeed the father of a 6-year-old, Diego Armando. The mother of the child is quoted:

> I am satisfied. After so many years, truth has finally won out. I do not want to destroy Maradona nor do I wish his money. But he must assume his responsibilities because it takes two to make children.

An accompanying article reported: "More than once the soccer star and his entourage tried in vain to persuade the woman to have an abortion."[6] Maradona's "solution" to the problem pregnancy is indicative of what I term "The Male as Model Theory" of human abortion. Put briefly: it regards killing as an acceptable solution to the problems of living. When feminists urge women to look upon the right to abortion as the great equalizer of men and women, they buy into the Male as Model Theory.

Who stole feminism? This question—the title of a recent book by Christina Hoff Sommers—is answered here by focusing on the one question Sommers glosses over in her volume, namely, abortion and contemporary feminism. Though we shall find ourselves doing so to some degree, my purpose in writing this book is not to examine Church teaching on abortion; it is rather to examine and evaluate recent feminist apologies for the practice. Nor is it my main aim to defend Christianity from the charge of misogyny. It is rather to subject the act of human abortion to an ethical evaluation; doing so, as we shall see, will involve us in recent uses of the charge of misogyny levelled by some Christian feminists that serve as a ground of sorts for their defenses of abortion.

"There are words as murderous as gas chambers." A not insignificant part of the reality of that life-and-death issue known as abortion is rhetorical. We shall see that Simone de Beauvoir, Mary Daly,

---

[6]The account of the Maradona paternity case is found in *Corriere della sera* (Thursday, May 7, 1992): "Diego Armando jr da ieri è figlio di Maradona." The accompanying story relating Maradona's proposed means of solving the problem pregnancy is on p. 19.

Carol Gilligan, and Beverly Wildung Harrison provide the rhetorical as well as theoretical foundations of a feminist case of sorts for the practice of human abortion. Beauvoir and Daly deal with the realities of killing and power, Gilligan and Harrison furnish the rhetorical devices of choice and rights. Put them together and this thesis emerges from our study of four feminist theoreticians of abortion: "The right to choose is the rhetoric, the power to kill is the reality." While their endorsement of abortion is a feminist case, it is not feminism, and it is not of necessity tied to feminism. Hence our first conclusion: "Atheism, not feminism, is the real root of the abortion rights mentality."

The atheism of Simone de Beauvoir is a good place to see the abortion idea on its native soil, as it were. How abortion works its way into Christion circles will be seen in our examination of the other three: Mary Daly is on the faculty of Jesuit-run Boston College, Beverly Wildung Harrison teaches Christian Ethics at Union Theological Seminary, and Carol Gilligan's work appears in anthologies of mainstream Roman Catholic moral theology texts. We shall argue that while there is a link between atheism and abortion, there is no such link between abortion and feminism.[7] Beauvoir and her cohorts are feminists, but their thought on abortion does not constitute feminism. Hence, our second conclusion: "There are many feminisms."

Abortion and "The Problem That Has No Name"

In Betty Friedan's *The Feminine Mystique,* a book considered by many as the launching of the contemporary feminist movement in the United States,[8] there is nary a hint of abortion.[9]   Chapter one of Friedan's book treats what the author labels the "Problem That Has No Name." Women, according to Friedan, were dissatisfied with life in the

---

[7]Some nuance on this point may be in order: there *does* exist a group known as "Atheists for Life," there *are* writers like Nat Hentoff.

[8]Betty Friedan, *The Feminine Mystique* (New York: Dell Books, 1963).

[9]Lee Epstein and Joseph F. Kobylka, *The Supreme Court and the Death Penalty* (Chapel Hill and London: The University of North Carolina Press, 1992), are commenting on Freidan's *Feminine Mystique:* "We should note, though, that neither the book nor its author (at least initially) viewed the issue of abortion as a particularly important one for the cause of women's rights" (p. 349, note 22).

comfortable concentration camp that was the suburban American home of the 60s. Women wanted more from life.[10] Lawrence Lader, a friend, suggested to Friedan that part of the problem was the fact that American women lacked the right to abortion.[11] Friedan was convinced and helped lead feminists in their battle against abortion laws.[12]

When in 1973 the United States Supreme Court handed down its Roe v. Wade decision, it seemed that Lader's and Friedan's ultimate freedom for women had arrived. Or had it? This present work urges feminists to reconsider their defining of abortion into feminism. Whatever the problem that has no name may be, abortion is not its solution.

A Word About the Title

In the course of this study we will encounter the "ghosts" and the "priests" found in the poem of Sylvia Plath, words which serve as the inspiration for the title of this present work. By defining abortion into feminism as they do Beauvoir and her companions give witness to the poet's intuition. Far from being a new and better way of doing ethics, a feminism with abortion as its linchpin is nothing more than business as usual, with male values masquerading in feminist language.

Speaking of himself and the other abortion advocates in the United States who helped repeal abortion laws in a scant six years, Lawrence Lader contended: "We knew that abortion wasn't just central

---

[10]Cf. Lisa Tuttle, *Encyclopedia of Feminism* (New York: Facts on File Publications, 1986), s. v. "Problem that has no name," p. 258: "The problem was that women were not allowed to be grown-up individuals, genuine human beings, but were expected to follow a false, infantile pattern of femininity and live through their husbands and children. She [Friedan] recognized that this was a genuine social problem, and not just the matter of individual maladjustment it was said to be. Subsequently, feminists have termed the problem sexism."

[11]Cf. Lawrence Lader, *Abortion II: Making the Revolution* (Boston: Beacon Press, 1973), pp. 36–39. It is not long before Friedan embraced Lader's vision, as we see in her 1966 article, "Our Revolution is Unique," reprinted in Mary Lou Thompson (ed.), *Voices of the New Feminism* (Boston: Beacon Press, 1975), pp. 31–43.

[12]According to Lader, Friedan was pushed along in the matter of abortion reform by the younger elements of radical feminism. Cf. *Abortion II*, pp. 36–37.

to a woman's right of choice. It was central to everything in life and how we wanted to live it" (*Abortion II*, p. 222). He then goes on to invoke the legacy of Jean-Paul Sartre as the inspiration of the abortion rights movement. It seems to me that Lader comes close to claiming the role of Sartre to Friedan's Beauvoir. If abortion is the ultimate female freedom, men like Lader and Sartre were largely instrumental in getting some women to see the connection.[13]

At confirmation hearings for a recent appointee to the Supreme Court of the United States, a front-page story from *The New York Times* quotes the nominee on the abortion question:

> It is essential to a woman's equality with man that she be the decision-maker, that her choice be controlling. If you impose restraints, you are disadvantaging her because of her sex. The state controlling a woman would mean denying her full autonomy and full equality.[14]

From her seat on the nation's highest tribunal, Ruth Bader Ginsburg is not only a judge; she is also a witness: "There sits no higher court/Than man's red heart."

---

[13]Cf. Lawrence Lader, *Abortion II*, pp. 221–223.

[14]Neil A. Lewis, "Ginsburg Embraces Right of a Woman to Have Abortion," *The New York Times* (Thursday, July 22, 1993).

From that pale mist
Ghost swore to priest:
"There sits no higher court
Than man's red heart."

Sylvia Plath
"Dialogue Between Ghost and Priest"
Collected Poems, p. 39

INTRODUCTION

"A FIGHT AGAINST THE WORK OF GOD"

SETTING THE STAGE

Herbert Marcuse once observed that the feminist revolution is in theory the most radical of all revolutions: the French and Russian revolutions were fought against works of human beings; the feminist revolution is a fight against the work of God.[1] We shall investigate the relevance of this observation as we view the work of four important feminist writers on abortion: Simone de Beauvoir, Mary Daly, Carol Gilligan, and Beverly Wildung Harrison.

Preliminary Considerations

At the outset we would do well to introduce a distinction regarded by many contemporary feminists as based on Beauvoir's distinction between woman *born* and woman *becoming*, encapsulated in the phrase: "One is not born, but rather becomes, a woman." This is the distinction between "sex" and "gender."[2] Kate Millett expresses it

---

[1] Herbert Marcuse, "Marxismus und Feminismus," *Jahrbuch für Politik* 6 (1974), p. 86, speaks of feminism as "possibly the most important and potentially radical movement of contemporary life." It is quoted in Jutta Burggraf, "The Mother of the Church and the Woman in the Church: a Correction of Feminist Theology Gone Astray," in Helmut Moll (ed.), *The Church and Women: A Compendium* (San Francisco: Ignatius Press, 1988), p. 239 note 7.

[2] According to Christina Hoff Sommers, *Who Stole Feminism? How Women Have Betrayed Women* (New York: Simon and Schuster, 1994): "Sex/gender feminism" ("gender feminism" for short) is the prevailing ideology among contemporary feminist philosophers and leaders" (p. 22). It is they who have stolen feminism, according to Sommers.

concisely: "Sex is biological, gender psychological, and therefore cultural"[3] According to Lisa Tuttle:

> Whereas *sex* refers to the biological, anatomical differences between male and female, *gender* refers to the emotional and psychological attributes which a given culture expects to coincide with physical maleness or femaleness.[4]

Beauvoir's text is often elaborated upon by contemporary feminists as a pithy statement of the problem of nature and culture, between *naturalism* and *culturalism*. Beauvoir herself provides a working definition of "culturalism":

> No biological, psychological, or economic fate determines the figure that the human female presents in society; it is civilization as a whole that produces this creature, intermediate between male and eunuch, which is described as feminine.[5]

If "culturalism" is the view that woman is virtually all environment and practically nothing of nature, "naturalism," on the other hand, is the view that innate sex differences have much to do with the broad structure of society.[6] Freud's "Biology is destiny" is an extreme expression of it. A way of presenting naturalism that avoids Freud's deterministic interpretation is summed up in the phrase "equal in dignity, complementary in nature," used at times in the teachings of

---

[3]Kate Millett, *Sexual Politics* (New York: Avon Books, 1970), p. 30. The author bases herself on observations made by Robert J. Stoller.

[4] Lisa Tuttle, *Encyclopedia of Feminism*, s.v. "Gender."

[5]Simone de Beauvoir, *The Second Sex*, p. 249. It is of some interest that Beauvoir regards the feminine as somewhere between the Male and Eunuch. We have here an instance of "The Male as Model Theory" appearing in the mother of contemporary feminism.

[6]What I have termed "naturalism" and "culturalism" is called "nativism" and "environmentalism" by Michael Levin, *Feminism and Freedom*, (New Brunswick, NJ: Transaction Books) p. 55. The definition of "naturalism" I have given is based on what he has to say on p. 3.

the Catholic Church to express the meaning of innate sex differences.[7]

Several other elements serve to frame the contemporary abortion problematic. Among them are the different varieties of feminism, the role of religion in general and Catholicism in particular, the question of technology and nature, the sexual revolution, and the issue of worldviews.

Abortion and the Different Waves of Feminism

Pace Catherine MacKinnon, feminism, assuredly, is not one doctrine. There are many feminisms. Alison Jaggar speaks of four basic contemporary varieties of feminism: liberal, Marxist, socialist and radical feminism.[8] Jean Bethke Elshtain treats five versions of feminism: liberal, Marxist, socialist, radical, and psychoanalytic.[9] Rosemarie Tong lists no fewer than seven varieties.[10] Lisa Tuttle, in her encyclopedia entry, "Feminism," mentions no fewer than fourteen variations of the theme of feminism.[11] Though a woman's right to abortion figures prominently in many varieties of feminism, it is by no means espoused by all.[12] Indeed, there is a morally formidable pro-life feminism.

---

[7] While Beauvoir remained a culturalist all her life, other feminists have moved from culturalism to naturalism as a better way of understanding the meaning of innate sex differences.

[8] Cf. Alison Jaggar, *Feminist Politics and Human Nature* (Totowa: Rowman and Littlefield, 1983).

[9] Cf. Jean Bethke Elshtain, *Public Man, Private Woman: Women in Social and Political Thought* (Princeton: Princeton University Press, 1981).

[10] Cf. Rosemarie Tong, *Feminist Thought: A Comprehensive Introduction* (Boulder and San Francisco: Westview Press, 1989). Tong discusses the following seven forms of contemporary feminism: liberal, radical, Marxist, socialist, psychoanalytic, existentialist, and postmodernist.

[11] Cf. Lisa Tuttle, *Encyclopedia of Feminism*, s. v. "Feminism." On the pluralism of contemporary feminism, see also Myra Marx Ferree and Beth B. Hess, *Controversy and Coalition: The New Feminist Movement* (Boston: Twayne, 1985).

[12] Cf. the words of Maurice Thorez in the May 2, 1956 *L'Humanité*: "The road of liberty for women takes the path of social reforms. . . . It does not lead to abortion clinics." Text found in Jean Toulat, *La droit de naître* (Paris: Pygmalion: Gérard Watelet, 1979), p. 195.

Because there *are* many feminisms, definitions of what is feminism and who is a feminist become parlous. One of the simplest definitions of feminism also has the added advantage of being acceptable to many: "Feminism is having excellent reasons for thinking that women suffer from systematic social injustice because of their sex."[13]

Earlier waves of feminism never spoke of abortion as a right. On the contrary, nineteenth-century feminists such as the American Elizabeth Cady Stanton (1815–1902) regarded abortion as degrading to the dignity of woman. Many twentieth-century feminists take a different view. Our study of four feminist authors will help us understand how the practice of human abortion could go from unspeakable crime to an absolute right,[14] in such a short time. Indeed, as recently as 1970, one feminist could write:

> It seems odd that no group of feminists (so far as the writer knows) has come out with the forthright claim that it should be an essential aspect of freedom of person for a woman to refuse to have an unwanted child.[15]

The four feminist authors whose thought on abortion we will scrutinize are not the only feminist theoreticians of abortion, to be

---

[13]Janet Radcliffe Richards, *The Sceptical Feminist: A Philosophical Inquiry* (Boston: Routledge and Kegan Paul), 1980, p. 1. Other definitions abound. According to Mary Anne Warren, *The Nature of Woman: An Encyclopedia and Guide to the Literature* (Inverness, CA: Edgepress, 1980), p. 662, feminism is "the thesis that male domination is morally wrong, and that women and men ought to enjoy equal moral, social, legal and political rights." To Catherine MacKinnon, *Toward a Feminist Theory of the State* (Cambridge, MA: Harvard University Press, 1989), p. 38: "Feminism is distinguished by the view that gender is a problem: that what exists now is not equality between the sexes."

[14]Regarding the expression "from unspeakable crime to absolute right," cf. James Reed, *From Private Vice to Public Virtue: The Birth Control Movement and American Society Since 1830* (New York: Basic Books, 1978).

[15]Constance Rover, *Love, Morals and the Feminists* (London: Routledge and Kegan Paul, 1970), pp. 162–163.

sure.[16] A major reason for our choice of the four is that all of them treat the abortion question in the context not only of their feminism but also of their perceptions of religion in general, Roman Catholicism in particular. While a solid case can be made for the overarching importance of each of the four, our study will show that the abortion seeds sown by Simone de Beauvoir in *The Second Sex* of 1949 bear fruit not only in Daly, Gilligan, and Harrison, but also in many others who follow in Beauvoir's wake.

Abortion and Religion

Religion is an important part of the current abortion debate. The rise of an abortion rights mentality can be regarded, on one level, as an instance of the rapid pace of secularization. On another level, it is part of a much older and long-standing problematic. Some authors regard the rise of an abortion rights mentality as a continuation of the individualism of the Protestant Reformation and an extension of the antitraditionalism of the Enlightenment.[17]

While there is indeed a sizeable segment of strictly secular feminists, the importance of religion for contemporary feminism is a theme much in evidence not only in the four authors we shall be treating but in others as well.[18] While some feminists may indeed show an antipathy toward religion, it is not the case that pro-choice feminism

---

[16]Among standard feminist defenses of abortion from a decidedly secular point of view, by far the most famous and certainly the most anthologized is that of Judith Jarvis Thomson, "A Defense of Abortion," *Philosophy and Public Affairs* 1 (1971), pp. 47–66. Other staple defenses of abortion include Mary Anne Warren, "On the Moral and Legal Status of Abortion," *The Monist* 57 (1973), pp. 43–61, and Rosalind Pollack Petchesky, *Abortion and Woman's Choice: The State, Sexuality, and Reproductive Freedom* (revised edition) (The Northeastern Series in Feminist Theory) (Boston: Northeastern University Press, 1990).

[17]Marilyn Falik, *Ideology and Abortion Policy Politics* (New York: Praeger Scientific Studies, 1983), sees the abortion question as a continuation of the Protestant Reformation.

[18]The importance of religion for feminism is also a theme in Mary Midgely and Judith Hughes, *Women's Choices: Philosophical Problems Facing Feminism* (New York: St. Martin's Press, 1983).

necessarily follows their lead.[19] I trust that perceptive readers will see that the argument I am attempting to elaborate in this book is *not* that pro-choice feminism is profoundly anti-religious. The point I *am* attempting to argue for is a different one: if and when *Christian* feminism holds pro-choice views, *this* I regard to be inconsistent with Christianity.[20]

To put it in another way: the abortion mentality is at home in atheism; it is out of place in Christianity. This opposition to the practice of human abortion comes about not because the Christian Church is misogynist, as some feminists such as Beverly Harrison will argue, but because the act of abortion does violence to both mother and child, creatures of a loving God in whose image both were made. While there is an undeniable link between the practice of abortion and the attitude of atheism, no such link exists between abortion and feminism. Here again we do well to remember: There are many feminisms.

Abortion and Catholicism

There are only two consistent attitudes to abortion: one is the extreme feminist one; the other is that held by Roman Catholics. The middle way, that abortion is all right sometimes, depending on the circumstances, and justified by situation ethics (i.e., it depends on the

---

[19]Gloria Steinem would be a good choice to lead the contingent of secular feminists. Belief in humanism understood as human potential for growth rather than transcendent religion is the wellspring of this approach. Hence Steinem's comment: "By the year 2000 we will, I hope, raise our children to believe in human potential, not God." Text found in Maggie Tripp (ed.), *Woman in the Year 2000* (New York: Arbor House, 1974), p. 50.

[20]One recent collection of Christian apologies for the practice of human abortion is that of Anne Eggebroten (ed.), *Abortion: My Choice, God's Grace—Christian Women Tell Their Stories.* (Pasadena: New Paradigm Books, 1994). Cf. Jeremy C. Jackson, "The Shadow of Death: Abortion in Historical and Contemporary Perspective," in Richard Ganz (ed.), *Thou Shalt Not Kill: The Christian Case Against Abortion* (New Rochelle: Arlington House, 1978), pp. 91–92: "What even radical feminists in the mid-nineteenth century attacked as immoral, an assault upon life, twentieth-century Christians have embraced with few questions asked."

situation), is morally and logically absurd.[21]

In a recent anthology of feminist theology, Ann Loades declares that all Christianity owes a debt of gratitude to the Roman Catholic Church because of the way the Church puts the issues "out front." The Catholic Church's teaching on the immorality of procured abortion stands in direct opposition to much of contemporary feminist ideology which maintains, in the words of Stella Browne, that "abortion must be the key to a new world for women."

During the tumultuous period of the 1960s when abortion as an absolute right was first proposed by some radical feminists, the teaching of the Roman Catholic Church on the immorality of directly procured abortion is clearly reiterated by the Second Vatican Council: "From the moment of its conception life must be guarded with the greatest care, while abortion and infanticide are unspeakable crimes."[22] Thus, we ought not to find it surprising that the Church's teaching on abortion is not far from the minds of feminist theorists. Indeed, the Church's teaching is regarded as the major moral obstacle to the feminist desire for a right to an abortion. Each of the four feminist thinkers will in her own way attempt to grapple with Roman Catholic moral teaching as she seeks to overcome the chief barrier to "a new world for women."[23]

Abortion, Technology, and Nature

Friedan and neofeminism erupted on a wave of technology. For it was the technology of contracep-

---

[21]Mary Kenny, *Abortion: The Whole Story*, (London and New York: Quartet Books, 1986), p. 2.

[22]Cf. Paragraph 51 of *Gaudium et spes*, also known as the "Pastoral Constitution on the Church in the Modern World." One readily available translation is that of Walter M. Abbott, S.J. (general editor), *The Documents of Vatican II* (New York: Guild Press, 1968). See also paragraph 27. Writing shortly before the start of the Second Vatican Council, J. Pilz, "Abtreibung," in *Lexikon für Theologie und Kirche* I (1957), cols. 96-100, regards Church teaching on the matter of abortion as so certain as to be practically a truth of faith.

[23]According to Kristin Luker, *Taking Chances: Abortion and the Decision Not to Contracept* (Berkeley: University of California Press, 1975), p. 45: the Catholic Church is often regarded as a "most significant other" in the abortion question.

tion, the birth control pill, that made possible the radicalization of women. Only when technology—and abortion is a crucial step in this process—allowed women to free themselves from the prison of incessant childbearing could they grapple with the possibility of achieving themselves on every plane.[24]

That abortion is sought as a right is owed in large part to the advances in the safety and efficiency of abortion technology. Abortion is often presented by feminist authors as safer than birth. Here, for instance, is Germaine Greer:

> Abortion is an extension of contraceptive technology, and the most promising extension of it at that. It is not an alternative standing in dichotomous relation to contraception, for contraception is too often abortion in disguise. Moreover, if we take women's right to life into consideration, the cruder forms of contraception, the condom and the diaphragm, coupled with early abortion, are the safest ways of conducting one's reproductive affairs in terms of life expectancy. Abortion is not a stopgap between here and some future perfect contraceptive; it can very well be the chosen method of birth control for more and more women[25] (*Sex and Destiny*, p. 231).

Hence, advances in technology have been a major reason why the *practice* of abortion has now been transformed into a *right* in Western societies. Not surprisingly, on the question of technology, we shall find elements of Roman Catholic moral theology, especially those pertaining to the natural law, becoming important factors in the

---

[24]Lawrence Lader, *Abortion II: Making the Revolution* (Boston: Beacon Press, 1973), p. 39.

[25]Germaine Greer, *Sex and Destiny: The Politics of Human Fertility* (New York: Harper & Row, 1984).

abortion question.[26]

Here, the much convoluted question of nature versus culture to which we have made reference earlier comes to the surface. Prescinding from talk of patriarchy and male domination plots to control the reproductive power of women, we can rephrase the terms of the debate to read: Is nature misogynist?

> I asked a friend, mother of six children, with a family income of £18 per week whether she thought financial or sexual inequalities were the greatest. After some thought, she said that *being a woman was the most unequal thing.*[27]

Is the fact that women bear the young of the species an injustice to be corrected by technological means?[28] If it is an injustice, it has been perpetrated not by men but by nature. In *The Dialectic of Sex* Shulamith Firestone elaborates an extreme radical feminist case for this position, severely upbraided by critics of feminism such as Carol McMillan as well as by culturalist feminists such as Christine Delphy.[29]

---

[26]Richard Gula, S.S., *What Are They Saying About Moral Norms?* (New York: Paulist Press, 1982), pp. 34–53, gives a succinct account of two current theories of natural law. The topic of natural law is featured in Charles E. Curran and Richard A. McCormick, S.J. (eds.), *Readings in Moral Theology No. 7: Natural Law and Theology* (New York: Paulist Press, 1991). Cf. the comments regarding Catholic natural law thinking made by James Childress, "The Meaning of the 'Right to Life,'" in Robert P. Davidow (ed.), *Natural Rights and Natural Law: the Legacy of George Mason* (The George Mason Lectures) (Fairfax, VA: George Mason Univ. Press, 1986), pp. 123–172.

[27]Text found in Juliet Mitchell, *Woman's Estate* (New York: Vintage Books, 1973), p. 178, note 1: my emphasis. Is nature misogynist? The theme is adumbrated in the context of abortion by Magda Denes, *In Necessity and Sorrow: Life and Death in an Abortion Hospital* (New York: Basic Books, 1976). Denes expresses astonishment at the meaning of being female; to her, it is the very essence of dependence and limitation (p. 126).

[28]Cf. Laurence H. Tribe, *Abortion: The Clash of Absolutes* (New York: W. W. Norton and Company, 1990), p. 132.

[29]Cf. Carol McMillan, *Women, Reason and Nature: Some Philosophical Problems With Feminism* (Princeton, NJ: Princeton University Press, 1982), pp. 115ff. She argues that Firestone is saying, in effect, that it is *nature* rather than *patriarchy* that is the great oppressor of women. As McMillan sees it, "the women's liberation movement

Irish author Edna O'Brien comes as close as anyone to reaching the heart of the question, "Is nature misogynist?" when she has a character in one of her novels say: "Oh God, who does not exist, you hate women, otherwise you'd have made them different."[30] This question is a leitmotif of sorts to which we return several times in the course of our study.[31] In O'Brien's one sentence we find the question of God, atheism, a misogynistic nature, the abortion issue, and the Male as Model Theory all rolled up into one neat feminist package.

Abortion and the Sexual Revolution

Though our discussion begins with Simone de Beauvoir's attitude toward the question of human abortion, the French existentialist feminist is certainly not the first to champion abortion. Canadian-born Stella Browne (1882–1955), a one-time Communist, life-long English Socialist, and devotée of Havelock Ellis's brand of sexual revolution, is speaking of abortion as a woman's *right* as early as 1915.[32]

---

is a rebellion against nature" (p. 118). Christine Delphy, *Close to Home: A Materialist Analysis of Women's Oppression* (Translated and edited by Diana Leonard) (Amherst: University of Massachusetts Press, 1984), p. 143, contends that Firestone's thesis is "outrageously biologistic." To feminists attached to a *culturalist* interpretation, the Firestone thesis, especially regarding *nature*, is anathema. Hence, the comment made by Lisa Tuttle, *Encyclopedia of Feminism*, s. v. "'Dialectic of Sex, The'", p. 83: "The book's conclusions alienated many feminists who are unwilling to locate the cause of women's oppression in anything inherent in women: and there is also an unwillingness to rely on technology—for so long used by men against women—to provide the means of liberation."

[30]Edna O'Brien, *The Country Girls Trilogy and Epilogue* (New York: Farrar, Straus, Giroux, 1986), p. 473.

[31]As in so many aspects of contemporary feminism, Simone de Beauvoir leads the way. *The Second Sex* provides a *locus classicus*: "Men tend to regard abortion lightly; they regard it as *one of the numerous hazards imposed on women by malignant nature*, but fail to realize fully the values involved. The woman who has recourse to abortion is disowning feminine values, and at the same time is in most radical fashion running counter to the ethics established by men. Her whole moral universe is being disrupted" (pp. 462–463), my emphasis.

[32]Regarding the 1915 date, see Lisa Tuttle, *Encyclopedia of Feminism*, p. 51, s. v. "Browne, Stella."

In Browne we find clear indication of some of the themes of contemporary feminist discourse on abortion.[33] She speaks quite clearly of the link she sees between abortion as an absolute right and the right of a woman to control the functions of her own body:

> Abortion must be the key to a new world for women, not a bulwark for things as they are, economically nor biologically. . . . It should be available for any woman, without insolent inquisitions, nor ruinous financial charges, nor tangles of red tape. For our bodies are our own.[34]

In their approaches to feminist issues, Browne and Beauvoir are alike in several ways. Both are adherents of a revolution in sexual mores. Both are aware of the economic issues confronting feminist analysis.[35] Both are enamored of a Marxist-inspired socialism. Neither believed in God.[36]

In the context of American jurisprudence, the sexual revolution becomes an important element in the attempt to make abortion into a right:

---

[33]Cf. Stella Browne, "The Right to Abortion," in Sheila Rowbotham, *A New World for Women: Stella Browne, Socialist Feminist* (London: Pluto Press, 1977), pp. 110–124.

[34]Stella Browne, "The Right to Abortion," p. 114. Here is Browne on abortion as a right: "Up to the viability of her child, it [abortion] is as much a woman's right as the removal of a dangerously diseased appendix" (p. 117). And on abortion as an *absolute* right: "The woman's right to abortion is an absolute right, as I see it, up to the viability of her child" (p. 113).

[35]In this sense, it is perhaps correct to say that the beginning of abortion as a right was owed at least as much to some forms of socialism, communism, and sexual libertinism as it was to feminism. There is an obvious sense in which we can quite readily discern the linking of feminist aims in general with Leftist political causes. The theme has been quite constantly treated in recent feminist writings. The last pages of Beauvoir's *The Second Sex* make clear the connection between an amelioration of woman's situation and Leftist analysis.

[36]Their adherence to Marxist thought requires atheism as a logical complement. In the case of Beauvoir, though she lost her faith in God when she was an adolescent, her atheism can also be seen as an extension of her espousal of Sartrian existentialism. In Browne's case, her commitment to Marxism would seem to entail atheism.

Without a right to abortion women are not equal to
men in the law. They are not equal to men with respect
to unburdened access to sex—with respect, that is, to
sexual freedom.[37]

Raising the issue of the sexual revolution and asking the
question: "Is Nature Misogynist?" at the same time is Laurence Tribe:

One powerful strand of feminist legal theory posits that
within our society even most nominally 'consensual'
sex, particularly in cases where the woman does not feel
free to use or to suggest the birth control, involves
coercion. But if one assumes a pregnancy that did not
result from any sort of coercion, then perhaps the
imposition of continued pregnancy on the woman may
not be unjust. But however voluntary the *sex* may have
been, the woman was, of course, not the sole
participant. Yet a ban on abortion imposes truly
burdensome duties *only* on women. Such a ban thus
places women, by accident of their biology, in a
permanently and irrevocably subordinate position to
men.[38]

What I would call "The Male as Model Theory" is much in
evidence. In this way of viewing things, there can be no equality
between men and women until women are equal to men in the area of
sexuality. Hence the link between the sexual revolution and the abortion
mentality.[39] Abortion is the great equalizer since it enables a woman's

---

[37]Guido Calabresi, *Ideals, Beliefs, Attitudes and the Law: Private Law Perspectives on a
Public Law Problem* (New York: Syracuse University Press, 1985), p. 101.

[38]Laurence Tribe, *Abortion: The Clash of Absolutes*, p. 132; author's emphasis. On the
themes of abortion, the sexual revolution, and Marxist theory, cf. two works of
Catherine A. MacKinnon, *Feminism Unmodified: Discourses on Life and Law*
(Cambridge, MA: Harvard University Press, 1987), and *Toward a Feminist Theory of
the State*.

[39]Cf. Susan Moller Okin, *Women in Western Political Thought* (Princeton, NJ:
Princeton University Press, 1979), p. 301: "Women cannot become equal citizens,
workers or human beings—let alone philosopher-queens—until the functionalist
perception of their sex is dead."

body to be more like a man's.

Abortion and the Worldviews

There are not a few authors, feminist and otherwise, who regard the abortion question with its attendant moral and metaphysical issues in the context of worldviews.[40] Indeed, it is particularly germane to discuss the abortion issue in this context since the concept of "worldview" possesses in itself that blend of ideology and religion that, when taken together, we associate with the abortion issue. One worldview is passing, another one is coming on the scene. Our age is one of tension and uncertainty, caught in the middle, as it were, as the two worldviews collide.

The worldview approach to the abortion question may take several forms: sanctity of life vs. quality of life, pro-life vs. pro-choice, religious vs. secular, traditional vs. progressive, and classical vs. historically conscious, the latter quite prominent among certain moralists.[41]

A certain liberal view of what constitutes "progress" animates

---

[40]On the question of worldviews in general, helpful is Ninian Smart, *Worldviews: Crosscultural Explorations of Human Belief* (New York: Charles Scribner's Sons, 1983). Feminist sociologist Kristin Luker is a proponent of the worldviews approach as she discusses the philosophies animating pro-lifers and pro-choicers in the abortion debate. See especially Luker's *Abortion and the Politics of Motherhood* (Berkeley: University of California Press, 1984), Chapter 7, "World Views of the Activists," pp. 158–191.

[41]The worldview thesis has worked its way into discussions of the revision of Roman Catholic moral theology as we see, for instance, in Charles E. Curran, "Absolute Norms and Medical Ethics," in Charles E. Curran (ed.), *Absolutes in Moral Theology?* (Washington, D.C.: Corpus Books, 1968), especially at pp. 125–126. He uses the worldview approach to support his case for a more historically minded moral theology in contrast to a classically oriented one. As his source for the idea, Curran credits an essay by Bernard Lonergan, S. J., "The Transition from a Classicist World-View to Historical-Mindedness," in James Biechler (ed.), *Law for Liberty: The Role of Law in the Church Today* (Baltimore: Helicon Press, 1967), pp. 126–133. John Finnis makes some critical observations regarding Lonergan's thesis in *'Historical Consciousness' and Theological Foundations* (Etienne Gilson Series 14) (Toronto: Pontifical Institute of Mediaeval Studies, 1992).

this sort of approach to the abortion controversy. A variation on this theme of Abortion as Progress finds some authors taking the line that on the question of abortion rights, one cannot turn back the clock.[42] They are countered, in true worldview fashion, by others who judge abortion as a regression, a step backward for humanity.[43]

The question of abortion takes center stage in a worldview approach expressed in this passage from an influential 1970 editorial:

> Since the old ethic has not yet been fully displaced it has been necessary to separate the idea of abortion from the idea of killing, which continues to be socially abhorrent. The result has been a curious avoidance of the scientific fact, which everyone really knows,[44] that human life begins at conception and is continuous whether intra- or extra-uterine until death. The very considerable semantic gymnastics which are required to rationalize abortion as anything but taking a human life would be ludicrous if they were not often put forth under socially impeccable auspices. It is suggested that this schizophrenic sort of subterfuge is necessary because while a new ethic is being accepted the old one has not yet been rejected.[45]

---

[42]One author who employs the *clock* simile in the sense that abortion is a mark of human progress is Judith Jarvis Thomson, *The Realm of Rights* (Cambridge, MA: Harvard University Press, 1990).

[43]On abortion as regress, cf. Sidney Cornelia Callahan, "A Christian Perspective on Feminism," in Sarah Bentley Doely (ed.), *Women's Liberation and the Church: The New Demand for Freedom in the Life of the Christian Church* (New York: Association Press, 1970), p. 46: "The feminist cry for abortion on demand is a throwback to an individualistic freedom-of-my-private-property concept of human life. It's difficult to see this as progress toward communal and co-operative models of life and life-giving growth."

[44]In the course of this work, we will have occasion to comment on the "killing" which takes place in abortion and "which everybody really knows."

[45]"A New Ethic for Medicine and Society," *California Medicine: The Western Journal of Medicine* 113 no. 3 (1970), pp. 67-68. It was cited at congressional hearings by Archbishop John R. Roach and Terence Cardinal Cooke, "Testimony in Support of the Hatch Amendment," in Patricia Beattie Jung and Thomas Shannon (eds.),

Abortion and the Four Feminists

Seen in this light, the four feminist thinkers we will study will be attempting to provide some of the "socially impeccable auspices"—Beauvoir in epistemology, Daly in metaphysics, Gilligan in psychology, and Harrison in theology—under which abortion has been wending its inexorable way into becoming "a linchpin of modern culture."[46] As we read them, we should keep in mind: they are feminists but their thought is not feminism. There are many feminisms.

While it would, no doubt, be an oversimplification to say that feminists who speak positively of Simone de Beauvoir automatically endorse all her views, no understanding of contemporary feminism is possible without a knowledge of Beauvoir.[47] Of the three American women whose thought on abortion we shall investigate, Mary Daly is the one who openly acknowledges her debt to Beauvoir. While Beverly Harrison and Carol Gilligan do not acknowledge any debt to Beauvoir, by the time they are writing, Beauvoir's ideas had become part of the fabric of what was called feminism. Indeed, Beauvoir's culturalist thesis casts a wide net: "No feminist questions the statement that women are manufactured by civilization, not biologically determined."[48]

An Overview

The first four chapters examine the thought of the four feminist theorists on abortion. In chapter 1 we show how Simone de Beauvoir

---

Abortion and Catholicism: The American Debate (New York: Crossroad, 1988), pp. 10–43. The prelates gave their testimony during congressional hearings that took place in 1981. The text appears in *Origins* 11 (1981), pp. 357–372.

[46]On abortion as a "linchpin of modern culture," the phrasing is that of H. Tristram Engelhardt, Jr., "Concluding Remarks," to William Bondeson et al. (eds.), *Abortion and the Status of the Fetus* (Dordrecht: D. Reidel, 1983), p. 334.

[47]While her book is a critique of what she calls "gender feminism" which is attributable in large part to Beauvoir, Christina Hoff Sommers, *Who Stole Feminism? How Women Have Betrayed Women*, nevertheless can acknowledge: "As an equity feminist I find much to admire in de Beauvoir's works" (p. 304, note 4).

[48]Simone de Beauvoir, *All Said and Done* (translated by Patrick O'Brian) (New York: G. P. Putnam's Sons, 1974), p. 455.

provides a feminist epistemology crucial for the abortion idea. Chapter 2 finds Mary Daly adding a dualist metaphysics to Beauvoir's theory of feminist knowledge. In Chapter 3 we examine Carol Gilligan as she provides the support of developmental psychology to the abortion project. Chapter 4 is an examination of the thought of Christian feminist ethicist Beverly Wildung Harrison in her effort to furnish a theological undergirding to support the abortion edifice. The aim of these first four chapters is to show how the essential feminist message, "the right of abortion," of the atheist Beauvoir, becomes "our right to choose" of the Christian Harrison.

"Whither feminism on the abortion issue?" The last two chapters attempt to answer that question. In chapter 5, we discuss pro-choice feminism, a feminism built upon the foundations laid by Beauvoir and her three companions; it is a feminism with abortion as its linchpin. Chapter 6 presents another and a better possibility, namely, that of a pro-life feminism. It is a feminism able to envisage "a new world for women" without abortion as its linchpin and bedrock. The aim of the final chapters is to show that "pro-choice feminism is a dead-end; pro-life feminism *is* feminism."

Transition to Simone de Beauvoir

Though showing a lifelong interest in religion, Simone de Beauvoir was an avowed atheist. As we shall see, it is in Beauvoir's existentialist atheism that we find the roots of the abortion mentality. If abortion and feminism are not inextricably linked, the same cannot be said of abortion and atheism. Speaking of our age's desire to possess total mastery of all aspects of the human condition, John T. Noonan, Jr. observes:

> These profound cultural drives toward absolute freedom and absolute control are comprehensible as expressions of an underlying atheism. If God does not exist, there are no limits—moral, social, or even biological. If God does not exist, it is each individual for himself or herself. If God does not exist, human control must replace divine providence. This underlying atheism is rarely articulated. Even many religious persons share the modern desires, breathing

them in from the surrounding atmosphere, without attending to the atheism which is their source. But when human beings in the name of human liberty assert the power to destroy innocent human life, it is plain that they have put themselves in the place of God as the Lord and Giver of Life. Abortion is atheism put into practice.[49]

As with many feminist issues of the twentieth century, we begin our study with Simone de Beauvoir. Two facts about her we do well to remember: first, much of what passes for contemporary feminism is inconceivable without her, and second, Simone de Beauvoir's atheism antedates her feminism by fifty years.

---

[49]John T. Noonan, Jr., *Abortion in Our Culture* (Washington, D.C.: National Conference of Catholic Bishops' Committee for Pro-Life Activities, 1980), p. 5.

CHAPTER ONE

SIMONE DE BEAUVOIR, 1908-1986

The Epistemology of Abortion

The immorality of women, favorite theme of misogynists, is not to be wondered at; how could they fail to feel an inner mistrust of the presumptuous principles that men publicly proclaim and secretly disregard? They learn to believe no longer in what men say when they exalt woman or when they exalt man; the one thing they are sure of is this rifled and bleeding womb, these shreds of crimson life, this child that is not there. It is at her first abortion that woman begins to "know." For many women the world will never be the same.[1]

The Mother of a Movement

Simone de Beauvoir's *The Second Sex* is the *sine qua non* of contemporary feminist readings.[2] Though she devotes a sizeable section of the book to the topic, Simone de Beauvoir spent her whole life avoiding motherhood.[3] Her attitude toward motherhood never

---

[1]Simone de Beauvoir, *The Second Sex*, pp. 463–464.

[2]Cf. Camille Paglia, *Sex, Art, and American Culture* (New York: Vintage Books, 1992), p. 112: "*The Second Sex* remains for me the supreme work of modern feminism. Most contemporary feminists don't realize to what degree they are merely repeating, amplifying, or qualifying its individual sections and paragraphs."

[3]Despite what Beauvoir said at the Bobigny trial, two recent biographers agree that Simone de Beauvoir herself never had an abortion. According to Deirdre Bair, *Simone de Beauvoir: A Biography* (New York: Summit Books, 1990), p. 547, even though

wavered: she never wanted to become a mother and spent much of her talent first as a writer and then as a feminist urging women either to avoid motherhood completely or else to choose the timing of it very carefully.[4]   Never a biological mother, Simone de Beauvoir has nevertheless become the mother of a movement.[5]

Depending on the classification and the varieties of feminism one wishes to use, Simone de Beauvoir is either at the source of the second feminist wave or else serves as a transition figure between the first and second feminist waves. Wherever she is situated, she is a formidable presence. She is the closest thing to a revered figure by modern feminists, as much for her lifestyle as for her thought, and this despite some recent studies strongly suggesting that she was more a pseudo-bourgeois housewife doing the best she could picking up the pieces after Sartre's love affairs than total mistress of her destiny.[6]

Beauvoir signed the Manifesto of the 343 and then led a pro-abortion march through the streets of Paris, the French feminist told Bair that she never had an abortion. Basing herself on comments made by Beauvoir's sister, Margaret Crossland, *Simone de Beauvoir: The Woman and her Work* (London: Wm. Heinemann, Ltd., 1992), reaches the same conclusion. Beauvoir's deposition at the Bobigny trial is found in Claude Francis and Fernande Gontier, *Les écrits de Simone de Beauvoir: La Vie. L'écriture: Avec en appendice textes inédits ou retrouvés* (Paris: Gallimard, 1979), pp. 510–513.

[4]Yolanda Astarita Patterson, *Simone de Beauvoir and the Demystification of Motherhood* (Ann Arbor: UMI Research Press, 1989), p. 188, points out texts in which Beauvoir spoke of writing as a sort of surrogacy for parenthood.

[5]Despite Beauvoir's inconsistencies and limitations, she *is* our first generation feminist mother. This is the view of Dorothy Kaufmann, "Simone de Beauvoir: Questions of Difference and Generation," *Yale French Studies* no. 72 (1986), p. 131. Cf. Lisa Appignanesi, *Simone de Beauvoir* (Lives of Modern Women Series) (London: Penguin Books, 1988), p. 2. She hints at the irony in Simone de Beauvoir's having no children yet being the mother of a movement.

[6]Cf. John Weightman, "Summing Up Sartre," *New York Review of Books* (August 13, 1984), pp. 42–46.

"La Grande Sartreuse"[7]

It is practically *de rigueur* that a study of Simone de Beauvoir must include her lifelong relationship with Jean-Paul Sartre.[8] While some feminists are uneasy with what they consider Beauvoir's somewhat subservient relationship with Sartre, others take comfort in the view that Sartre's existential philosophy is congenial to feminist aims and demands them as its logical complement. Her devotion to Sartre is complete. In her posthumously published *Letters to Sartre* Beauvoir often speaks of Sartre as "my little absolute."[9] It is probably not coincidental that Simone de Beauvoir, despite the acclaim heaped on her by grateful legions of feminist admirers, accepted the label of "feminist" only in 1973 as Sartre's own health declined.[10]

At the end of *Force of Circumstance*, Simone de Beauvoir treats at some length the oft-raised question: did she owe her success to Sartre? Jean Guitton had said that with another man, Beauvoir may well have become a mystic. The French feminist takes umbrage, seeing in the Catholic critic's comments nothing more than the old ideas of her

---

[7]On the epithets "la grande Sartreuse" and "Notre-Dame de Sartre," see Simone de Beauvoir, *Force of Circumstance*, p. 46: "Not that I was oversensitive; when people called me 'la grande Sartreuse' or 'Notre-Dame de Sartre' I just laughed, but certain looks men gave me left their mark; looks that offered a lewd complicity with the Existentialist, and therefore dissolute, woman, they took me for."

[8]On the success of her relationship with Sartre, see Beauvoir's comments in *Force of Circumstance*, p. 643.

[9]Cf. the two volumes of Simone de Beauvoir, *Lettres à Sartre* (édition presentée, établie et annotée par Sylvia le Bon de Beauvoir) (Paris: Gallimard, 1990), *passim*. A shortened English edition is *Letters to Sartre* (translated and edited by Quintin Hoare) (New York: Arcade, 1992). Cf. the comment made by Elaine Marks, *Simone de Beauvoir: Encounters with Death*, who, after citing a text from *The Prime of Life*, in which Beauvoir declares that Sartre's existence justified the world for her, goes on to add: "What Simone de Beauvoir is in fact saying is God is dead; long live Sartre" (p. 30). According to Toril Moi, *Simone de Beauvoir: The Making of an Intellectual Woman* (Cambridge, MA: Blackwell, 1994), Sartre was God for Beauvoir (p.224).

[10]Alice Schwarzer, *After 'The Second Sex': Conversations With Simone de Beauvoir* (Translated by Marianne Howarth) (New York: Pantheon, 1984), contains the interview, "I Am a Feminist," which appeared in *Le Nouvel Observateur* in 1972.

father,[11] namely, that woman is made by others: "But people in our society really do believe that a woman thinks with her uterus—what low-mindedness, really!"[12] She then goes on to lament the fact that while Sartre earned fame, she reaped only opprobrium.[13]

Simone de Beauvoir and Jean-Paul Sartre began writing on abortion at approximately the same time, and they think along the same lines. Not only was *The Second Sex* written by Beauvoir to follow up on a suggestion made to her by Sartre; what passes for a plot in Sartre's novel *The Age of Reason* revolves around its protagonist's finding the money for his lover's abortion.[14] As we shall see, Simone de Beauvoir's first literary attempts to write about abortion were also by means of fiction.

Beauvoir once remarked of herself and Sartre that freedom was their very substance.[15] If liberty was their substance, then death was their message. This was precisely as it had to be, according to Simone de Beauvoir. In point of fact, as "Notre-Dame de Sartre" read the evidence of women's oppression in her key of existentialism as filtered through Sartre's gaze, violence and killing were regarded as the keys to the whole mystery of woman's secondary status.[16] For those who accept in

---

[11]The role of her father in the shaping of Simone de Beauvoir's perspective toward life is especially prominent in her first autobiographical volume, *Memoirs of a Dutiful Daughter* (New York: Penguin Books, 1963). Her relationship with her father and its importance upon her eventual feminism is emphasized by Francis Jeanson, *Simone de Beauvoir ou l'enterprise de vivre: Suivi de deux entrétiens avec Simone de Beauvoir* (Paris: Éditions du Seuil, 1966), pp. 100ff.

[12]*Force of Circumstance*, p. 644.

[13]Cf. *Force of Circumstance*, pp. 643ff.

[14]According to Joseph McMahon, *Humans Being: The World of Jean-Paul Sartre* (Chicago: University of Chicago Press, 1971), p. 119, in Sartre the desire to abort is the desire to destroy what one cannot possess or dominate.

[15]Cf. Simone de Beauvoir, *The Prime of Life* (translated by Peter Green) (Cleveland: The World Publishing Company, 1962), p. 17: "We had no external limitations, no overriding authority, no imposed pattern of existence. We created our own links with the world, and freedom was the very essence of our existence."

[16]When reading Beauvoir, the reader should be on the lookout for the word "mystery." Beauvoir's rationalism impels her to contest and unravel mysteries wherever she finds them. Hence Yolanda Astarita Patterson can write about "Simone de Beauvoir and the Demystification of Motherhood," *Yale French Studies* no. 72

principle and live out in practice the sexual revolution, abortion is regarded as a routine hazard of sex life. In another sense, especially in the hands of existential philosophy, it was to be nothing less than the harbinger of the entrance of woman into full humanity.

Beauvoir and Ethics

In 1947 Simone de Beauvoir presents an elaboration of existential ethics.[17] Here we find some of the key strands of what will pass for her moral philosophy. In this work she defends atheistic existentialism against the charge of being amoral. On the contrary, says the French existentialist, it is precisely because God does not exist that human actions take on an absolute character. God is able to pardon and compensate for sins, but "if God does not exist, man's faults are inexpiable."[18] She attempts a definition of the sort of humanism she espouses: the moral world is not a world that is given but rather a world as it is *willed* by human beings, precisely as their will expresses its authentic reality. Being moral and being free is the same choice.

Existentialist ethics is an effort to become aware of and then to avoid *mauvaise foi*, bad faith, bad willing, the free choice to let others shape one's destiny, resulting in the anomaly of a free adult human being living in an infantile world. How is it possible? As Descartes observed, children have no choice but to live in this way (*The Ethics of Ambiguity*, p. 35). Women, on the other hand, *do* have a choice, yet they often choose to live in bad faith. That women, free and rational beings, choose freely to live in bad faith is a theme to which Simone de Beauvoir will return in her later works.[19]

Several times in *The Ethics of Ambiguity* Beauvoir discusses three

---

(1986), 87–105.

[17]Simone de Beauvoir, *Pour une morale de l'ambiguité* (nouvelle édition) (Les essais xxvi) (Paris: Gallimard, 1947), translated into English by Bernard Frechtman as *The Ethics of Ambiguity* (New York: Philosophical Library, 1948). A recent attempt to resurrect the philosophical validity of Beauvoir's book is that of Monika Langer, "A Philosophical Retrieval of Simone de Beauvoir's *Pour une morale de l'ambiguité*," *Philosophy Today* 38 1 (Spring 1994), pp. 181–190.

[18]Simone de Beauvoir, *The Ethics of Ambiguity*, p. 16.

[19]See, for example, Beauvoir's comments in *The Second Sex*, p. xxviii.

categories of persons that she will examine in greater detail in *The Second Sex*: the infant, the slave, and the woman. As she nears the end of her treatise on existential ethics, after discovering the complexity of human ethical behavior, Beauvoir tells her readers that ambiguity is not to be confused with absurdity.[20]

Though the terminology is ours and not hers, if we were to question Simone de Beauvoir for a moral methodology, it seems clear that hers would be decidedly teleological. In discussing a question pertaining to violence, for example, she observes that human beings can never judge the good in a given situation *a priori*.[21] As the very title of the work suggests, Beauvoir is also mindful of the difficulty of the subject matter of human ethical action: "What makes the problem more complex is that the freedom of one man almost always concerns that of other individuals" (*The Ethics of Ambiguity*, p. 143).

Is existential ethics open to the charge of individualism? Yes, but then again, opines Beauvoir, so is Christianity, so is Kantianism. Free human beings find their law in freedom (p. 156). The volume ends with a plea for an existential ethics cut to human and earthly standards; her atheism will not permit her to admit that there are any others.

When we slice through the existential rhetoric of *The Ethics of Ambiguity*, Simone de Beauvoir's existential ethics looks remarkably like the ethics of secular humanism.[22] Both are enamored with the perfectible human subject, both pin their hopes on the power of modern technology to bring about a more just, humane society, and both herald the advance of secular civilization despite notable religious obscurantism. The atheism that animates both is by no means the least of their likenesses.[23]

---

[20]Cf. *The Ethics of Ambiguity*, p. 129.

[21]Cf. *The Ethics of Ambiguity*, p. 142. Despite her teleological leanings, Beauvoir will nevertheless aver a few pages later: "Lynching is an absolute evil (p. 146)."

[22]While Monika Langer, "A Philosophical Retrieval of Simone de Beauvoir's *Pour une morale de l'ambiguité*," laments the fact that Beauvoir's book on ethics has been forgotten, I believe it is safer to say that its ideas live on in the works of those feminists who follow the French feminists. Mary Daly will make much of ambiguity, and Carol Gilligan's contextual relativism is another way of expressing the central contentions of Beauvoir's ethics.

[23]Cf. Paul Kurtz, *A Secular Humanist Declaration* (Buffalo: Prometheus, 1981), a

Beauvoir, Atheism, and Religion

Always religious as a young girl, Simone de Beauvoir stopped believing in God when she was fourteen, as she recounts at some length in the first volume of her autobiography. The loss of faith in God was gradual. The foundations of her girlish faith were weakened in an episode that took place with her confessor, Abbé Martin.[24] The example given by her father continued the gradual process of unbelief. Her faith in God finally toppled one evening at Meyrignac. Reading the forbidden Balzac and realizing just how much she loved the world, the precocious fourteen-year-old Simone de Beauvoir became an atheist:

> "I no longer believe in God," I told myself, with no great surprise. . . . For a long time now the concept I had had of Him had been purified and refined, sublimated to the point where He no longer had any countenance divine, any concrete link with the earth or therefore any being. His perfection cancelled out His reality. That is why I felt so little surprise when I became aware of His absence in heaven and in my heart. I was not denying Him in order to rid myself of a troublesome person: on the contrary, I realized that He was playing no further part in my life and so I concluded that he had ceased to exist for me.[25]

We might find it strange, therefore, that despite her atheism, and even if only indirectly, Simone de Beauvoir tells us that her Catholic faith had a large hand in shaping her vision of the world.[26] Her social consciousness, for example, she attributes to her Catholic faith:

---

reprint of an article which appeared in the first issue (Winter 1980) of *Free Inquiry*.

[24]Recounted in *Memoirs of a Dutiful Daughter*, pp. 134–135. Konrad Bieber, *Simone de Beauvoir* (Boston: Twayne, 1979), pp. 25–26, suggests that this episode was the beginning of the end of religion for Beauvoir.

[25]Simone de Beauvoir, *Memoirs of a Dutiful Daughter*, p. 137.

[26]Soon after God died for her, the young Simone de Beauvoir made another discovery: "One afternoon, in Paris, I realized that I was condemned to death. I was alone in the house and I did not attempt to control my despair: I screamed and tore at the red carpet" (*Memoirs of a Dutiful Daughter*, p. 137).

My Catholic upbringing had taught me never to look upon any individual, however lowly, as of no account: everyone had the right to bring to fulfilment what I called their eternal essence. My path was clearly marked: I had to perfect, enrich, and express myself in a work of art that would help others to live.[27]

In a volume which includes several interviews, French critic Francis Jeanson reiterates what Beauvoir has related regarding the great lessons her faith taught. Chief among them is the infinite worth of the individual, women as well as men.[28] Perhaps it is this religious upbringing that haunts Simone de Beauvoir when she approaches the question of abortion.[29]

The Writings of Simone de Beauvoir on Abortion: Two Early Fictional Accounts

Simone de Beauvoir has written extensively: novels, philosophical and literary essays, autobiographical volumes. While her most elaborate statement regarding abortion is found in *The Second Sex*, the topic of abortion is treated in several of her other writings, at times in passing, at other times in hopes of elucidating her treatment in *The Second Sex*. It is in the pages of her fiction that she first comes to grips with the abortion question.

---

[27]*Memoirs of a Dutiful Daughter*, p. 191. On Catholicism's legacy to Simone de Beauvoir, Renée Winegarten, *Simone de Beauvoir: A Critical View* (Oxford: Berg Publishers Limited, 1988) comments: "It was all or nothing, now or never. With a kind of spiritual absolutism preserved from her Catholic childhood, she (Beauvoir) wanted the absolute perfection of the ideal—something to be striven for, no doubt, but scarcely likely to be attained overnight in an imperfect world" (p. 96).

[28]Cf. Francis Jeanson, *Simone de Beauvoir ou l'enterprise de vivre*, pp. 257–258.

[29]Beauvoir's atheism should cause us to be wary when she handles religious topics. According to Ruth Colker, *Abortion and Dialogue: Pro-choice, Pro-life, and American Law* (Bloomington and Indianapolis: Indiana University Press; A Midland Book, 1992), identifying Beauvoir with religious feminists is as misleading as saying that Franklin Delano Roosevelt and George Wallace were both Democrats (p. xiii).

When Things of the Spirit Come First, ca. 1937

Written, as Beauvoir remarked, "a little before I was thirty," but not published until 1979,[30] *When Things of the Spirit Come First* is Beauvoir's taking issue with what she considers the hypocrisy of her bourgeois milieu, including the Catholicism which she blamed for bringing about the death of her best friend, Elizabeth Mabille, affectionately known as Zaza.[31] In this youthful work we find the first mention in the writings of Simone de Beauvoir of the child developing in the womb.[32] In the story "Chantal," we find one of the characters, Monique, facing an unplanned pregnancy. It is she who is speaking to her friend, Andrée, about the father of the child, Serge:

> "I went to bed with him three months ago and I'm pregnant. I don't know what will happen to me."

> Andrée gazed at her friend with horror, though she could not yet quite believe her. It seemed impossible that a mysterious bit of rot should be spreading in that slim, graceful body. . . .

> Andrée shivered. She looked at Monique's familiar face but without being able to overcome an immense disgust. Under the blue silk dress, under her belly's satiny skin there was something shapeless, something living, that grew and swelled with every minute. . . .[33]

---

[30]Simone de Beauvoir, *Quand prime le spirituel* (Paris: Gallimard, 1979), p. vii. Beauvoir acknowledges the youthful character of the work, yet decides it is valuable enough to be published forty years after it was written. There is an English translation by Patrick O'Brian, *When Things of the Spirit Come First* (New York: Pantheon, 1982).

[31]Was it Catholicism or a Jansenist substitute that passed for Catholicism in the milieu of the Beauvoir family? Hilda Graef, *Modern Gloom and Christian Hope* (Chicago: Regnery, 1959), and A. M. Henry, O.P., *Simone de Beauvoir ou l'échec d'une chrétienté* (Paris: Arthème Fayard, 1961), agree on the infantile and rationalistic religion known to the Beauvoirs.

[32]Cf. *When Things of the Spirit Come First*, pp. 85–89.

[33]*When Things of the Spirit Come First*, pp. 85–86.

The two friends decide to go to their teacher, Plattard,[34] in hopes of coming up with a way out of the embarrassing situation. Andrée reassures Monique of their teacher's help:

> "Let me tell her; she'll understand," said Andrée, gently stroking Monique's hot, feverish hand. "She has no prejudices. She will be able to advise us—tell us about something you can take, the address of a midwife. They say it's easy: all you have to know is what to do."[35]

Approaching Plattard on behalf of her friend, Andrée tells her of the disaster that has befallen Monique. Believing initially that Monique is in fact Serge's mistress, Plattard agrees and asks Andrée: "'What will her parents say? There will be the most appalling scandal.'" Beauvoir continues the narrative:

> The trouble and the look of reprobation that Andrée saw in Plattard's eye froze her heart; in a hesitant voice she said, "But isn't there a way of not having babies? Don't you know any? Or people that could tell us?"
>
> Plattard looked at her with a kind of horror. "God, what filth!" she said in a deeply shocked voice. "To think that such an idea can have come into Monique's head, and into yours, Andrée. It's unbelievable."
>
> Andrée went white. . . . "But why?" she cried passionately. "Why is it wicked? Monique can't have her whole life ruined because of this nonsense."
>
> Plattard's features grew sharp. "Who has been influencing you? Have you no moral sense at all? It's monstrous!"[36]

---

[34]"Plattard" is the name which Andrée uses for the "Chantal" of the story. Elizabeth Fallaize, *The Novels of Simone de Beauvoir* (New York: Routledge, 1988), is helpful to understand the shifts that take place in this youthful work.

[35]*When Things of the Spirit Come First*, p. 86. For a real-life parallel, see the episode recounted by Beauvoir in *Force of Circumstance*, p. 191.

[36]*When Things of the Spirit Come First*, p. 88.

Much of Simone de Beauvoir's subsequent writing is an attempt to exonerate Andrée and silence what Beauvoir considers the false moralizing and hypocrisy of Plattard who, in Beauvoir's eyes, is guilty of bad faith. These themes of hypocrisy and bad faith recur in Beauvoir's other treatments of abortion, most notably in *The Second Sex*.

The Blood of Others

Another fictional treatment of abortion follows, an abortion undergone by the heroine, Hélène Bertrand, who dies at the end of *The Blood of Others*, not of the abortion but while fighting in the French Resistance in World War II.[37] She is perhaps the most heroic female protagonist in all of Beauvoir's writings.[38] Ironically, her death is practically an act of self-sacrifice on behalf of the male protagonist, Jean Blomart.[39]

The description of the abortion scene has some parallels to her earlier treatment. In both instances, the abortion is sought because there is no true love between the man and the woman. (In fact, Blomart is not even the father of Hélène's child.) The language Beauvoir uses is also similar, especially that of refusing to acknowledge any sort of human standing to what Beauvoir calls "that thing in the womb." It is Jean Blomart who is doing the narrating:

> She [Hélène] stood outside my room with a timid expression that I had not seen before; she carried a big parcel under her arm. My last hope faded: Yvonne had not lied, it was no jest. Under Hélène's blue dress, beneath her childish skin, was that thing which she fed

---

[37]Simone de Beauvoir, *Le sang des autres* (Paris: Gallimard, 1945). It has been translated into English as *The Blood of Others* (translated by Roger Senhouse and Yvonne Moyse) (New York: Pantheon, 1948).

[38]See Yolanda Astarita Patterson, *Simone de Beauvoir and the Demystification of Motherhood*, p. 90, who takes note of the favorable picture Beauvoir paints of Hélène; Jean Leighton, *Simone de Beauvoir on Woman* (Foreword by Henri Peyre) (Rutherford, NJ: Fairleigh Dickinson University Press, 1975), p. 131, comments that Hélène is the only character in the novel to engage in heroic masculine action.

[39]Elizabeth Fallaize, *The Novels of Simone de Beauvoir*, pp. 44–66, analyzing *The Blood of Others*, p. 63, makes this observation.

with her blood.[40]

And again:

> But in a room there was Hélène with that thing in her
> womb. . . . Her teeth were chattering violently and her
> hands were clutching the sheet. "Do I disgust you?"
> "My poor child, what do you take me for?" "But it's
> disgusting," she said brokenly. A tear rolled down her
> cheek.[41]

Beauvoir paints a bleak and somewhat contrived picture in
detailing the abortion episode. Nine references to *blood* and *red* occur in
the five pages of the abortion scene. There is talk of disgust, things
feeding on blood, vague odors filling the room, a practically blind old
abortionist, unsanitary conditions, and guilt on the part of both
protagonists.[42]

Blomart regards the pregnancy experience and the abortion
which Hélène will shortly undergo as her coming of age:

> How young she was! She liked chocolate and bicycles
> and she went forward into life with the boldness of a
> child. And now she lay there, in the midst of her red
> woman's blood, and her youth and her gaiety ebbed
> from her body with an obscene gurgling (*The Blood of
> Others*, p. 118).

Hélène feels relief after the abortion: "'It's all over,' she said. 'I
can't believe it. I feel so well!'" There follows an exchange on freedom
and choice. Hélène tells Blomart:

> "I'm not a little dog. . . . You have said to me so often
> that you respect other people's liberty. And you made
> decisions for me and treat me like a thing" (p. 120).

---

[40]Simone de Beauvoir, *The Blood of Others*, p. 113.

[41]*The Blood of Others*, p. 114. Catherine Savage Brosman, *Simone de Beauvoir Revisited*
(Boston: Twayne Publishers, 1991), p. 60, speaks of the "metaphysical disgust"
permeating the abortion scene.

[42]Cf. *The Blood of Others*, pp. 118–119.

Blomart replies: "I didn't want you to be unhappy."

Hélène answers:

> "And if I prefer to be unhappy? It's for me to choose."
> She leaned her cheek against my hand. "I have chosen."
> She repeats once again: "It's for me to choose."[43]

Simone de Beauvoir's first attempts to deal with the abortion issue are remarkably similar: in fictional narratives, Beauvoir describes situations in which there is no love between the man and the woman who conceive the child; there is disgust at the situation, dehumanizing language is utilized to refer to the child in the womb, and in both accounts we discover a suffused, smoldering rage at the human condition. *When Things of the Spirit Come First* points out the hypocrisy of bourgeois morality on abortion; *The Blood of Others* uses the abortion decision to make a point about woman's power to choose. The stage is set for Beauvoir's existential musings in *The Second Sex*.

Abortion in *The Second Sex*

A seminal work to some, the bible of modern feminism to others,[44] *The Second Sex* stands as the source of much of contemporary

---

[43] *The Blood of Others*, p. 120. In a sense, Beauvoir is giving a fictional and individualistic account of a popular feminist pro-choice chant: "Our bodies, our lives, our right to decide." In an attempt to establish a right to abortion, American feminist Gloria Steinem, "A Basic Human Right," *Ms.* 18 (July/August 1989), begins with the words: "The most crucial question of democracy, feminism, and simple self-respect is not: *What* gets decided? That comes second. The first question is: *Who* decides?" (p. 39). That Steinem is being faithful to Beauvoir we see in the the final words of Beauvoir's first novel, *L'Invitée* (Paris: Gallimard, 1943), appearing in English translation as *She Came to Stay* (translated by Yvonne Moyse and Roger Senhouse) (Glasgow: Fontana/Collins, 1975), pp. 408–409: "Alone. She had acted alone: as alone as in death. One day Pierre would know. . . . But even his cognizance of this deed would be merely external. No one could condemn or absolve her. Her act was her very own. 'It is I who will it.' It was her own will which was being acccomplished, now nothing at all separated her from herself. She had at last made a choice. She had chosen herself."

[44] In the view of Alice Schwarzer, *After 'The Second Sex': Interviews With Simone de Beauvoir*, p. 23: "*The Second Sex*, her (Beauvoir's) physiological, psychological,

feminist ideology relating to abortion and abortion rights.[45] It was
written by Simone de Beauvoir as a follow-up to a suggestion made by
Jean-Paul Sartre.[46] Beauvoir wrote *The Second Sex* while financially
totally dependent on Sartre.[47] Ironically, it is not in his own works but
in one of Simone de Beauvoir's that Sartre finally produces a book that
offers the possibility of changing the world.[48] A change in the way some
human beings come to view human abortion is a major piece in this
drama.

    "One is not born, but rather becomes, a woman."[49] With these
words Simone de Beauvoir opens up book two of *The Second Sex*, the
most controversial section of the volume. Beauvoir herself remarked
that while book one earned critical acclaim, book two netted her insults

---

economic and historical study of the internal and external reality of women in a
male-dominated world, is a pioneering work without parallel. Even today,
thirty-three years after it was first published, it is still the most exhaustive and
far-reaching theoretical work on the new feminism!"

[45]Cf. L. W. Sumner, *Abortion and Moral Theory* (Princeton: Princeton University
Press, 1981), pp. 49–50.

[46]The standard reading of the philosophical relationship holding between Sartre and
Beauvoir is that she was dependent upon him. Several authors try to show that Sartre
also benefitted from his philosophical relationship with Beauvoir; in fact, some of his
thought is dependent on hers. See the articles by Margaret A. Simons, "Beauvoir and
Sartre: the Philosophical Relationship," *Yale French Studies* no. 72 (1986), pp. 165–179,
and Linda Singer, "Interpretation and Retrieval: Rereading Beauvoir," *Women's
Studies International Forum* 8 no. 3 (1985), pp. 231–238.

[47]In interviews given to Alice Schwarzer, *After 'The Second Sex,'* p. 56, Beauvoir is
quite explicit that she was living off Sartre's money as she wrote *The Second Sex*.
Suzanne Lilar (avec la collaboration du Professeur Gilbert-Dreyfus), *Le malentendu
du 'deuxième sexe'* (Paris: Presses universitaires de France, 1969), pp. 31–32, emphasizes
Sartre's influence upon Beauvoir in writing *The Second Sex*. The unequal roles of men
and women in procreation are mirrored in this little drama: Sartre gives Beauvoir the
idea for the writing of a treatise on woman's condition; she labors two years to bring
it to the light of day. Cf. Beauvoir's comment in *Force of Circumstance*, p. 644: "It has
been said by some people that Sartre writes my books."

[48]On Beauvoir's influence being greater than that of Sartre, see Jacques J. Zéphir, *Le
néo-feminisme de Simone de Beauvoir: trente ans après 'Le deuxième sexe': Un
post-scriptum* (Paris: Denöel/Gonthier, 1982), p. 220.

[49]Simone de Beauvoir, *The Second Sex*, p. 249. Alice Schwarzer, *After 'The Second Sex,'*
p. 77, contends that this is Simone de Beauvoir's most famous statement.

and at times derision: "Unsatisfied, frigid, priapic, nymphomaniac, lesbian, a hundred times aborted, I was everything, even an unmarried mother."[50] One reason for this is not surprising: the French existentialist begins her chapter on "Motherhood" with a long section on abortion.

In *The Second Sex* Hegel and Sartre are among Beauvoir's philosophical mentors, providing her with several key notions.[51] One of them is the notion of *otherness* as a fundamental category of human thought;[52] another is the fundamental hostility of each consciousness to every other consciousness.[53] How she uses these notions in the context of mother, child, and abortion is Beauvoir's own legacy.

To prepare us to understand Simone de Beauvoir's treatment of abortion in *The Second Sex*, there are three key themes—all bound up with the existential philosophy she espouses[54]—that will be helpful to bear in mind:

1. the problematic nature of the human body in general and of the

---

[50]*Force of Circumstance*, p. 187.

[51]In addition to Hegel and Sartre, Nietzsche and the Marquis de Sade also exert notable influence upon Beauvoir. For more on Nietzsche in Beauvoir, see Donald L. Hatcher, *Understanding 'the Second Sex'* (American University Studies, Series V Philosophy, Vol. 8) (New York: Peter Lang, 1984). Cf. the remarks regarding Beauvoir and Nietzsche made by Mary Midgely and Judith Hughes, *Women's Choices: Philosophical Problems Facing Feminism* (New York: St. Martin's Press, 1983), p. 215.

[52]Cf. *The Second Sex*, pp. xviff. Carol Ascher, "On 'Clearing the Air': My Letter to Simone de Beauvoir," in Carol Ascher, Louise DeSalvo, and Sara Ruddick (eds.), *Between Women: Biographers, Novelists, Critics, Teachers and Artists Write About Their Work on Women* (Boston: Beacon Press, 1984), pp. 97–99, notes the importance of the concept of the *other* to understand Simone de Beauvoir's work in general. Ascher sees in Sartre's and Beauvoir's concept of the *other* the conflation of jealousy and hatred into a worldview.

[53]Woman is oppressed, according to Beauvoir, by what she calls in Hegelian terms "the imperialism of the human consciousness" (*The Second Sex*, p. 52). It is perhaps worth noting that *She Came to Stay*, Simone de Beauvoir's first novel, has as its epigraph Hegel's comment: "Each consciousness pursues the death of the other." The fundamental hostility of human beings toward each other remains constant in Beauvoir's works all her life long. In a sense, her whole literary output as well as her life can be regarded as a long, running commentary upon *She Came to Stay*'s epigraph.

[54]It is helpful to keep in mind that Simone de Beauvoir was an existentialist much longer than she was a feminist.

female body in particular;
2. the lack of any maternal instinct; and
3. the passive nature of motherhood.

The Body As Problematic

If the body and dualism are problems for Sartre's existentialism in general, these will also prove troubling in Simone de Beauvoir's version of Sartre's existential philosophy. While she speaks in *The Second Sex* of rejecting Cartesianism and its accompanying mind/body split, not all believe she succeeded.[55] Contemporary feminist thinking has wrestled with few questions for so long and with such intensity as it has with the question of the female body.[56]

Simone de Beauvoir takes a rather disparaging view of the female body.[57] Her critics as well as her supporters attest to this feature in Beauvoir's thought.[58] Some texts from *The Second Sex* illustrate her attitude:

The female is the victim of the species (p. 18).

The mammary glands, developing at puberty, play no role in women's individual economy: they can be

---

[55] According to Mary O'Brien, *The Politics of Reproduction* (Boston: Routledge and Kegan Paul, 1981), p. 67, dualism may be a specifically masculine experience which Beauvoir accepted uncritically.

[56] Cf. Adrienne Rich, *Of Woman Born* (New York: Bantam, 1977), p. 276, who gives the classic expression of this dis/ease with the female body: "I know no woman. . . for whom her body is not a fundamental problem."

[57] Cf. *Memoirs of a Dutiful Daughter*, p. 289.

[58] Taking Beauvoir to task for her denigration of the female body is Jean Bethke Elshtain, *Public Man, Private Woman: Women in Social and Political Thought*, pp. 306–310. An admirer of Beauvoir who is also aware of the validity of Elshtain's critique (at least to a certain extent) is Rosemarie Tong, *Feminist Thought: A Comprehensive Introduction*, pp. 211ff. According to Iris Marion Young, *Throwing Like a Girl and Other Essays in Feminist Philosophy and Social Theory* (Bloomington: Indiana University Press, 1990), p. 143: "By largely ignoring the situatedness of the woman's actual bodily movement and orientation to its surroundings and its world, Beauvoir tends to create the impression that it is woman's anatomy and physiology *as such* that at least in part determine her unfree status."

excised at any time of life (p. 24).

Woman, like man, *is* her body; but her body is something other than herself.[59]

Gestation is a fatiguing task of no individual benefit to the woman but on the contrary demanding heavy sacrifices. It is often associated in the first months with loss of appetite and vomiting, which are not observed in any female domesticated animal and which signalize the revolt of the organism against the invading species (*The Second Sex*, p. 26).

Her harsh perspective upon the female body helps us at least begin to approach Beauvoir's cryptic comment: "Feminine sex desire is the soft throbbing of a mollusk."[60]

Regarding women as childbearers, Simone de Beauvoir has this to say:

The conflict between species and individual, which sometimes assumes dramatic force at childbirth, endows the feminine body with a disturbing frailty. It has been well said that women "have infirmity in the abdomen." They have within them a hostile element—it is the species gnawing at their vitals" (p. 27).

With all the respect thrown around it by society, the function of gestation still inspires a spontaneous feeling

---

[59] *The Second Sex*, p. 26: author's emphasis. Beauvoir is not infrequently cited as espousing a masculine ideal. See for example Catriona Mackenzie, "Simone de Beauvoir: Philosophy and/or the Female Body," in Carole Pateman and Elizabeth Gross (eds.), *Feminist Challenges: Social and Political Theory* (The Northeastern Series in Feminist Theory) (Boston: Northeastern University Press, 1986), pp. 144–156. In the opinion of Jean Leighton, *Simone de Beauvoir on Woman*, *The Second Sex* seems to have been written by a misogynist.

[60] Simone de Beauvoir, *The Second Sex*, p. 362. There are sections of Jean-Paul Sartre's *L'être et le néant: Essai d'ontologie phénoménologique* (Bibliothèque des idées) (Paris: Gallimard, 1943), and translated as *Being and Nothingness*, which treat the viscous, the slimy, and the disgusting, linking them to the female body in general. Beauvoir is his faithful follower here.

of revulsion (p. 136).

In the mother-to-be the antithesis of subject and object
ceases to exist; she and the child with which she is
swollen make up together an equivocal pair
overwhelmed by life. Ensnared by nature, the pregnant
woman is plant and animal, a stockpile of colloids, an
incubator, an egg; she scares children proud of their
young, straight bodies and makes young people titter
contemptuously because she is a human being, a
conscious and free individual, who has become life's
passive instrument (p. 467).

Women who delight in being pregnant are characterized in this fashion:

Such women are not so much mothers as fertile
organisms, like fowls with high egg-production. And
they seek eagerly to sacrifice their liberty of action to
the functioning of their flesh: it seems to them that
their existence is tranquilly justified in the passive
fecundity of their bodies.[61]

Here is Beauvoir describing pregnancy:

She knows that her body is destined to transcend itself;
day after day a growth arising from her flesh but
foreign to it is going to enlarge within her; she is the
prey of the species, which imposes its mysterious laws
upon her, and as a rule this subjection to strange outer
forces frightens her, her fright being manifested in
morning sickness and nausea (p. 469).

The mother and the unborn child, the two major protagonists
in the drama of pregnancy, are described by Beauvoir in similar fashion:
both are parasites.[62]

It is not only the female body that Simone de Beauvoir distrusts.

-----

[61]*The Second Sex*, p. 467. Jean Bethke Elshtain, *Public Man, Private Woman*, p. 309, is
critical of Beauvoir for using what Elshtain calls "silencing terms."

[62]On the *woman* as parasite, see *The Second Sex*, p. 454, p. 639, and again on p. 682.
Regarding the *fetus* as parasite, see p. 466.

Human sexuality is suspect in her existentialist phenomenological analysis. Heterosexuality itself is problematic: "Furthermore, however deferential and polite the man may be, the first penetration is always a violation."[63]

The Lack of Maternal Instinct

The anti-nature views of existential philosophy are another legacy of Sartre to Beauvoir, a legacy of that anti-essentialism encapsulated in the formula: "Existence precedes essence." In the existentialist view of Sartre and Beauvoir, talk of nature brings in the possibility that freedom might be in some way circumscribed. If, as Beauvoir noted, freedom was their very essence, this cannot be allowed. Hence, we find the reason for the attack on nature. Beauvoir's lifelong criticism of what she considers the myth of the eternal feminine goes hand-in-hand with the totally cultural character of motherhood.[64]

Years after writing *The Second Sex*, Beauvoir comments upon her many attempts to demythologize maternalism:

> I think that by changing the concept of motherhood, by changing the idea of maternal instinct, of the feminine vocation, society will change completely. Because it is through this idea of feminine vocation that women are enslaved.[65]

---

[63]*The Second Sex*, p. 359. With a view that basically comes down to asserting that all heterosexuality is rape, American feminists Catherine MacKinnon, *Feminism Unmodified: Discourses on Life and Love* (Cambridge, MA: Harvard University Press, 1987), and Andrea Dworkin, *Intercourse* (New York: Free Press, 1987), build upon and eventually outdo Beauvoir on this point. In fairness to Beauvoir, she did attempt to move away from her rather extreme position. See her comments in *All Said and Done*, p. 458.

[64]Beauvoir's battle against the myth of the eternal feminine reaches its apogee in Part Three of *The Second Sex* as she discusses the myths surrounding woman. See pp. 129ff. Feminist theologian Rosemary Radford Ruether, *New Woman, New Earth: Sexist Ideologies and Human Liberation* (New York: Seabury Press/Crossroad Book, 1975), follows Beauvoir faithfully regarding the eternal woman myth.

[65]Text cited in Yolanda Astarita Patterson, *Simone de Beauvoir and the Demystification of Motherhood*, p. 308. Following Beauvoir's lead regarding the need to desacralize the maternal function are Margaret Farley, "Feminist Theology and Bioethics," in Earl

Coupling the problematic nature of the female body with the freedom that existentialism regards as the essence of the individual leads Beauvoir to conclude that there is no such thing as maternal instinct. The culturalist interpretation at the heart of Beauvoir's analysis of the feminine condition is summed up well in her well-known phrase: "One is not born, but rather becomes, a woman."

If everything about humanity is cultural and nothing natural, Beauvoir reasons, then and only then can human beings do something about it.[66] If the relationship between the sexes is allowed any sort of natural standing, changes in the *status quo* become harder to bring about;[67] hence, the postulate of *culturalism* that lies at the heart of Simone de Beauvoir's vision.[68] Supposedly natural instincts such as

---

E. Shelp (ed.), *Theology and Bioethics: Exploring the Foundations and Frontiers* ("Philosophy and Medicine, no. 20) (Dordrecht: D. Reidel, 1985), pp. 163–183, especially p. 178, and Beverly Wildung Harrison, *Our Right to Choose* (Boston, Beacon Press, 1983). *Desacralizing* is a much less formidable task for an atheist like Simone de Beauvoir, of course, than it would be for believers such as Farley and Harrison.

[66]Cf. Donald DeMarco, "Men and Women, Their Difference and Its Importance," *Thought* 56 no. 223 (1981), pp. 449-462.

[67]I have always been intrigued by a remark made by Evelyne Sullerot, (ed.), *Le fait féminin* (Paris: Fayard, 1978), to the effect that, given the possibilities of modern science, it is easier to change the facts of *nature* than those of *culture* (p. 23).

[68]Elisabeth Badinter carries the torch of her countrywoman's thoroughgoing culturalism in two works: *L'amour en plus: histoire de l'amour maternel: XVIIe–XXe siècle* (Paris: Flammarion, 1980), and *L'un est l'autre: des relations entre hommes et femmes* (Paris: Éditions Odile Jacob, 1986). Among the authors who note the importance of Beauvoir's text as a key to understanding contemporary feminism are Ruth Bleier, *Science and Gender: A Critique of Biology and Its Theories on Women* (The Athene Series) (New York: Pergamon Press, 1984), and Ginette Castro, *American Feminism: A Contemporary History* (Feminist Crosscurrents Series), (Translated by Elizabeth Loverde-Bagwell) (New York: New York University Press, 1990); Jacques Ehrmann, "Simone de Beauvoir and the Related Destinies of Woman and Intellectual," *Yale French Studies*, no. 27 (1961), pp. 26–32; Sara Ruddick, *Maternal Thinking: Toward a Politics of Peace* (New York: Ballantine Books, 1989); Beatrice Slama, "Simone de Beauvoir: Feminine Sexuality and Liberation," in Elaine Marks (ed.), *Critical Essays on Simone de Beauvoir*, pp. 218–234; Evélyne Sullerot (ed.), *Le fait féminin*; Odette Thibault, *Débout les femmes* (Collection: L'Essentiel) (Lyon: Chronique sociale, 1980); and Anne Whitmarsh, *Simone de Beauvoir and the Limits of Commitment* (Cambridge: Cambridge University Press, 1981). Feminists are not

motherhood have to be combatted, and they are.[69]

After citing several examples, Simone de Beauvoir comments: "These examples all show that no maternal 'instinct' exists: the word hardly applies, in any case, to the human species" (*The Second Sex*, p. 482). " As she nears the end of her work, Beauvoir reiterates:

> There is one feminine function that it is actually impossible to perform in complete liberty. It is maternity. . . . She frequently finds herself responsible for an unwanted child that can ruin her professional life. . . . It must be said in addition that in spite of convenient day nurseries and kindergartens, having a child is enough to paralize a woman's activity entirely. [70]

Despite her total theoretical culturalism, on occasion Beauvoir does show herself aware of the power of nature. At times this philosopher of freedom seems fearful that women will use this freedom in unenlightened ways, ways that almost seem *natural*. In 1975 Betty Friedan interviewed Simone de Beauvoir. In the course of that exchange of views, Beauvoir states flatly that women should not receive money for housework:

> Women should not have that choice, precisely because if there is such a choice, too many women will make

---

alone in seeing the importance of Beauvoir's culturalist credo. See also Piersandro Vanzan, S.I., "Il femminismo contemporaneo: crisi, rilancio e prospettive," *La Civiltà Cattolica* 134, v. II, no. 3187 (7 maggio 1983), p. 263. He regards Beauvoir's sentence as the *key* culturalist text of contemporary feminism, an observation made a quarter of a century earlier by Lucius F. Cervantes, S. J., *And God Made Man and Woman: A Factual Discussion of Sex Differences* (Chicago: Regnery, 1959).

[69]Note the subtitle of Judith Wilt's book, *Abortion, Choice, and Contemporary Fiction* (Chicago: University of Chicago Press, 1990): "*The Armageddon of Maternal Instinct.*" Wilt explains what she means by the term and concludes: "These are the last days, not of maternity, but of maternity as instinct" (p. 34).

[70]Simone de Beauvoir, *The Second Sex*, p. 655. Yolanda Astarita Patterson, a mother herself, chides Beauvoir on this point (*Simone de Beauvoir and the Demystification of Motherhood*, p. 310).

that one. It is a way of forcing women in a certain direction.[71]

The exchange with Friedan helps explain this comment which we find in *The Second Sex*:

What is extremely demoralizing for the woman who aims at self-sufficiency is the existence of other women of like social status, having at the start the same situation and the same opportunities, who live as parasites. A man may feel resentment toward the privileged, but he has solidarity with his class; on the whole, those who begin with equal chances reach about the same level in life. Whereas women of like situation may, through man's mediation, come to have very different fortunes. A comfortably married or supported friend is a temptation in the way of one who is intending to make her own success; she feels she is arbitrarily condemning herself to take the most difficult roads; at each obstacle she wonders whether it might not be better to take a different route.[72]

The Passivity of Mothering

Having children, according to Simone de Beauvoir's existentialist analysis, is a passive, not a creative, task:

But in any case giving birth and suckling are *activities*, they are natural functions; no project is involved; and

---

[71]Beauvoir's comments appear in an interview with Betty Friedan, "Sex, Society and the Female Dilemma," *Saturday Review* 2 19 (June 14, 1975), p. 18. Yolanda Astarita Patterson, *Simone de Beauvoir and the Demystification of Motherhood*, p. 306, understates when she observes that the dialogue did not translate well.

[72]*The Second Sex*, pp. 657–658. Is Beauvoir saying in effect: a mother with children is a naturalist affront to a culturalist interpretation of reality? Could her advocacy of abortion have anything to do with the texts we have just read? Maggie Gallagher, *Enemies of Eros: How the Sexual Revolution Is Killing Family, Marriage, and Sex and What We Can Do About It* (Chicago: Bonus Books, 1989), p. 146, raises this and other pertinent questions regarding Beauvoir's purposes in writing this text.

that is why woman found in them no reason for a lofty affirmation of her existence—she submitted passively to her biological fate. [73]

Men are the true creators in Simone de Beauvoir's view. This creativity is accomplished in works of transcendence:

> But man assures the repetition of life while transcending Life through Existence; by this transcendence he creates values that deprive pure repetition of all value (p. 59).

Woman also wants a share in transcendence, yet as Beauvoir views the matter:

> Her misfortune is to have been biologically destined for the repetition of Life, when even in her own view Life does not carry within itself its reasons for being, reasons that are more important than the life itself.[74]

Simone de Beauvoir hates repetition. This theme is constantly repeated in the pages of *The Second Sex*. Housework, for example, is likened to the tortures of Sisyphus (p. 425). In her existentialist analysis, bringing children into the world is nothing more than the mere repetition of life.[75] No project is involved. Women can have children without even willing it.[76] Beauvoir's elitism shows here: for while it may

---

[73]*The Second Sex*, p. 57. Virginia Held, "Birth and Death," *Ethics* 99 no. 2 (1989), pp. 362–388, criticizes Beauvoir for contending that birth is a mere natural process.

[74]*The Second Sex*, p. 59. Catriona Mackenzie, "Simone de Beauvoir: Philosophy and/or the Female Body," pp. 144–156, says that Beauvoir in this passage denies women's reproductive powers in order to align herself with masculinism as the ideal of subjectivity. It is not the first charge of masculinism to be made against her. Beauvoir herself states that enlightened women do indeed have "masculine pretensions"; see, for example, *The Second Sex*, p. 676: "The 'modern' woman accepts masculine values."

[75]Virginia Held, "Birth and Death," takes Beauvoir and Hannah Arendt to task for seeing in reproduction nothing more than a mere repetition of life.

[76]Linda Bird Francke, *The Ambivalence of Abortion* (New York: Laurel Book, 1982), quotes a remark of one her interviewees who is speaking in reference to fetal life: "Hell, you can make one of those things every month" (p. 147).

be true that any woman can have children, only superior ones can write books.[77]

We can detect this attitude quite clearly in an incident that took place between Beauvoir and her closest friend, Zaza, Elizabeth Mabille:

> Zaza shocked me when she declared, in a provocative tone of voice: "Bringing nine children into the world as Mama has done is just as good as writing books." I couldn't see any common denominator between these two modes of existence. To have children, who in their turn would have more children, was simply to go on playing the same old tune *ad infinitum*; the scholar, the artist, the writer, and the thinker created other worlds, all sweetness and light, in which everything had purpose.[78]

If we keep in mind the distaste Simone de Beauvoir felt with repetition and couple it with her staunch atheism, a text such as the following becomes more clear: "In a sense the mystery of the Incarnation repeats itself in each mother; every child born *is* a god who *is* made man" (*The Second Sex*, p. 468).

Beauvoir's Case for Abortion in *The Second Sex*

Once granted these premises, Beauvoir's case for abortion follows relentlessly. Abortion is culture taking aim at the blind forces of nature. Since the myth of a maternal instinct is likewise a cultural creation,[79] abortion is a way of taking charge, of taking power into one's

---

[77]On Beauvoir's elitism, see especially *The Second Sex*, p. 671. Cf. Maggie Gallagher, *Enemies of Eros*, pp. 146–147. She sees the elitism of feminism leading to the creation of the *Überwench*, trampling on the bodies and dreams of the majority of women who marry, have children, and try to find happiness in maternal pursuits. Gallagher believes that Beauvoir regarded such women with disdain.

[78]Beauvoir recounts the episode in *Memoirs of a Dutiful Daughter*, pp. 140–141.

[79]Simone de Beauvoir comments toward the end of *The Second Sex*: "'Women will always be women,' say the skeptics. Other seers prophesy that in casting off their femininity they will not succeed in changing themselves into men and will become monsters. This would be to admit that the woman of today is a creation of nature; *it must be repeated once more that in human society nothing is natural and that woman,*

own hands. It is no longer being passive. Abortion is, rather, an active shaping of one's own destiny by one's own free choice.

In the pages of *The Second Sex* many of the standard pro-abortion arguments used by feminists and other abortion rights advocates begin to take shape. In fact, L. W. Sumner regards Simone de Beauvoir's pro-abortion arguments in *The Second Sex* as the paradigm of the standard feminist approaches to the topic.[80] In a variation on Sumner we list the following:

1. The right to an abortion is based on reproductive freedom, a notion that includes birth control as well as abortion. Technology in the area of sexuality is the key to women's liberation, according to Simone de Beauvoir.

2. Religion is the chief moral obstacle to abortion reform.

3. Anti-abortion laws are the work of patriarchal institutions. Here the patriarchal family serves as Simone de Beauvoir's *bête noire*.[81]

4. Social reasons for abortion are likewise adumbrated by the French feminist. For example, as long as maternity is enforced, as long as it is not a freely chosen existential project, for so long will unwanted children be brought into a cold and inhospitable world.[82]

The Total Package of Reproductive Freedom

Regarding the first point, Simone de Beauvoir to all intents and purposes buys into the sexual revolution's promise of sex without consequences. Here the breaking of the link between the procreative and the unitive aspects of human sexuality is obvious. Speaking of woman, Simone de Beauvoir comments: "Her most difficult problems are going to be posed in the field of sex" (*The Second Sex*, p. 644.) Why? In the

---

like much else, is a product elaborated by civilization" (p. 682: my emphasis).

[80] L. W. Sumner, *Abortion and Moral Theory*, pp. 49–50.

[81] Cf. *The Second Sex*, p. 103: "All forms of socialism, wresting woman away from the family, favor her liberation."

[82] Cf. *The Second Sex*, p. 457. Abortion as a class crime likewise finds its way into Beauvoir's analysis. The rich can afford abortions. The poor cannot. The legal system must be changed to help the poor (p. 459).

simplest terms, sex is not as dangerous for man as it is for woman.

> In order to be a complete individual, on an equality
> with man, woman must have access to the masculine
> world as does the male to the female world, she must
> have access to the *other*; but the demands of the *other*
> are not symmetrical in the two symmetrical cases.[83]

Male sexuality as the norm is Simone de Beauvoir's ideal here
as well.[84] Woman, like man, has a right to recreational sex. Woman's
eroticism also has its needs.[85]

For those who choose to express themselves in a *heterosexual*
manner, given Simone de Beauvoir's view of sex as primarily for
pleasure, birth control is an obviously important element. Indeed,
reading Beauvoir one gets the impression that the major danger the
author of *The Second Sex* sees in heterosexuality for women is precisely
to be found in its procreative element.[86]

Same-sex relations are perfectly acceptable choices in Beauvoir's
culturalist universe. Writing in her chapter, "The Lesbian," Beauvoir
asserts: "A woman who wishes to enjoy her femininity in feminine arms
can also know the pride of obeying no master" (*The Second Sex*, p. 394).
At the end of the chapter, she adds:

> The truth is that homosexuality is no more a

---

[83] *The Second Sex*, p. 644. The lack of symmetry is one way that Beauvoir asks the
question: Is nature misogynist?

[84] American sociologist Alice Rossi, "A Biosocial Perspective on Parenting," *Daedalus*
106 (Spring 1977), p. 14, comments on the male model of sexuality as the preferred
paradigm of some feminists: "Sexual liberation, then, seems to mean that increasing
numbers of women are now following male initiatives in a more elaborate,
multi-partner sexual script." Rossi cites one feminist who claims that "a feminist goal
is total freedom of choice in sex partners throughout one's life."

[85] *The Second Sex*, p. 646: "A woman who expends her energy, who has responsibilities,
who knows how harsh is the struggle against the world's opposition, needs—like the
male—not only to satisfy her physical desires but also to enjoy the relaxation and
diversion provided by agreeable sexual adventures."

[86] Note Beauvoir's comment in *The Second Sex*, p. 362: "Finally, there is another factor
that often gives man a hostile aspect and makes the sexual act a serious menace: it is
the risk of impregnation."

perversion deliberately indulged in than it is a course of
fate. It is an attitude chosen in a certain situation—that
is, at once motivated and freely adopted.[87]

For those women, those "maternal amazons" (*The Second Sex*,
p. 466) who may conceivably want children, Simone de Beauvoir tells
them that liberated women ought to live by the code which says in
effect: "Sex is for play, artificial insemination's the way."

> If the idea of artificial insemination interests many
> women, it is not because they wish to avoid
> intercourse with a male; it is because they hope that
> freedom of maternity is going to be accepted by
> society.[88]

Perhaps the main reason why Simone de Beauvoir seeks control
over the reproductive process is best understood as we see it aligned with
her existentialism; it comes down to a question of control and a feeling
of independence. As Beauvoir sees it, pregnant women are not in control
of their destinies; contraceptors and aborters are.

Commenting on the fact that human females, like certain
domesticated animals, need help in giving birth, the author of *The Second*

---

[87] *The Second Sex*, p. 398: author's emphasis. The question of lesbianism is much
discussed in feminist circles. Cf. Maggie Humm, *The Dictionary of Feminist Theory*,
(Columbus: Ohio State University Press), s.v. "Feminism is the theory; lesbianism
is the practice." The expression, according to Humm, was "coined by Ti-Grace
Atkinson in the 1970s to affirm that lesbianism was the radical political practice and
experience of the feminist movement" (p. 75). The posthumously-published two-
volume work, *Lettres à Sartre* (Paris: Gallimard, 1990), shows us a Simone de Beauvoir
as quite bisexual, an observation made by Quintin Hoare who translated and edited
the abbreviated English translation, *Letters to Sartre* (with a preface by Sylvie Le Bon
de Beauvoir) (New York: Arcade Publishing, 1992).

[88] *The Second Sex*, p. 655. Earlier in the book, Beauvoir opined: "Artifical insemination
completes the evolutionary advance that will enable humanity to master the
reproductive function" (p. 111). See also p. 464. Basing her argument in large part on
the work of Beauvoir, Shulamith Firestone, *The Dialectic of Sex: The Case for Feminist
Revolution* (New York: Bantam, 1970), makes artificial insemination and
reproductive technologies central elements of her "cybernetic socialism." See
Beauvoir's generally favorable comments on Firestone in *All Said and Done*, pp.
454–456.

Sex ruminates:

> It is significant that woman—like the females of certain
> domesticated animals—requires help in performing the
> function assigned to her by nature. . . . At just the time
> when woman attains the realization of her feminine
> destiny, *she is still dependent*: proof again that in the
> human species nature and artifice are never wholly
> separated.[89]

The Religious-Moral Argument Against Abortion

As Simone de Beauvoir views the issue through her existentialist
eyes, there are really no *practical* arguments against the practice of
human abortion; all such are dismissed as being without value. Turning
next to the *moral* arguments against abortion, Beauvoir refers explicitly
to abortion and the Catholic faith:

> As for the moral considerations, they amount in the
> end to the old Catholic argument: the unborn child has
> a soul which is denied access to paradise if its life is
> interrupted without baptism (*The Second Sex*, p. 458).

Earlier in her book, Beauvoir contended that most peoples have
viewed abortion as a normal event. It was Christianity that
revolutionized this view; it did so by endowing the embryo with a soul
(p. 110). While states may have mitigated their rigor toward abortion,
the Church has not relented. Beauvoir goes on to cite statistics that lead
her to conclude that there are 800,000 to a million abortions every year
in France.[90]

---

[89] *The Second Sex*, p. 476: my emphasis. If we follow Beauvoir, she is saying in effect
that giving birth is not a project for a free human being but that having an abortion
is. We might want to look at the way our language handles abortion. Is a woman
aborted by another or does she abort herself? It would seem that the second is a
project but the first is passive. The act by which an individual human being enters the
world is regarded as passive; the act by which one is dispatched is seen as active.
Hence, the priority given to the killers in Beauvoir.

[90] Beauvoir, in a "Préface" she wrote to Dr. Lagroua Weill-Halle, *Le planning familial*
(Paris: Librairie Maloine S.A., 1959), p. 3, has the number of abortions in France

The Church has evolved a just war theory to justify killing; Simone de Beauvoir is not above using sarcasm when she comments that the God of the Christians did not object during the epochs when the infidels were piously slaughtered (*The Second Sex*, p. 458). Yet the Church remains intransigent on abortion. Indeed, continuing in her sardonic vein, the French feminist observes of the Church: "It reserves its uncompromising humanitarianism for man in the fetal condition."[91]

However, as Simone de Beauvoir continues her analysis, the appearance of morality traditionally attached to the Church's position turns out in her eyes to be deceptive. In her existentialist language, the attitude of the Church is an example of *mauvaise foi*, an illustration of what she calls "masculine sadism."[92] Strictures against abortion, be they

----

down to half a million. The use of statistics in the abortion question is open to the charge of abuse. Abortionist turned pro-life advocate Bernard Nathanson, *Aborting America* (Toronto: Life Cycle Books, 1979), tells how pro-abortion groups fabricated figures for purposes of selling abortion to the American public by way of an accommodating press.

[91] *The Second Sex*, p. 458. Feminists (Mary Daly and Robin Morgan, for two) are fond of this text.

[92] See *The Second Sex*, p. 458. Beauvoir brought in the theme of *sadism* in *The Second Sex*, p. 375. In a sense it is not odd that she bring in Sade. The "divine marquis" fascinated her. She wrote an extended essay on Sade, "Faut-il brûler Sade?" which first appeared in *Les Temps Modernes* 7 no. 75 (janvier 1952), pp. 1197–1230. There is an English translation, "Must We Burn Sade?", which is reprinted in Austryn Wainhouse and Richard Seaver (compilers and translators), *The Marquis de Sade* (New York: Grove Press, 1966), pp. 3–64. Beauvoir writes of Sade: "The original intuition which lies at the basis of Sade's entire sexuality, and hence his ethic, is the fundamental identity of coition and cruelty" ("Must We Burn Sade?," p. 20). So sympathetic is Beauvoir's portrait of her countryman that radical feminist Andrea Dworkin, *Pornography: Men Possessing Women* (New York: Perigee Books, 1981), p. 70, speaks of it as an apologia of sorts for Sade. Dworkin contends that the French feminist author's treatment makes Sade's crimes nearly invisible (p. 81). John T. Noonan, Jr., "An Almost Absolute Value in History," in John T. Noonan, Jr., (ed.), *The Morality of Abortion: Legal and Historical Perspectives* (Cambridge, MA: Harvard University Press, 1970), notes that "the Marquis de Sade had attacked restrictions on abortion as the result of religious superstition, and had exulted in the delight of destroying an embryo" (p. 37). According to Noonan, Sade's book, *La philosophie dans le boudoir*, is the "first in Western Europe to praise abortion." Might Beauvoir's espousal of abortion owe anything to Sade's views on the matter? Beauvoir does show herself acquainted with Sade's *Philosophie dans le boudoir*. See *The Second Sex*, p. 375. Several

from Church or state, turn out to be nothing more than other ways of making women suffer.

To be against abortion is to be against the emancipation of women: "How lively antifeminism is can be judged by the eagerness of certain men to reject everything favorable to the emancipation of women."[93]

While she criticizes the Catholic positions on birth control and abortion as both hypocritical, she argues the case for hypocrisy only in the case of birth control.[94] By associating the Church with the institutions of patriarchy and by means of the charge of masculine sadism, Beauvoir is able to avoid the moral question of abortion. In this approach, many feminists will follow Beauvoir's lead.

Abortion and the Question of Patriarchal Control

Modern technology offers women some control over nature by means of what we may call "the birth control-abortion package." Opposing birth control and abortion is to oppose the liberation of women, in Beauvoir's sense of liberation.

The rich weather the storm caused by an unplanned, unwanted pregnancy rather well; they can afford the best medical facilities for their abortions. Indeed, "some of these privileged persons assert that the little accident is good for the health and improves the complexion" (*The Second Sex*, p. 460). Liberated women, of course, pay no heed to the moral teachings of the Church. Their disdain for all traces of bourgeois morality makes abortion nothing more than an inconvenience, or as she matter-of-factly phrases it: "There is a more or less disagreeable moment

---

authors touch upon the link of Sade and the rise of the abortion mentality. Among them are Luigi Lombardi Vallauri, "Abortismo libertario e sadismo," in *Sul Problema dell'aborto: Aspetti medico-giuridici* reprinted from *Jus* 22 fasc. 3-4 (luglio-dicembre 1975) (Milano: Vita e Pensiero, 1976), pp. 279-326, and John Attarian, "Abortion and the Marquis de Sade," *Human Life Review* 20, no. 3 (Summer 1994), pp. 59-68. On Sade's hatred for God, his misotheism, cf. Dr. Iwan Bloch, *Marquis de Sade: His Life and Works* (New York: Brittany Press, 1931).

[93] *The Second Sex*, pp. 458-459. I would contend this apparently innocuous text is momentous because in it we find Beauvoir, in effect, defining the right of abortion *into* her idea of feminism.

[94] Cf. *The Second Sex*, pp. 110-111.

to live through, and it must be lived through, that is all."[95]

The woman who suffers most is the one who has been unable to get out of the bind of traditional morality, a woman who cannot conform to it yet still respects it. For such a woman, acknowledges Beauvoir, abortion can be a harrowing, haunting experience:

> She is divided against herself. Her natural tendency can well be to have the baby whose birth she is undertaking to prevent. Even if she has no positive desire for maternity, she still feels uneasy about the dubious act she is engaged in. For if it is not true that abortion is murder, it still cannot be considered in the same light as a mere contraceptive technique; an event has taken place that is a definite beginning, the progress of which is to be stopped.
>
> Some women will be haunted by the memory of this child which has not come into being (*The Second Sex*, p. 462).

In this text Beauvoir tries to come to grips with the reality of abortion as it affects the majority of women, touching on both the ambivalence as well as the ambiguity of abortion,[96] themes that will be much discussed as they work their way into the current abortion literature.

Men and women view abortion differently, according to Beauvoir:

> Men tend to take abortion lightly; they regard it as one of the numerous hazards imposed on women by malignant nature, but fail to realize fully the values involved. The woman who has recourse to abortion is disowning feminine values, and at the same time is in most radical fashion running counter to the ethics

---

[95]*The Second Sex*, p. 461. Jean Toulat, *L'avortement: crime ou libération* (Paris: Fayard, 1973), pp. 28-29, opines that Beauvoir herself may have been haunted by the children she did not have.

[96]As we are using the terms, "ambivalence" refers to the subjective side of the abortion experience; "ambiguity" refers to the objective side.

established by men. Her whole moral universe is being disrupted.[97]

When men ask—nay, demand—that women abort their children, Simone de Beauvoir is quite clear about the meaning for women: masculine hypocrisy is shown in all its uncaring and unfeeling cynicism. It is a moment pregnant with meaning. Men may mouth the words about abortion but they soon forget them; women will have to interpret these words in pain and blood.

> They learn to believe no longer in what men say when they exalt woman or when they exalt man; the one thing they are sure of is this rifled and bleeding womb, these shreds of crimson life, this child that is not there. It is at her first abortion that woman begins to know. For many women the world will never be the same.[98]

As Simone de Beauvoir sees the matter, the abortion decision is an epistemological watershed for women. "It is at her first abortion that woman begins to 'know'."

Abortion and Killing as the Key to the Whole Mystery

As these texts clearly indicate, Simone de Beauvoir is quite aware of the nature of the abortion procedure. She knows what it is and what it does. It is a violent procedure.[99] It is taking a life. It is killing.

---

[97] *The Second Sex*, pp. 462–463. In passing, we note that what Beauvoir's American translator renders as "her whole moral *universe* is being disrupted" is more precisely translated as "her whole moral *future* is being disrupted" (my emphasis). The text in French: "Tout son avenir moral en est ébranlé" (*Le deuxième sexe*, II, p. 341).

[98] *The Second Sex*, p. 464. After citing Beauvoir's text, Carol McMillan, *Women, Reason and Nature*, p. 129, observes: "The general horror people have of abortion, then, is not as irrational as Beauvoir suggests at first" and goes on to point out the contradictory character of Beauvoir's position. We remember Beauvoir's early language denigrating the child in the womb as "that thing." In this text, it is the very humanity of "that thing" which makes abortion such a horror. In a very real sense, then, Beauvoir acknowledges that abortion destroys a human life. Her argument for killing would seem to demand that that which is killed be human. Otherwise, it loses its force.

[99] Beauvoir treats violence in some detail in her section on "The Young Girl" in *The*

Indeed, it is precisely the fact that abortion *is* killing that makes it such a crucial element in her existentialist analysis.[100] Why has man always been superior to woman? Beauvoir answers:

> It is not in giving life but in risking life that man is raised above the animal; that is why superiority has been accorded in humanity not to the sex that brings forth but to that which kills (*The Second Sex*, p. 58).

Simone de Beauvoir then adds the pregnant comment: "*Here we have the key to the whole mystery.*"[101]

Abortion allows women to know these things. As the power to take life, the power to kill, has made men superior, it will be by women's sharing in this power by means of abortion that the wrong of past patriarchal injustices will be righted.[102] Seen in this light, the right

---

Second Sex. See for example, pp. 308–309. We have already observed Beauvoir's fascination with the Marquis de Sade. On the predilection for violence in the existentialism of Sartre and Beauvoir, consult Carol Ascher, *Simone de Beauvoir: A Life of Freedom* (Boston: Beacon Press, 1981), p. 216. She quotes Beauvoir: "It is only in violence that the oppressed can attain their human status." Yolanda Astarita Patterson, *Simone de Beauvoir and the Demystification of Motherhood*, p. 73, cites Beauvoir to the effect that the murder committed at the end of her novel, *She Came to Stay*, though contrived, had to take place because, in Beauvoir's words, "I preferred any other alternative to that of being submissive." Patterson also relates Sartre's acceptance of murder as the ultimate existential choice. See especially p. 73 and p. 119.

[100]On the importance of killing in Beauvoir's analysis of women's condition, cf. Claude Alzon, *Femme mythifiée, femme mystifiée* (Paris: Presses universitaires de France, 1978), pp. 70ff; Dorothy Kaufmann McCall, "Simone de Beauvoir, the 'Second Sex,' and Jean-Paul Sartre," *Signs* 5 (1979), pp. 209–222; and Peggy Reeves Sanday, *Female Power and Male Dominance: On the Origins of Sexual Inequality* (New York: Cambridge University Press, 1981).

[101]*The Second Sex*, p. 58: my emphasis.

[102]Cf. Una Stannard, *Mrs Man* (San Francisco: Germainbooks, 1977), pp. 333–334. She deals with the theme of killing in the context of the equal roles of man and woman in procreation and draws out the same implications regarding abortion as did Beauvoir; the power to kill that belonged exclusively to males is now to be shared with females. Nancy Hartsock, "The Feminist Standpoint: Developing the Ground for a Specifically Feminist Historical Materialism," in Sandra Harding and Merrill B. Hintikka (eds.), *Discovering Reality: Feminist Perspectives on Epistemology, Metaphysics, Methodology, and Philosophy of Science* (Dordrecht: D. Reidel, 1983), pp. 283–310, asks—it seems to me—a very sensible question: why give pride of place to killing?

to abortion—the right to kill, if you will—serves as the first stage of a feminist discourse on method. It is the first feminist certainty, its Cartesian, or perhaps better, its Beauvoirian starting-point.

Toward the end of *The Second Sex*, Beauvoir observes: "Woman is in any case deprived of the lessons of violence by her nature" (pp. 670–671). As we have seen Beauvoir's analysis unfold, it would seem that what takes place in abortion will begin to provide some of what, in her words, are "the lessons of violence."[103]

Her culturalist analysis of abortion in terms of the killing that she regards as the "key to the whole mystery" of woman's subjugation will prove a recurring theme in the abortion controversy right up to the present. In fact, the killing that takes place in abortion might well be the key to understand the intractable nature of the abortion debate. This is especially seen when some link woman's full humanity with the right to abortion, that is, with the right to kill.[104]

---

[103]Cf. Catherine Keller, "Feminism and the Ethics of Inseparability," in Barbara Hilkert Andolsen et al. (eds.), *Women's Consciousness, Women's Conscience* (New York: Seabury, 1985), pp. 251-263. Notes Keller: "Ironically 'The Second Sex,' which could be described as a single protest against the Freudian essentialism (that 'anatomy is destiny'), lets echo in its very foundations another Freudian axiom: that of the 'primary mutual hostility of human beings'" (p. 255). To Keller, it is precisely because of the harsh, violent, "masculine" aspects embedded in Beauvoir's analysis that the thought of Carol Gilligan holds out such promise for the establishing of a sound feminist ethics.

[104]Following in Beauvoir's footsteps, other feminists attempt defenses of the killing that takes place in abortion. Linda Gordon, *Woman's Body, Woman's Right: a History of Birth Control in America* (New York: Grossman Publishers, 1976), p. 415, in speaking of anti-abortion advocates, says that "they oppose the specific forms of 'killing' that amount to women's self-defense." Another explanation of sorts meant to justify women's absolute right to abortion in terms of killing is given by Andrea Dworkin, *Letters from a War Zone: Writings 1976–1989* (New York: E. P. Dutton, 1988), but as the following passage shows, Dworkin would have us understand *killing* in a unique way: "I want to talk about abortion, only abortion. Killing is central to it: the killing that takes place in forced sex. The killing is in sex that is forced, and every single synonym for sex in this society says so. . . . So the practical reality is that as long as sex is forced on women, women must have the right to abortion, absolutely, no matter what it means, no matter what you think it means" (p. 144). On the reasoning that unless women can abort unwanted pregnancies, they are not allowed to be fully human, cf. Betty Friedan, "Our Revolution Is Unique," in Mary Lou Thompson (ed.), *Voices of the New Feminism* (Boston: Beacon Press, 1975), pp.

Summary of Abortion Arguments in *The Second Sex*

Let us sum up the arguments we have seen so far. Motherhood must be totally free if it is to be worthy of the liberated woman. Technology is the great advance in this area: it is freeing women more and more from slavery to nature. Religion is a relic of the past; technology is the hope of the future. Simone de Beauvoir regards abortion as an essential component of the liberated woman's approach to equality with men.

In Beauvoir's estimation, the religious arguments marshalled against abortion, while more solid than the secular reasons against it, are ultimately discredited, tied in as they are with the reigning patriarchal institutions. While hinting broadly that abortion is a right, Simone de Beauvoir is honest enough to relate the ambivalence which many women experience in facing the complexity of the abortion decision. She portrays this existential angst of sensitive (albeit unliberated) women with some nuances.

In Beauvoir we find abortion being treated as a power issue, as a control issue, as a reproductive rights issue, as a choice issue. It touches themes of metaphysics, epistemology, sociology, religion, and anthropology as well. Beauvoir even outlines a pro-abortion argument based on social utility: unwanted children live unhappy lives, so why not spare them the agony of a miserable life? Abortion as a class issue, abortion as a religious issue, as a moral issue, all are treated in some fashion by Simone de Beauvoir.

Abortion serves as an epistemological moment of insight for enlightened women; Simone de Beauvoir puts it this way in *The Second Sex*: "It is at her first abortion that woman begins to 'know'" (p. 464).

Abortion in the Autobiographical Volumes

If we keep in mind the whole thesis of *The Second Sex*, especially its penultimate chapter "Toward Liberation," while perhaps it is true to say that we should not put too much stress on Beauvoir's musings on the ambivalence, ambiguity and angst that abortion stirs up in the hearts of middle-class women, she *does* nonetheless show herself aware that

---

34–35.

abortion is a matter of great moment for many women. But when she writes about abortion after 1949, it is more as a sloganeer, a pamphleteer, a birth control and abortion activist and not as an essayist. Indeed, after *The Second Sex*, Simone de Beauvoir has become a name.

Memoirs of a Dutiful Daughter

It was as a name that she began to recount her life in several autobiographical volumes. In *Memoirs of a Dutiful Daughter*, we find a passage which contains the kernel of the bodyright argument, the chief pro-abortion argument used by feminists.

> Current notions of sexual morality scandalized me both by their indulgence and their severity. I was stupefied to learn from a small news item that abortion was a crime: what went on in one's body should be one's own concern; no amount of argument could make me see it differently (*Memoirs of a Dutiful Daughter*, p. 190).

On this point of the bodyright argument for abortion, Simone de Beauvoir helps point the feminist way.[105]

Force of Circumstance

In *Force of Circumstance*, Beauvoir recounts the storm of protest that greeted the publication of volume two of the French edition of *The Second Sex*. Yes, there were differences between men and women, but no, these differences were based not on nature but rather on culture.[106] Her critics were especially vitriolic because she began her chapter on motherhood with a discussion of abortion. Yet had she not treated the topic in *The Blood of Others*? Had Sartre not made it part of the plot of

---

[105]The lineage of the bodyright argument is much older than the writings of Simone de Beauvoir. Havelock Ellis seems to be the source of the pro-abortion argument that is elaborated by Stella Browne. Among many feminists the bodyright argument reigns supreme. Gloria Steinem, *Outrageous Acts and Everyday Rebellions* (New York: Holt, Rinehart and Winston, 1983), p. 18, says: "How much power would we ever have if we had no power over the fate of our own bodies?"

[106]Cf. Simone de Beauvoir, *Force of Circumstance*, pp. 186ff.

The Age of Reason? She even tells of becoming annoyed when a young man approached her, asking for the address of an abortionist.[107]

Later on in *Force of Circumstance*, Simone de Beauvoir recounts her fight for birth control and abortion. When married women are denied access to birth control, abortion is the result. Reproductive freedom is a *sine qua non* for women's liberation: "'For a woman, freedom begins with the womb,' one woman had written me. I agreed with her."[108]

The role of language and vocabulary is an important component of the contemporary abortion debate.[109] Simone de Beauvoir shows herself aware that the issues of birth control and abortion have to be treated by means of a careful choice of words. Reporting on a press conference she attended for Doctor Lagroua Weill-Halle's *La grande peur d'aimer*, Beauvoir observes:

> The vocabulary employed was edifying in the extreme. They talked, not about birth control but about the joys of maternity, not about contraception but about orthogenesis. At the word abortion, faces were turned away; as for sex, that wasn't allowed in the room at all.[110]

The Shorter Pieces on Abortion

As a name, Simone de Beauvoir was much in demand to follow up on the success of *The Second Sex* by lending her name and writing talents to aid those causes she championed in her 1949 volume, especially birth control and abortion. In her brief pieces, there is little if any concern with ambiguity or ambivalence. In these shorter pieces, Simone de Beauvoir is fully the pamphleteer, selling abortion and the reproductive rights package, as it were, to her reading public.

The preface she writes for a book on family planning gives a

---

[107]Cf. *Force of Circumstance*, p. 191.

[108]*Force of Circumstance*, p. 499.

[109]Cf. Celeste Michelle Condit, *Decoding Abortion Rhetoric: Communicating Social Change* (Urbana: University of Illinois Press, 1990), for a recent treatment of the power of language to shape the abortion debate.

[110]*Force of Circumstance*, p. 500.

feeling for the genre.[111] Is it true, asks Beauvoir, that untrammeled technological progress is everywhere in evidence in human endeavors? Not quite. Beauvoir regards as obscurantism the view that the question of human population control is best left to the blind workings of nature. Such a view she considers "aberrant."

Most of the half-million abortions in France are performed upon mothers of families who find themselves pregnant "against their will." Abortion, when done clandestinely, can cause physical and psychological problems. When performed in sanitary conditions, abortions are called "benign" by Beauvoir.

Beauvoir paints a bleak picture of the typical marriage. Women with too many children battle despair; their husbands are weighed down with concern for their support. The spontaneity of marriage relations is poisoned by the fear of additional children. Borrowing from the thought of Sartre, Beauvoir continues: "As a result, many family situations turn into living hells after several years of marriage." Into this gloomy picture Simone de Beauvoir introduces family planning as a way out. Human beings take charge in all other areas of their lives. Why not in the area of family life?

Two years later, Beauvoir writes another preface for Doctor Weill-Hallé.[112] Some themes remain constant: the statistics on abortion, the absurdity of nature still controlling woman regarding human natality, and the talk of hell. Yet we do detect a switch in Beauvoir's tactics. She begins to play off the woman against the man: the woman in her body feels the fatigue of pregnancy and motherhood; the man is able to evade the domestic hell that consumes the woman.[113] In her writings,

---

[111]Simone de Beauvoir, "Préface" to Docteur Lagroua Weill-Halle, Le planning familial (Paris: Librairie Maloine S.A., 1959), pp. 3–5.

[112]The preface written by Beauvoir for Docteur Lagroua Weill-Hallé, La grand peur d'aimer: Journal d'une femme médecin is reprinted in Claude Francis and Fernande Gontier, Les écrits de Simone de Beauvoir. La Vie. L'écriture (Paris: Gallimard, 1979), pp. 397–400.

[113]Is nature unjust (misogynistic?) in the way it apportions the duties and delights of sexual intercourse? Richard Roach, S.J., "Moral Theology and the Mission of the Church: Idolatry in Our Day," in William E. May (ed.), Principles of Catholic Moral Life (Chicago: Franciscan Herald Press, 1980), p. 35, comments on the different roles assigned in procreation: "This is either a dispensation of profound spiritual significance or it is the damnedest injustice in creation."

Beauvoir has made much of the fact that the battle of the sexes had no meaning for her.[114] On this occasion, at least, she goes against her earlier injunctions.

In a preface she writes for the Bobigny abortion trial, Beauvoir speaks of what she considers the positive abortion experience taking place in New York State.[115] Laws *against* abortion are criminal, not laws in favor of it. Five thousand Frenchwomen die every year, victims of the unenlightened French legal system. There are no new valid arguments against abortion; her earlier work had disposed of the old ones. To consider the fetus as a human being is nothing more than metaphysical mumblings. Science disproves that possibility, states Beauvoir, citing several scientists as her authorities.

Why the refusal to change the laws? Anti-abortion laws are an essential piece of a society that is oppressive to women. Women remain subordinate as long as laws against abortion are on the books. Motherhood is part of a vast conspiracy to keep women relegated to second-sex status since time immemorial. *Choisir*, a pro-abortion organization she co-founded, is fighting for the right of all women to choose the timing of their births, to choose birth control and abortion as their rights.

Simone de Beauvoir concludes by appealing to the bodyright argument: it is only when women have total right over their own bodies that they will be free enough to engage in the other battles that have to be fought to bring about a more just society. Here she totally embraces the bodyright argument as the linchpin of her pro-abortion feminist vision.

Commentary on Simone de Beauvoir

Everywhere one looks in the current abortion controversy, one will find Simone de Beauvoir's presence. To those who lionize her, Beauvoir's life is a valiant struggle against enforced motherhood. To

---

[114]See especially *The Second Sex*, p. 685. In *Force of Circumstance*, p. 645, Beauvoir speaks of the bad faith involved in pitting one sex against the other.

[115]Simone de Beauvoir, "Préface" to Association Choisir, *Avortement: une loi en procès, L'affaire de Bobigny* (Sténotype intégrale des débats du Tribunal de Bobigny 8 novembre 1972) (Paris: Gallimard, 1973), pp. 9–15.

others who believed in her message at least for a moment in their lives, the cost of Beauvoir's atheistic existential battle against motherhood has been high, leaving them with a feeling of emptiness. Others find themselves in a sort of "no man's land" on the issue, aware of how much they owe Beauvoir, both positively and negatively, on the abortion question.[116] Elisabeth Badinter may well have spoken better than she knew when she exclaimed at Beauvoir's funeral, "Women, you owe everything to her!"[117]

Simone de Beauvoir was an existentialist much longer than she was a feminist. We have seen how much importance Beauvoir attached to killing or the lack of it as the key to the whole mystery of woman's secondary status. This comes from her existentialism: it will shortly become an integral part of her feminism. No feminist who follows Beauvoir on abortion will speak of killing as the key to the whole mystery with the frankness of the French existentialist; no honest discourse on abortion can avoid it either. In this regard, no one will trace the connections between killing and secondary status, abortion and woman's dignity in any more detail. In this sense, then, Simone de Beauvoir's thought on the matter is a watershed.[118]

I believe it is true to say that the roots of the abortion mentality are planted more firmly in Beauvoir's atheistic existentialism than in her feminism. Indeed, Beauvoir's atheism would seem to be an integral part of her abortion vision. Why abortion despite all the pain and anguish it causes in the lives of many women? As Dostoevsky phrased it, "if God does not exist, everything is permitted." In Beauvoir's existential vision,

---

[116]The bittersweet abortion legacy from Beauvoir is touched upon by Carol Ascher, "On 'Clearing the Air': My Letter to Simone de Beauvoir," p. 94. She speaks about a time in her life when she was unintentionally pregnant. Hinting (but not saying) that she had an abortion, Ascher observes that she, just as Simone de Beauvoir, is childless. She is sad she will not be a mother because giving birth is an act of optimism in oneself and in the world.

[117]Text found in Deirdre Bair, *Simone de Beauvoir: A Biography*, p. 617.

[118]In effect, others—among them Betty Friedan and Beverly Wildung Harrison—will go heavy on the connections they see between the right to abortion and full humanity for women, but tread lightly if at all on the killing that is concomitant with it. Beauvoir, as we have seen, goes heavy on the killing that men do and women heretofore have not engaged in, which she regards as the key to the whole mystery of woman's second-class status.

it reads: "Without God, all things are possible."[119]

Though it is in her feminism that Beauvoir finds her chief claim to fame, it is in her thoroughgoing atheism that her pro-abortion position finds its strongest appeal. "Without God, all things are possible." To paraphrase John Noonan: "Atheism is the theory, abortion is the practice."

Transition to Mary Daly

If the safest general characterization of what passes for contemporary feminist thought is that it consists in a series of footnotes to Beauvoir, the three American feminists to whom we shall now turn—Mary Daly, Carol Gilligan, and Beverly Wildung Harrison—write many of the notes on abortion. Indeed, as we shall see, each of their attempts to establish women's right to abortion is, when all is said and done, little more than an elaboration of the themes found in Simone de Beauvoir.

We have attempted to show that Beauvoir's atheism is by no means the least important element of her analysis of woman's actual situation. Mary Daly's importance resides precisely in this: she serves as a conduit of sorts for the ideas of the atheist Simone de Beauvoir to become more widely disseminated among certain believing Christian women. We do well to remember that of the three American feminists whose thought on the matter we shall examine, Daly is the only one to acknowledge her indebtedness to Beauvoir. It is to her interpretation of *la grande Sartreuse* that we now turn.

---

[119]In *The Ethics of Ambiguity*, p. 15, Beauvoir shows herself aware of the famous Dostoevsky observation. In the words of Judith Butler, "Sex and Gender in Simone de Beauvoir's 'Second Sex.'" *Yale French Studies* 72 (1986), pp. 35–49. "If motherhood becomes a choice, then what else is possible?" (p. 42). Abortion, for one.

CHAPTER TWO

MARY DALY, 1928–

The Metaphysics Of Abortion

"One hundred per cent of the bishops who oppose the repeal of anti-abortion laws are men and one hundred per cent of the people who have abortions are women." I thought it clear and obvious—and outrageous—that men had appropriated the right to dictate to women in this matter. I saw that the main issue was really power over women[1]

M ary Daly was born in 1928, a generation after Simone de Beauvoir, who was born in 1908. In many ways Daly continues the French existentialist philosopher's efforts begun in *The Second Sex*. As we shall see, Daly will be more faithful to the French atheist than she is to the faith of her parents, to whom she dedicates *The Church and the Second Sex*. At any rate the importance of religion to feminism can be seen as an atheist, Beauvoir, and a believer (at least at the time), Daly, continue to regard religious issues as of central importance to feminist concerns.

Some Signposts for the Journey

As we begin our investigation of Mary Daly, some signposts may be helpful to the reader, especially because Daly herself has become rather difficult to understand as she seeks to fashion a new reality for

---

[1]Mary Daly, *Outercourse: The Be-Dazzling Voyage: Containing Recollections from My 'Logbooks of a Radical Feminist Philosopher' (Be-ing an Account of My Time/Space Travels and Ideas, Then, Again, Now and How* (San Francisco: Harper SanFrancisco, 1992), p. 142.

women. If Beauvoir attempts to exorcise death with words, then Daly is on a linguistic crusade to slay the dragons of patriarchy. Indeed, Daly endeavors to construct a new feminist language to reclaim the power of naming stolen from women by patriarchal institutions.[2]

Who are those thinkers she counts as influences upon her? Of classical authors, Daly often refers to St. Thomas Aquinas and Scholastic thought in general. At times she even gives the Common Doctor some faint praise as the best of a bad lot.[3] On occasion Daly will use Scholastic categories to help her explain the most recent feminist subtlety. If St. Thomas is the medieval doctor most used by Mary Daly, Paul Tillich is the contemporary thinker she calls upon the most to help explain her evolving feminist themes, though he too is not presented without a discussion of his faults.[4]

On occasion Daly speaks with some approbation of process thought in general and of Alfred North Whitehead in particular.[5]

----

[2]One of her attempts to construct a new language is found in Mary Daly with Jane Caputi, *Webster's First New Intergalactic Wickedary of the English Language* (Boston: Beacon Press, 1987).

[3]Cf. Mary Daly, "Feminist Postchristian Introduction" to *The Church and the Second Sex* (New York: Harper Colophon Books, 1975; reissue of the 1968 edition), p. 24, notes that Thomas's remarks on *esse* were helpful for her in coming to the realization that *being* is better described as a verb than as a noun, and that this insight would have to hold her until feminist thought blossoms on the scene. Thomas Aquinas's thought served her as "starvation rations from the best of the Christian philosophers."

[4]There is a lengthy discussion of the good and the weak points Daly unearths in Tillich's elaboration of Western philosophy in *Pure Lust: Elemental Feminist Philosophy* (Boston: Beacon Press, 1984), pp. 155–161. Read this along with Daly's charge in her earlier book, *Gyn/Ecology: The Metaethics of Radical Feminism* (Boston: Beacon Press, 1978), pp. 94–95, that Tillich was addicted to pornography, a charge stemming from Hannah Tillich, the theologian's widow. Daly returns to Tillich once again in *Outercourse*, p. 101 and pp. 431–432. For more on the Daly-Tillich connection, see Mary Ann Stenger, "A Critical Analysis of the Influence of Paul Tillich on Mary Daly's Feminist Theology," in John J. Carey (ed.), *Theonomy and Autonomy: Studies in Paul Tillich's Engagement with Modern Culture* (Macon, GA: Mercer University Press, 1984), pp. 243–265.

[5]Cf. Mary Daly, *Beyond God the Father: Toward a Philosophy of Women's Liberation* (Boston: Beacon Press, 1973), p. 21: "This detachment from the problem of relevance of God-language to the struggle against demonic power structures characterizes not

Herbert Marcuse fits into Daly's overall plans and is cited with approval for his contention that a new type of human being has to emerge from the current struggles with alienating structures.[6] Paracelsus, Nietzsche, Teilhard de Chardin, Jacques Maritain, Leslie Dewart, Gabriel Moran are also employed on occasion. Of feminist authors who have exerted an influence on Daly, Simone de Beauvoir certainly comes first. Others include Rosemary Lauer, Rosemary Radford Ruether, and Betty Friedan.

For all practical purposes, St. Thomas Aquinas and Paul Tillich are the two thinkers, in addition to Simone de Beauvoir, whose thought has exercised the most influence upon Mary Daly. While acknowledging her indebtednes to the disciplines of philosophy, theology and feminism, Daly has expressed quite serious reservations about the value of psychology and psychiatry, especially as practiced by Freud and his disciple Hélène Deutsch.[7]

---

only Tillich but also other male theoreticians who have developed a relatively nonsexist language for transcendence. Thinkers such as Whitehead, James, and Jaspers employ God-language that soars beyond sexual hierarchy as a specific problem to be confronted in the process of human becoming." See also Daly's "The Courage to Leave: a Response to John Cobb's Theology," in David Roy Griffin and Thomas J. J. Altizer (eds.), *John Cobb's Theology in Process* (Philadelphia: The Westminster Press, 1977), pp. 84–98. That feminist aims and process thought are basically compatible is the theme of several authors in the collection of articles edited by Sheila Davaney as *Feminism and Process Thought* (The Harvard Divinity School/Claremont Center for Process Studies Symposium Papers) (Lewiston: Edwin Mellen Press, 1981). See for example John B. Cobb, Jr., "Feminism and Process Thought: a Two-Way Relationship," pp. 32–61. Mary Daly's espousal of process thought as preferable to static thinking is a point made by Judith Plaskow and Carol P. Christ (eds.) *Weaving the Visions: New Patterns in Feminist Spirituality* (San Francisco: Harper and Row, 1989), p. 216.

[6]*Beyond God the Father*, pp. 98–99. If we recall, it is Marcuse who regards the feminist revolution as in theory the most radical of all revolutions because it is nothing less than a fight against the work of God.

[7]Daly has an animus against psychology in general, Freud in particular, though Jung is not spared, as we see in this text from *Pure Lust*, p. 280: "Tokenism is embedded in the very fabric of Jung's ideology—in contrast to the more obvious misogynism of Freud's fallacious phallocentrism. Thus it is possible for women to promote Jung's garbled gospel without awareness of betraying their own sex, and even in the belief that they are furthering the feminist cause."

Early Efforts

A look at some of Daly's early efforts will help us understand the general orientation of her theological thought. In one of her earliest efforts, we see two quite clear themes emerging: first, theology is to be open to *change* or else it will die; and second, *experience* is an important key to indicate the direction of theology's change. Theology is to be open to change by being open to new experiences. Daly will follow these early ideas all the way through to their radical feminist conclusions in the works which follow.[8]

Her feminist writing begins with an article in *Commonweal*.[9] Gone are the theological courtesies of *The Thomist* article in this more or less overtly polemical piece which, as Daly later observed, got her noticed by a publisher and led to her first book, *The Church and the Second Sex*.[10]

Drawing on the existentialism of Jean-Paul Sartre and Simone de Beauvoir enables Mary Daly to outflank, as it were, the thought of St. Augustine and St. Thomas Aquinas on the question of human nature in general and woman's nature in particular. According to Daly, erroneous biological and philosophical theories have melted away in this brave new technological age of progress. With them has gone the static immutable female nature so despised by Simone de Beauvoir, leading as it does to

---

[8]Mary Daly, "The Problem of Speculative Theology," *The Thomist* 29 no. 2 (1965), pp. 172–216. Cf. Sidney Callahan, *Christian Family Planning and Sex Education* (Notre Dame: Ave Maria Press, 1969). She cautions against the mystique of experience. The concept of *experience* is notoriously ambiguous, of course. *Whose* experience is to count? One way of trying to get beyond this difficulty is found in Carol P. Christ and Judith Plaskow (eds.), *Womanspirit Rising: A Feminist Reader in Religion* (San Francisco: Harper and Row, 1979), p. 8. There, a distinction is made between *feminist experience* and *traditional female experience*.

[9]Mary Daly, "The Forgotten Sex: a Built-in Bias," *Commonweal* 81, no. 16 (1965), pp. 508–511, and reprinted in Gertrud Heinzelmann (ed.), *Wir Schweigen Nicht Langer! We Won't Keep Silence Any Longer. Women Speak Out to Vatican Council II* (Zurich: Interfeminas-Verlag, 1965).

[10]In her "Autobiographical Preface to the Harper Colophon Edition" which she wrote for a re-edition of her first book, *The Church and the Second Sex* (New York: Harper Colophon Books, 1975; reissue of the 1968 volume), p. 11, Daly recounts the story of how her first book came to be written.

the myth of the eternal feminine.

Talk of static, immutable essences calls to mind what we have referred to earlier as the worldview thesis. Almost from the time she begins writing, Daly utilizes the worldview hypothesis in the sense of the static-classical opposed to the dynamic-progressive. *Nature* is an appalling stereotype to be overcome; modern technology gives us the wherewithal to bring about this transformation. These early works suffice to show the sort of theologizing Daly was doing during the 1960s.

A Creature of the Sixties

Mary Daly is likewise a creature of a rather turbulent era. As she puts it: "I sort of belonged in the 1960s."[11] After *The Church and the Second Sex* was published and she was dismissed from her teaching position at Boston College, student petitions, protests, and marches led to her being rehired, and with tenure, in the summer of 1969, an event she herself describes as "absurdly improbable." She remains to this day on the faculty. In the confusing times following the close of the Second Vatican Council, Mary Daly finds her niche in what she considers a male bastion of patriarchy.[12] From that position she still seems to exert some influence upon certain Roman Catholic women and organizations.[13]

---

[11]Mary Daly, *Outercourse*, p. 419 note 18.

[12]As such, Daly is at times sought out by the American press. See for example how Kathryn Marchocki, "Issues of God's Gender Causes a Stir on Earth," *Boston Sunday Herald* (June 23, 1991), p. 16, pits Mary Daly against Cardinal John O'Connor of New York on the question of the gender of God.

[13]There is agreement regarding Daly's continuing influence. See Rosemary Rader, O.S.B., "Catholic Feminism: Its Impact on United States Catholic Women," in Karen J. Kennelly, C.S.J., *American Catholic Women: A Historical Exploration* (Part of the Bicentennial History of the Catholic Church in America Series) (New York: Macmillan, 1989), pp. 182–197, especially at p. 192, and Sandra M. Schneiders, *Beyond Patching: Faith and Feminism in the Catholic Church* (The Anthony Jordan Lectures, 1990, Newman Theological College in Edmonton) (Mahwah: Paulist Press, 1991), p. 31. Cf. the comments on Daly made by Mary E. Hines and M. Carmel McEnroy, "Feminism and Theological Language—a Report of Convention Workshops on the Theme, 'The Linguistic Turn and Contemporary Theology," *Proceedings of the Catholic Theological Society of America* 42 (1987): "Women attending the CTSA today in increasing numbers, presenting papers, and hearing some of our questions being addressed in major sessions need to remember our brave foresister, Mary Daly, that

While few follow Daly's extreme version of radical feminism,[14] many feminists profess to be in awe of her for being the one to get them to think beyond traditional categories.[15] Rosemarie Tong has a hard time finding the words to explain what Mary Daly has meant to the feminist movement. To Tong, Daly has "out-Nietzsched" Nietzsche![16]

Other feminists are more circumspect, thanking Daly for her efforts but observing that contemporary feminism for the most part has relegated Daly to the sidelines, especially because of the extreme nature of her brand of radical lesbian separatism. Some of her feminist critics are much less kind.[17] And yet, to many feminists, Daly remains a

---

crone, hag, witch, spinster, fury, amazon who dared to change the character of the CTSA" (p. 135). In the view of Marilyn Bowers, "Women's Liberation: A Catholic View." *Theology Today* 28 1 (April 1971), p. 33: "Mary Daly is the outspoken Joan of Arc of the lobbyists." Less favorably disposed toward Daly is Donna Steichen, *Ungodly Rage: The Hidden Face of Catholic Feminism* (San Francisco: Ignatius Press, 1991), especially pp. 297–301. Though extremely critical, Steichen does in a roundabout way acknowledge Daly's influence.

[14]There are some comments in Daly's "Feminist Postchristian Introduction" to *The Church and the Second Sex* (New York: Harper Colophon Books, 1975), in which she appears to be proclaiming herself a witch: "For women, concerned with philosophical/theological questions, it seems to me, this implies the necessity of some sort of choice. One either tries to avoid 'acceptable' deviance. . . or else one tries to make the qualitative leap toward self-acceptable deviance as ludic cerebrator, questioner of everything, madwoman, and witch. . . . I do mean witch" (p. 50). See also her remarks in *Beyond God the Father*, pp. 65–66.

[15]Daly's continuing influence is seen in Mary Hunt, *Fierce Tenderness: a Feminist Theology of Friendship* (New York: Crossroad, 1991). See also Mary Jo Weaver, *Springs of Water in a Dry Land: Spiritual Survival of Catholic Women Today* (Boston: Beacon Press, 1993).

[16]Cf. Rosemarie Tong, *Feminist Thought: A Comprehensive Introduction*, p. 102. See also Rosemarie Tong, *Feminine and Feminist Ethics* (Belmont, CA: Wadsworth, 1993), p. 225. We remember the attraction Nietzsche exerted upon Simone de Beauvoir.

[17]Cf. Jean Bethke Elshtain, *Public Man, Private Woman: Women in Social and Political Thought*, p. 224, who is evaluating Daly's attempt to fashion a new linguistic medium: "Again, conceptual similarities to fascism, which also insisted that the old language and reason was thoroughly false, debased, and unacceptable, arise. Language must no longer serve, *as it must* for otherwise it would not be language, as a 'divisive instrument,' as an expression of diversity and variability. Perhaps the apogee of this mistrust of language is Daly's insistence that Lesbians must imitate/learn from the language of 'dumb' animals, 'whose nonverbal communication seems to be superior

prophet of sorts, and hence they are able to put up with what may be considered a certain outlandishness.[18] She occupies an important position in their eyes. She was a Catholic. She earned the highest ecclesiastical degrees. She continues to hold a tenured position on the faculty of Boston College.

Daly's Debt to Simone de Beauvoir

In her autobiography, Daly maintains that she understood Beauvoir's *The Second Sex* immediately; indeed, she "welcomed it with unspeakable gratitude."[19] Daly's 1968 book, *The Church and the Second Sex*, can be regarded as a continuation of the Beauvoirian theme of the Church as a foe of human and female progress. From Beauvoir, a one-time believer turned atheist existentialist, such an approach is not surprising. Coming from a Catholic,—at least Daly says she is one at the time she writes *The Church and the Second Sex*,—we *are* surprised to see the impact Simone de Beauvoir's analysis made upon some Roman Catholic women at the time of the Second Vatican Council.

What is also evident is Daly's admiration for Simone de Beauvoir. Again and again, the Catholic Daly accepts major contentions of the atheist Beauvoir. She agrees, for example, with the French feminist on the danger to women posed by the perpetuation of the myth of the eternal feminine. Daly's leanings toward personalism and humanism are also in the best Beauvoirian tradition.[20] She likewise

---

to androcratic speech.' Daly cites several conversations she has had with animals and translates a few of those conversations; needless to say, all the animals shared her perspective and none contested her position." The quote within the quote is from p. 414 of Daly's *Gyn/Ecology*. For more on Daly and the animals, especially her philosophical cats, see *Outercourse*.

[18]To see how gently feminists treat Daly and her work, cf. two reviews of *Outercourse*: Mary Jo Weaver, "Notes of a Nag-Gnostic," *New York Times Book Review* (January 24, 1993), p. 15, and Carol J. Adams, "Mary, Mary Quite Contrary," *The Women's Review of Books* 10 6 (March 1993), pp. 1–3. Personal appearances by Daly are counted as events by her admirers and are duly reported as such. See for example Kitty Axelson-Berry, "Awesome Nag-Gnostic: Local Hags Be-dazzled by Pirate Mary Daly," *Valley Advocate* (Springfield, MA) (April 15, 1993), p. 11.

[19]Cf. Mary Daly, *Outercourse*, p. 112.

[20]See *The Church and the Second Sex*, p. 83 and p. 184.

makes a bow toward Simone de Beauvoir's *locus classicus* for her thoroughgoing culturalism: "One is not born, but rather becomes, a woman."[21]

On another point Daly shows herself to be a faithful disciple of Beauvoir. As we saw in treating the French feminist philosopher, Simone de Beauvoir was a rationalist who regarded the body, especially the female body, as an inconvenience, if not a downright embarrassment, to her philosophy.[22] Daly, in her quest for women's spiritual liberation, takes a similar position *vis-à-vis* the human body.[23] Other similarities between the American theologian and the French philosopher are often detected by contemporary feminists.[24]

Mary Daly's anger at the Church explodes on the pages of *The Church and the Second Sex*.[25] One of the reasons for her anger is that she sees the Church as irrelevant. Over and again, Daly indicts the Church for being out of touch with what she considers the real needs of women: birth control, abortion, divorce, and ordination among them.

In *The Church and the Second Sex* Daly considers Simone de Beauvoir to be making the following case against Christianity. The first

---

[21]Mary Daly, *The Church and the Second Sex*, after noting, in the context of Beauvoir's atheism, the meaning of "One is not born, but rather becomes, a woman" (p. 70), says in her own right: "As to whether one is born or becomes man or woman, dogmatic assertions about an unchanging feminine essence do not find anything like general acceptance among those who follow developments in modern philosophy and in the social sciences and psychology. In fact, our awareness of the profound and subtle effects of conditioning upon the human personality is continually increasing. There is an impressive stock of evidence in support of de Beauvoir on this point, and despite the tenacious hold of the 'eternal feminine' upon the popular mind, the concept of woman is changing, whether one is existentialist or not" (pp. 71–72).

[22]The charge of rationalism is made against Beauvoir by Carol McMillan, *Women, Reason and Nature: Some Philosophical Problems With Feminism*, p. 129.

[23]Moira Gatens, *Feminism and Philosophy: Perspectives on Difference and Equality* (Bloomington: Indiana University Press, 1991), pp. 82–84, notes that Daly's list of atrocities in *Gyn/ecology* is directed for the most part against female corporeality.

[24]Cf. Letty M. Russell, *Human Liberation in a Feminist Perspective. A Theology* (Philadelphia: Westminster, 1974).

[25]The anger (as well as the pride and hope) she felt in writing *The Church and Second Sex* is mentioned by Daly herself in the "Autobiographical Preface to the Colophon Edition," p. 5.

four points are negative, the fifth is somewhat positive.

1. The Christian religion has been an instrument of the oppression of women.
2. Church doctrine implicitly conveys the idea that women are naturally inferior.
3. Certain moral doctrines, including Church teaching on abortion, are harmful to women.
4. Exclusion from the hierarchy is damaging to women.
5. Women can achieve transcendence through religion.

While she does not gloss over the fact of Beauvoir's atheism and its relevance to the positions taken in *The Second Sex*, at the end of her detailed analysis of Beauvoir's critique of Christianity, Daly concludes that the French existentialist has not overstated the feminist case against the Church.[26]

Daly And Abortion

As a faithful disciple of a woman without faith, Mary Daly will continue to expound some of the standard Beauvoirian themes, including the role of religious belief and the question of human abortion. At least at the time when she is most under Beauvoir's influence, Daly likewise regards technology as the great deliverer of women from the tyranny of nature in the reproductive process. There is a similar linking of birth control and abortion into one reproductive rights package.[27] Both the French existentialist philosopher and her American feminist follower regard Christianity as one of the chief obstacles to women's liberation.

In a *Commonweal* article which even Daly describes as controversial,[28] she attempts to explain strictures against abortion as

---

[26]Mary Daly, *The Church and the Second Sex* with a new "Feminist Postchristian Introduction" (New York: Harper Colophon Books, 1975; reissue of the 1968 volume), esp. pp. 69–73.

[27]As Daly moves toward lesbian separatism, she moves away from the "pill-poppers" as another instance of male perfidy. See for example her comment in *Gyn/Ecology*, p. 278.

[28]Cf. Mary Daly, *Outercourse*, p. 142.

instances of what she calls "sexual caste," a notion she appropriates from Jo Freeman.[29] Daly contends that women deserve the right to abortion as a way of making up for past patriarchal injustices. She makes of "sexual caste" an important feature of her radical feminist edifice.

Daly's argument in "Abortion and Sexual Caste": male authors on abortion—what can they know? All are unobjective. Hence the need for abortion to right past wrongs. Nature is out, culture is in. Elements of a bodyright argument, the wanted and unwanted child argument, the ambiguity of the situation, all work their way into Daly's abortion analysis. Patriarchy is the great foe; it is in the Church, to be sure, but Daly sees patriarchal tentacles everywhere. Her indebtedness to Beauvoir's treatment of abortion is present throughout.

As Daly herself makes clear, her lesbian separatist version of feminism is the reason why the abortion question is by no means the most important feminist issue.[30] After she recounts the "vitriolic response" her abortion article occasioned, Daly tells her readers that, in effect, the episode convinced her to say good-bye not only to *Commonweal* but also to Catholicism.[31] Yet Daly is important, as we have noted, because of her influence upon the rank and file of women who show an interest in feminism, religion, and reproductive rights. Daly signed a pro-abortion "amicus curiae" brief somewhat akin to the French Feminist Manifesto of the 343 and testified in 1971 on behalf of abortion reform before a welfare committee of the Massachusetts State Legislature.[32]

---

[29]Cf. Mary Daly, "Abortion and Sexual Caste," *Commonweal* 95 no. 8 (1972), pp. 415–419.

[30]Cf. *Outercourse*, pp. 142–144. On lesbianism, Daly has this to say in *Outercourse*: "The insight that *Lesbianism* implies *Feminism* and that *radical feminism* implies *lesbianism* has been shared by many women" (p. 435, note 10). There is an entry in Maggie Humm, The Dictionary of Feminist Theory, p. 75: "Feminism is the theory; lesbianism is the practice."

[31]Ideas, of course, have consequences. Immediately after describing how her feminism and its pro-abortion position led her to a definitive break with the Church, Daly in the very next section of *Outercourse* deals with what she calls "Volcanic Taboo-Breaking: Recalling My Lesbian Identity."

[32]We learn about the "Amicus curiae" brief from Marian Faux, *Roe v. Wade: The Untold Story of the Supreme Court Decision That Made Abortion Legal* (New York: Macmillan, 1988), p. 226. The document known as "The Women's Brief" was signed

If abortion is the starting point of a feminist discourse on method as Simone de Beauvoir would have it with her contention: "It is at her first abortion that woman begins to 'know,'" one of the first lessons it imparts is that abortion is a humiliating experience. Daly's emphasis on this is fully in line with the thought of Beauvoir.[33] Writes Mary Daly:

> As for *feminist consciousness*: abortion is hardly the "final triumph" envisaged by all or the final stage of the revolution. There are deep questions beneath and beyond all this, such as: Why should women be in situations of unwanted pregnancy at all? Some women see abortion as a necessary measure for themselves but no one sees it as the fulfillment of her greatest dreams. Many would see abortion as a humiliating procedure.[34]

From one point of view, it is true, Mary Daly is simply not all that interested in the question of abortion: there is not much demand for it in the radical lesbian separatist vision she has elaborated in the years since she wrote *The Church and the Second Sex*. But write about it she will, if only because the Church she has left takes the strong position it does on the issue of abortion.[35]

Despite her lesbian leanings, Daly latches on to the Beauvoirian theme of abortion as an important epistemological moment for enlightened women in the know, as it were, in their fight against the

---

by, among others, sociologists Alice Rossi and Margaret Mead, as well as by the wife of then-United States Senator from New York Jacob Javits. Daly tells of her appearance before the Massachusetts legislature in *Outercourse*, pp. 136–137.

[33]Cf. *The Second Sex*, p. 464.

[34]Mary Daly, *Beyond God the Father: Toward a Philosophy of Women's Liberation*, p. 112.

[35]In the second chapter of *Beyond God the Father*, Daly regards the Fall as a good; she styles it a "Fall into Freedom." She is reversing values: if the Church is *for* something, then Daly must be *against* it. Randall A. Lake, "The Metaethical Framework of Anti-Abortion Rhetoric," *Signs* 11 no. 3 (1986), pp. 478–499, reads Daly in this fashion.

demons of patriarchy.[36] In her autobiography, Daly explains:

> It was not because of a personal/private agenda that
> I took on this issue. I have never needed an abortion.
> But my commitment was and is to the cause of
> women as women (*Outercourse*, p. 142).

Abortion in *The Church and the Second Sex*

In a section of *The Church and the Second Sex* entitled "Harmful
Moral Teaching," as Daly is explaining Beauvoir's hostility toward the
Roman Catholic doctrine on woman, she touches briefly on the
abortion question, doing so only after treating the question of female
sexuality. There is a double standard at work in the patriarchal world of
which the Church is a major player. In the sexual arena men can play
around, women cannot. Men are measured by standards other than
sexuality, but such is not the case with women. This is the way Daly
expresses the case made by Simone de Beauvoir.[37]

Where Beauvoir finds hypocrisy and unconscious sadism in
Christian attitudes, we can expect Daly will find it as well. Indeed, as her
proof she cites the *bon mot* to the effect that the Church "reserves an
uncompromising humanitarianism for man in the fetal condition."[38]
Adverting to the fact that it is often the husbands and the lovers who
force their women to abort, Daly sees that Church opposition to
abortion means that women are forced to get their abortions in

---

[36]Cf. Mary Daly, *Pure Lust*, p. 323: "At certain times and places, for example, some
women have focussed upon the abortion issue. This can be seen as a microcosm of
female oppression, since it is the autonomy of women that is the target of
anti-abortionists." Daly's practically exclusive focus on the woman in the abortion
issue is not shared by all lesbian feminists. For example, Sarah Lucia Hoagland,
Lesbian Ethics: Toward a New Value (Palo Alto: Institute of Lesbian Studies, 1988), p.
97, speaks of the special nature of the fetus and cautions feminists against regarding
it as a mere clump of cells.

[37]Cf. *The Church and the Second Sex*, p. 64. Do we detect traces of the question, "Is
nature misogynist?" in Daly's text?

[38]Cf. *The Church and the Second Sex*, p. 64, citing Beauvoir's *The Second Sex*, p. 458.
That the Church reserves its "uncompromising humanitarianism" for man in the fetal
condition is a Beauvoirian passage Daly is fond of quoting. See Mary Daly, "After the
Death of God the Father," *Commonweal* 94 no. 1 (1971), pp. 7–11.

unhealthy facilities, often scarring them for life.

The opposition of the Church in the area of birth control is particularly to blame, opines Daly. Not that the Church is to be held accountable for the basic facts of male and female biology, of course, but following in Beauvoir's footsteps, Daly is angry because the Church has not bought into the total women's liberation package of reproductive rights which would allow women to undertake their maternities in freedom (p. 65). Work can free women. Birth control can free women from unwanted pregnancies and allow them to work. In a real sense, therefore, it is through male occupations such as work that women can transcend.

While Daly is aware of discussion among Catholics on issues such as birth control and divorce (p. 135), she also points out that Catholics of both Left and Right are united on the abortion question, though she notes at least one Bishop, Francis Simons of Indore in India, willing to speak of the moral ambiguity and complexity of an abortion necessary to save the mother's life (p. 135). It is in her next book that we find Daly's most extensive treatment of the abortion issue.[39]

Beyond God the Father

In *Beyond God the Father*, Mary Daly links Beauvoir's epistemology of abortion to her own incipient dualist metaphysics. She also makes a definitive break with the Catholic faith and embraces a new one, radical feminism.[40] One European commentator is impressed at Daly's success in *Beyond God the Father*, a most important book not only because of its sustained attack on the institutions of patriarchy but also because in its pages Daly is able to overcome "Americanism." In fact, Daly's book is regarded in some circles as a truly universalist feminist

---

[39]Daly continues writing about the abortion issue from 1968 to 1973, the year in which she publishes *Beyond God the Father*. See, for example, an interview with Edward Maron, "Mary Daly and the Second Sex," *U.S. Catholic* 34 no. 5 (1968), pp. 21–24.

[40]"Autobiographical Preface," p. 5. We have already seen texts in Beauvoir noting the importance of religion, understood in a proper feminist sense, for women's liberation.

primer for the new feminist religion of the future.[41] Adrienne Rich is extravagant in praising *Beyond God the Father*, calling it "the first philosophy of feminism, the first psychology of feminist experience."[42]

Though Daly in *Beyond God the Father* is hopeful that an androgynous world might come into being as men and women re-evaluate traditional sex roles, she—ever the metaphysician[43]—is also working her way toward a theory which amounts to separate ontologies for men and women:

> Men and women inhabit different worlds. Even though these are profoundly related emotionally, physically, economically, socially, there is a wall that is visible to those who *almost have managed* to achieve interplanetary communication with the opposite sex.[44]

While she is working her way toward her dualist metaphysics, Daly is convinced of the need not only for an *ethics* but also an *ontology* of women's experience.

---

[41]Cf. Ginette Castro, *American Feminism: A Contemporary History*, p. 40.

[42]Rich's comments are found on the back cover of the paperback edition of *Beyond God the Father*.

[43]Cf. *Beyond God the Father*, p. 6: "For my purpose is to show that the women's revolution, insofar as it is true to its own essential dynamics, is an ontological, spiritual revolution, pointing beyond the idolatries of sexist society and sparking creative action in and toward transcendence." Commenting on her 1973 book, Daly insists that the basic theme of *Beyond God the Father* is that "the movement for women's liberation is an ontological movement" (*Outercourse*, p. 159).

[44]*Beyond God the Father*, pp. 171–172: Daly's emphasis. She holds out some hope in 1973 that a "cosmosis," a change in attitudes is possible: "It will require in men as well in women a desire to become androgynous, that is, to become themselves" (*ibid.*). There is in *Beyond God the Father* a certain tension between these two views of androgyny on the one hand, in which Daly is somewhat optimistic, and metaphysical dualism on the other, in which we find her rather more pessimistic. Daly dismisses all talk of androgyny by 1978 and fully embraces the separate ontologies thesis in *Gyn/Ecology*.

Abortion in *Beyond God the Father*

Hypocrisy is rife in male morality. With this decidely Beauvoirian beginning, Mary Daly begins her Nietzschean section on ethics, "Transvaluation of Values." Patriarchal authoritarianism sees moral issues in black and white; women's experiences, however, are in shades of gray. "The fact that all of the major ethical studies of the abortion problem, both Catholic and Protestant, have been done by men is itself symptomatic of women's oppressed condition" (*Beyond God the Father*, p. 106). A truly feminist ethics does not yet exist and will have to be formulated to deal with complex situations such as abortion.

At the beginning of a section entitled "Abortion and the Powerlessness of Women," we see Daly's incipient ontologies at work: "One hundred percent of the bishops who oppose repeal of anti-abortion laws are men and one hundred percent of the people who have abortions are women."[45] Daly pursues this line of argument throughout what amounts to her most detailed examination of the abortion issue. Abortion and abortion law repeal are not single issues but parts of a larger whole: "They must be seen within the context of sexually hierarchical society."[46]

The Anti-Abortion Devices of Patriarchy

Daly touches upon several sorts of anti-abortion arguments used by moralists which all serve the interests of the sexually hierarchical society that her radical feminist analysis of patriarchal institutions has uncovered. On the surface these anti-abortion arguments seem reasonable and objective. Viewed from the perspective of the planetary sexual caste system, they prove to be, in Daly's view, "rationalizations of a system that oppresses women. . . incongruous with the experience and needs of women" (p. 107). Daly endeavors to show that abortion is

---

[45]See also *Outercourse*, p. 142. Cf. the observation made by Catherine MacKinnon, *Toward a Feminist Theory of the State*, p. 184: "Most women who seek abortions became pregnant while having sexual intercourse with men." We note in passing Daly stating the case for abortion in the terms of Catholic *hierarchy* versus the unwillingly pregnant woman. She will return to this theme of the Catholic *hierarchy* again on p. 113.

[46]*Beyond God the Father*, p. 106.

not a single action but comprises part of the fabric of a woman's life and experience. The *social context* within which abortions take place is most important to give an adequate evaluation. Arguments against abortion are the devices of patriarchy.

Though Daly's argument is not totally systematic, the following would seem to be the anti-abortion devices of patriarchy:

1. The Loaded Language Argument.
2. The Women Can't Be Trusted Argument.
3. The Wedge Argument.
4. The Unanswerable Argument.
5. The Almost Absolute Value Argument.

"The Loaded Language Argument" is seen when anti-abortionists use expressions such as "the *murder* of the unborn *child*." Such rhetorical devices, while plausible and cogent superficially, serve in reality to mask a system oppressive to women's experiences. As Daly views the matter, "there has been a planned and concerted tactic on the part of the hierarchy to use inflammatory language such as 'murder' rather than 'abortion,' and 'child' rather than 'fetus'" (p. 113).

"The Women Can't Be Trusted Argument" is critical of George Huntston Williams's approach to the abortion question.[47] The supposed sharing in the abortion decision envisioned by Williams is deemed illusory since "it becomes evident that the woman's judgment is submerged in the condominium" (p. 107). Women work under a double handicap in the politics of abortion. On the *cultural* level, the level of sexual politics, men and women are *not* social equals and hence men cannot be assumed to judge in such matters without bias. On the *biological* level, Daly observes that "the 'progenitors' do not have equal roles in the entire reproductive process, since it is obviously the woman who has the burden of pregnancy."[48]

"The Wedge Argument" goes by many names; Daly captures its essence in a pithy way: "If the fetus can be destroyed, who will be the

---

[47]George Huntston Williams, "The Sacred Condominium," in John T. Noonan, Jr. (ed.), *The Morality of Abortion: Legal and Historical Perspectives*, pp. 146–171, is the article to which Daly refers.

[48]Mary Daly, *Beyond God the Father*, p. 107. The rest of the passage is vintage Beauvoir.

next victim?"[49] Daly appropriates the reply made to this sort of anti-abortion device by Jean MacRae. In Daly's words:

> The death of the fetus is significantly different from that of a more actualized human being. . . . The question of abortion has to do with a *unique* struggle between two living beings, for it is only in the case of an unwanted pregnancy that the *body* and the whole well-being of a person is controlled by another being.[50]

As she answers "The Wedge Argument" against abortion, Mary Daly does so in terms that are remarkably akin to the bodyright argument for abortion.

"The Unanswerable Argument" is the one that "consists in posing such a question as, 'When does human life begin?' Since no unanimous response is forthcoming, the conclusion drawn is that women must passively submit to the situation until they can produce the impossible answer" (p. 111). Daly merely states the device of the "unanswerable argument" and leaves it at that. At any rate, it would appear that Simone de Beauvoir's influence is in evidence, especially in the phrase regarding women *passively submitting to the situation*.[51]

"The Almost Absolute Value Argument" contends that defense of the fetus' right to life has been an important part of Christian moral reflection from the very beginning:

> Still another tactic is that employed by John Noonan in asserting that the moral condemnation of abortion has been an almost absolute value in history. The question that is unasked is: Whose history? The fact

---

[49] *Beyond God the Father*, p. 111. She also calls it "the domino theory" (*ibid.*). She quotes a text from Ralph Potter in which she finds the argument clearly employed.

[50] *Beyond God the Father*, p. 111. We do detect a switch in Daly's linguistic usage in the two scenarios outlined by MacRae. In the first, the fetus is characterized as less than a *more actualized human being*; in the second, it is the well-being of a *person* that is being controlled by another *being*.

[51] Cf. Simone de Beauvoir, *The Second Sex*, p. 57: ". . . Giving birth and suckling are not *activities*, they are natural functions; no project is involved. . . . she [the pregnant woman] submitted passively to her biologic fate" (author's emphasis).

that history written by men has ignored the historical
experience of women is not taken into account
(*Beyond God the Father*, p. 111).

Once again we find Mary Daly taking issue with those who oppose the
practice of human abortion by the tactic of dismissing all arguments as
a priori invalid or at the very least highly suspect precisely because they
have been elaborated by men. A hermeneutics of suspicion, indeed.[52]

Abortion as an Issue of Power

The influence of the author of *The Second Sex* is much in
evidence in this passage as we see Mary Daly distilling the abortion
question down to power and control:

Women did not arbitrarily choose abortion as part of
the feminist platform. It has arisen out of the realities
of the situation. On its deepest level, the issue is not
as different from the issue of birth control as many,
particularly liberal Catholics, would make it appear.
There are deep questions involved which touch the
very meaning of human existence. Are we going to let
'nature' take its course or take the decision into our
own hands? In the latter case, who will decide? What
the women's movement is saying is that decisions will
be made affecting the processes of 'nature,' and that
women as individuals will make the decision in
matters most intimately concerning ourselves (*Beyond
God the Father*, p. 113).

After an attempt to explain what she considers an enlightened religious
attitude on reproductive rights—the standard Beauvoirian fare of better

---

[52]Feminist theology often employs a hermeneutic of suspicion. We see it, for instance,
in Elisabeth Schüssler Fiorenza, "Toward a Feminist Biblical Hermeneutics: Biblical
Interpretation and Liberation Theology," in Charles E. Curran and Richard A.
McCormick, S.J. (eds.), *Readings in Moral Theology, No. 4: the Use of Scripture in Moral
Theology* (New York: Paulist Press, 1984), pp. 354-382. Susan Welch, *Communities
of Resistance and Liberation: a Feminist Theology of Liberation* (Maryknoll: Orbis
Books, 1985), extols Daly as a master of suspicion.

birth control, better sex education, free access to safe and legal abortion and the omnipresent "technological creativity" to which Daly adds her own contribution, vasectomy—the American feminist goes on to avow that "patriarchal power structures, whether civil or ecclesiastical, of course do not operate in this humanizing way" (p. 114). Thus the abortion question becomes an issue of power.

Abortion, she warns, is neither the summit of feminist consciousness nor the apex of religious consciousness; feminism ought not to fixate on it as if it were. Abortion is never an isolated issue. It is of a piece with a host of other issues, and feminism must continue to search out these connections. Among these interlinked issues Daly lists rape and war.[53]

Seen in this new feminist light, the question of abortion law repeal is no longer to be regarded as peripheral. Drawing on Simone de Beauvoir once again, Daly contends:

> At this moment in history the abortion issue has become a focal point for dramatic conflict between the ethic of patriarchal authoritarianism and the ethic of courage to confront ambiguity. When concrete decisions have to be made concerning whether or not to have an abortion, a complex web of circumstances demands consideration. There are no adequate textbook answers. Essentially women are saying that because there is ambiguity surrounding the whole question and because sexually hierarchical society is stacked against women, abortion is not appropriately

---

[53]Cf. *Beyond God the Father*, pp. 107–109. Is it possible that Daly's discussion of rape harks back to Beauvoir's suggestion that, all things considered, heterosexual intercourse is akin to rape? There is a tolerance for complexity in war and in cases of capital punishment in the Christian moral tradition. Why has this not been translated into the complexity of the abortion decision? Daly seems to be asking for a theory of the just abortion to go along with the theory of the just war. This is clearly the question posed to the United States Catholic Bishops by Mary C. Segers, "The Catholic Bishops' Pastoral Letter on War and Peace: a Feminist Perspective," *Feminist Studies* 11 no. 3 (1985), pp. 619–647.

a matter of criminal law.[54]

As Daly sees the matter, abortion is affirmative action in practice. Abortion is a necessary palliative to atone for past patriarchal injustices.

Women, including many Christian women, have aborted. Did all feel guilty? No. And if some did, it can be explained as well by cultural conditioning as by anything else. The guilt is produced by society, not by any immorality. Daly's indebtedness to Beauvoir's culturalist hypothesis is apparent:

> Indeed, it is clear that even within Christian societies multitudes of women have by their actions repudiated the assumption that the life of the fetus is an absolute value. The argument that all or most of these women have suffered great guilt feelings is first of all false as an alleged statement of fact, and second it is dishonest in not recognizing that even if such guilt feelings exist in some cases, they may be explained by social conditioning.[55]

---

[54]Mary Daly, *Beyond God the Father*, p. 110. We note the reference to Beauvoir's *The Ethics of Ambiguity*. In 1970 Richard Cardinal Cushing of Boston said: "Catholics do not need the support of civil law to be faithful to their religious conviction." Text found in Kate Maloy and Maggie Jones Patterson, *Birth or Abortion? Private Struggles in a Political World*, p. 96. At about the same time, Jesuit Robert Drinan was saying the same about the decriminalization of abortion laws. Pro-choice advocates found such views helpful for their own ends. We note *en passant* that at about the same time as the American Jesuit was urging a decriminalization of all abortion statutes, a group of Jesuits was attempting something similar in France. See for example the collective article edited by Bruno Ribes, S. J., "Pour une réforme de la legislation française relative à l'avortement," *Études* 338 (janvier 1973), pp. 55–84.

[55]Cf. *Beyond God the Father*, pp. 111–112. Compare Daly regarding the status of the fetus with the remarks made by another professor at Boston College, Lisa Sowle Cahill, "Abortion, Autonomy and Community," in Sidney and Daniel Callahan (eds.), *Abortion: Understanding Differences*, p. 262: "My theoretical position on abortion (that the fetus deserves serious but not absolute consideration) has been confirmed by my experiences of pregnancy and parenthood with the difference that my view of the mother-fetus relation is now 'from the inside out' rather than from detached observation. Motherhood has heightened my sensitivity to the vulnerability of the fetus and its concomitant need for protection, as well as to the 'otherness' of the fetus and the burden that it imposes when the needs of mother and fetus are incompatible."

At this point Daly enlists the aid of two male authors on abortion: Daniel Callahan and Lawrence Lader. While neither is without flaw, each proves serviceable in showing the cracks in the anti-abortion structures of patriarchy.[56]

Some Conclusions from *Beyond God the Father*

While Mary Daly begins her feminism by siding with Simone de Beauvoir and taking issue with her Church on the matters of birth control, abortion, divorce, and the ordination of women, the examination of the abortion issue leads Daly to see that the Church is not the whole of the problem but only a part. In fact, she finds mainline Protestantism is no better than Catholicism in responding to feminist concerns.[57] The *real* problem is sexism, the sexual caste system that currently is in power all over the globe. What is the importance of the abortion issue in Daly's radical feminist perspective?

> Feminism cannot be reduced to an isolated "issue".
> . . . The very issue of abortion is revelatory of the
> fact that feminism is not merely an issue but rather a
> new mode of being (*Beyond God the Father*, p. 113).

Her radical feminist analysis has led to the discovery of a patriarchal world order; this enables Daly to see the abortion question not only in terms of power politics but also in terms of a metaphysics, as we see in her contention that feminism is "a new mode of being." Men have power, women want it. Abortion is no minor issue. Thinking her way out of the Church means that Mary Daly can now see the abortion question for what it is in a radical feminist perspective: a male attempt to control women's reproductive powers.

Daly, it is true, does mention the ambiguity of the act of abortion and the ambivalence experienced by many women regarding

---

[56]Cf. *Beyond God the Father*, pp. 112–113 and notes 22 through 24.

[57]Cf. *Beyond God the Father*, pp. 120–121, where Protestant ethicians Paul Ramsey and James Gustafson are criticized by Daly, the former for his defense of war, the latter for hinting that "abortion (though sometimes permissible) is a more serious aberration than war, and that fetuses are more to be mourned than adult human beings."

the abortion decision, but, as we have seen, she calls on Beauvoir's culturalism to explain them away.[58] Having crossed the abortion Rubicon, Daly is well aware that all her links to the Roman Catholic Church are severed. She will not treat the abortion issue any more extensively than she has done in *Beyond God the Father*.

In her "Feminist Postchristian Introduction," which Daly writes for a re-issue of *The Church and the Second Sex*, she gives a book review of sorts, the newer radical feminist Daly critiquing the early Christian Daly who wrote *The Church and the Second Sex*. She castigates her earlier self for thinking that the Christian tradition was worth saving. As an indication of how far she has traveled in such a short time, she notes that what was scarcely thinkable before—a Catholic writing about abortion, for example—has led to greater insights as well. Not only the role of women in marriage but also the corrupt roots of the institution of marriage itself are now seen for what they are. Daly, in effect, with this critique on marriage, has come to accept the views of Simone de Beauvoir on the matter of reproductive rights, of birth control and abortion, and of marriage as an unnatural institution, one of the chief obstacles to the liberation of women. Homosexuality was part of Beauvoir's program, and it makes its way into Mary Daly as well; she accepts it as a value-free part of post-patriarchal culture (p. 36). Now that she sees the world in a radical feminist perspective, choices have to be made.

Abortion in *Gyn/Ecology*

Gyn/Ecology is a chronicling of male horrors—psychological, anthropological, cultural, religious, and medical—perpetrated upon females.[59] Although abortion is not a central concern, it does make an

---

[58]Cf. *Beyond God the Father*, pp. 111–112. Since she avails herself of the thesis of separate ontologies for men and women, perhaps the question can be raised: is the explanation to be found in nature or in culture? Is Daly being totally consistent here? On the charge of inconsistency, cf. Denise Lardner Carmody, *Feminism and Christianity: A Two-Way Reflection* (Nashville: Abingdon Press, 1982), p. 86: Daly's demonization of males has made her lose her grip on objective reality.

[59]Mary Daly, *Gyn/Ecology: The Metaethics of Radical Feminism*, is an attempt to forge a feminist ethic as well as a new feminist language. Claudia Card (ed.), *Feminist Ethics* (Lawrence: University Press of Kansas, 1991), regards *Gyn/Ecology* as the most

appearance in a section entitled "Flying Fetuses: Myth-ological/Technological Necrophilia" which begins with a description of Fordham Law Professor Robert Byrn's attempt to save fetuses from destruction in the state of New York.

After noting that Byrn's attorney argued that "the fetus might well be described as an astronaut in a uterine spaceship," Daly quotes Ellen Frankfurt to the effect that male perfidy is especially in evidence here because "there is a desire to see the fetus as controlling the woman" (*Gyn/Ecology*, p. 50). In Daly's power analysis, such a view is intolerable. The reason for this reaches into the heart of the feminist pro-abortion position: "Our bodies, our lives, our right to decide" is at stake.[60]

Men feel fetal. They identify with the fetus. Daly cites Jean-Paul Sartre as leading her to the source of this "fetal identification syndrome."[61] Such an identification of males with fetuses will become a standard part of feminist bodyright arguments in favor of abortion, overlooking Simone de Beauvoir's observation that it is often the man who urges the woman to get an abortion.[62]

---

important work in feminist ethics in twenty years. Harsher is the critique of John Gordon, *The Myth of the Monstrous Male, and Other Feminist Fables* (New York: Playboy Press, 1982): for a man to read Daly's book without murmur is like a Jew reading *Mein Kampf* for its imagery (p. 134).

[60]Cf. Letty M. Russell, *Household of Freedom: Authority in Feminist Theology* (The 1986 Annie Kinkead Warfield Lectures) (Philadelphia: Westminster, 1987), p. 53. Speaking of the feminist equivalent to the Midas Touch in which everything turns to a question of power and authority, Russell cites with approval Daly's line from *Beyond God the Father*: "If god is male, then the male is God," arguably the most famous line in Daly's writings. Daly's statement is examined and criticized in many of the articles appearing in Alvin Kimel, Jr., (ed.), *Speaking the Christian God: The Holy Trinity and the Challenge of Feminism* (Grand Rapids: Eerdmans, 1992).

[61]*Gyn/Ecology*, p. 431, note 30: "A striking admission of male identification with fetuses is made by Jean-Paul Sartre in *Being and Nothingness*, translated and with an introduction by Hazel E. Barnes (New York: Washington Square, 1966), p. 198: 'We can conceive of the ontological meaning of this shocking solidarity with the foetus, a solidarity which we neither deny nor understand.'"

[62]Cf. *The Second Sex*, p. 463: "And now here is man asking woman to relinquish her triumph as female in order to preserve his liberty, so as not to handicap his future, for the benefit of his profession!" Historian James Mohr, *Abortion in America: The Origins and Evolution of National Policy, 1800–1900* (New York: Oxford University Press, 1978), notes the hostility of nineteenth-century American feminists to

Daly's Separatist Metaphysics

The upshot of all this leads into the heart of Daly's separatist vision: men are necrophilic, women are biophilic. She redefines "necrophilia" to mean "love for those victimized into a state of living death."[63] Men are childless by their very nature, interested in reproducing their male selves, and they can do so only by living off the reproductive powers of females.[64]

Daly by now has come to see male plots everywhere. To reverse the theory of penis envy with one of womb envy as Karen Horney did is nothing but an instance of male fixation and fetishism:

> The problem with such a theory is that the implied criticism stops short of being a genuine feminist analysis. Hags must learn to double-double unthink (Andrea Dworkin's phrase)—that is, to go past the obvious level of male-made reversals and find the underlying Lie.[65]

Men's alleged creativity is bogus to Daly, a form of parasitism, in fact,

---

abortion. Matilda Joslyn Gage (1826–1898), for example, lays the blame for abortion squarely on the doorstep of the male sex. The Foreword for a re-issue of Gage's 1893 book, *Women, Church and State: The Original Exposé of Male Collaboration Against the Female Sex* (Watertown, MA: Persephone, 1980) was written by Mary Daly.

[63] *Gyn/Ecology*, p. 59. In *Pure Lust*, pp. 36–50, in an attempt to show that *all* men are necrophilic, Daly does a deconstruction of sorts upon several revered male figures, including Mahatma Gandhi, T. E. Lawrence, Robert Oppenheimer and Dag Hammarskjöld.

[64] Cf. Mary O'Brien, *Reproducing the World: Essays in Feminist Theory* (Boulder: Westview Press, 1989), p. 14. She picks up on this Beauvoirian theme: "Paternity is fundamentally ideal, and is a matter of knowing rather than doing." And a bit later: "Mater semper certa est; pater is est quem nuptiae demonstrant" (p. 21). In O'Brien's Marxist-inspired analysis of the reproductive situation: if fatherhood is ungrounded idealism, motherhood is grounded materialism.

[65] *Gyn/Ecology*, p. 60. Claude Alzon, *Femme mythifiée, femme mystifiée* (Paris: Presses universitaires de France, 1978), pp. 94–98, praises for the most part the thought of Simone de Beauvoir and upbraids French feminists, such as Annie LeClerc, who tend to make too much of female bodily differences. In Alzon's estimation, LeClerc has written one of the most reactionary feminist books ever.

because "this envy is not necessarily a desire to *be* creative but rather to draw—like fetuses—upon another's (the mother's) energy as a source" (*Gyn/Ecology*, p. 60). They wish to control women just as fetuses are thought to control the pregnancy. Men/fetuses regard women with contempt, regarding them as nothing more than spaceships which they relegate "to the role of controlled containers, and later discard as trash" (p. 61).

In a departure from the standard Beauvoir line, Mary Daly begins to see technology as not quite the savior that the French feminist thought that it was. In fact, technological creation manifests the profoundly necrophilic tendencies of technocracy (p. 61). While the benefits of the birth control pill, extolled by the earlier and excoriated by the later Daly, fall under this anti-technological rubric, regarding abortion, however, Daly makes no such correction in course, leaving us to conclude that she regards the technology of abortion as no such threat to women.

Abortion in *Pure Lust*

The last book to interest us is the 1984 volume with the oxymoronic title, *Pure Lust*.[66] In it Mary Daly continues her attempt to refashion a new feminist language in order to reclaim for women what patriarchy has stolen: the power of naming.[67]

---

[66]Mary Daly, *Pure Lust: Elemental Feminist Philosophy* (Boston: Beacon Press, 1984). The title refers more to erraticism than to eroticism, notes Daly, who adds that the latter meaning is by no means excluded (p. x). Aware that her thought is being regarded—and not only by 'snools' (p. 20)—as more and more out of touch with reality, Daly answers: "We are proud that our published works are, according to phallic fixations ('standards'), utter *errata*" (p. xi).

[67]*Pure Lust*, pp. 449–453, contains an index of words usages, new and old, and how they are to be understood in the specific sense meant by Mary Daly. Robin Morgan, *Going Too Far: The Personal Chronicle of a Feminist* (New York: Vintage Books, 1978), approves of Daly's efforts to give back to women the power of naming, the loss of which is described as the ultimate degradation. Less sanguine is Moira Gatens, *Feminism and Philosophy: Perspectives on Difference and Equality*, p. 80, who cautions that Daly's views on naming, especially in *Gyn/Ecology*, verge on the magical. (For a sample, psychiatry's "therapist" becomes to Daly "The/Rapist.") When Daly, *Gyn/Ecology*, p. 239, urges her followers to get a "misterectomy" rather than use the Pill, this is more than Alice Echols, "The Taming of the Id: Feminist Sexual Politics,

With her separate ontologies for women and men, Daly seems to take for granted the fact that because the Church has a male priesthood, it *must* be part of the planetary patriarchal conspiracy. As a result, seeing male plots everywhere, Daly sees the Eucharistic doctrine of the Church as an instance of one of the "less obviously sex-related dogmas which have undermined psychic integrity," with effects that make themselves felt not only in the hearts of millions of Catholics but "also, in a more subliminal way, the whole of Western society. For training in doublethink and doubt of one's own perceptions is psychically contagious" (*Pure Lust*, pp. 50–51). Daly opines that the Catholic doctrine of the Eucharist has had an impact on the abortion wars being fought in America.[68]

Daly criticizes American conservative Phyllis Schlafly, who led the successful fight against passage of the Equal Rights Amendment, calling Schlafly "a sort of female Doctor Strangelove," loving as she does the Bomb and hating all forms of life on earth, except life in fetal form, a passage which seems an evocation of Beauvoir's barb about the Church's "uncompromising humanitarianism for man in the fetal condition" (*Pure Lust*, p. 212). Though not treated quite so harshly, Mother Teresa of Calcutta is next. After citing the Nobel Peace Prize winner on the evils of abortion, Daly interprets in feminist terms what women like Mother Teresa and Phyllis Schlafly are really accomplishing:

1968–1983" in Carole Vance (ed.), *Pleasure and Danger: Exploring Female Sexuality* (Boston: Routledge and Kegan Paul, 1984), p. 53, can bear. Daly's lesbianism, Echols seems to be saying, would derail the sexual revolution which Echols equates, more or less, with the feminist revolution. The question of how far the sexual revolution is to be linked to the feminist revolution is, of course, the point at issue.

[68]Does Daly mean to say that to see the human person present in a fetus is akin to seeing Christ present in the Eucharist? Be that as it may, on one point Daly is certainly right: Catholic teaching on the sacrament of Christ's body and blood *will* have repercussions on the Church's moral teaching on abortion as well as other issues. We remember Simone de Beauvoir touching on this issue in *The Second Sex*, p. 468: "In a sense the mystery of the Incarnation repeats itself in each mother; every child born *is* a god who *is* made man; he cannot find self-realization as a being with consciousness and freedom unless he first comes into the world; the mother lends herself to this mystery, but she does not control it; it is beyond her power to influence what in the end will be the true nature of this being who is developing in her womb." (Keep in mind what Beauvoir understands by *repetition* to make a proper exegesis of the text.)

The point here is not to question Mother Teresa's good intentions but to see how her well-meaning but inherently woman-destroying simple views are massively used against women, eliciting not only guilt but also despair that there might be another way of be-ing. Thus the publicly legitimated alternatives seem to be the pseudoself-serving, woman-betraying politics of a Schlafly on the one hand, and the self-sacrificing, unconsciously woman-betraying beliefs of a Mother Teresa on the other (p. 214).

Such women serve the masters of patriarchy. While Daly's desire is not to "attack" these women, she explains that she has had to shed light on such matters lest her sisters' search for their true selves be impeded if they followed the lead of Schlafly and Mother Teresa:

My intent is to Name the foreground fixing of female Passion, the forces at work to freeze our Fire. For these mutilating messages infect *all* women, killing the possibility of Elemental E-motion (p. 214).

Daly beyond Beauvoir

True enough, says Daly, abortion does serve as a sort of microcosm of female oppression (*Pure Lust*, p. 323), but feminists must not spend too much energy on this one issue. It is not the be-all and end-all of feminine liberation. Given the lesbianism which animates Daly's feminist universe, it is obvious that too much focus on abortion recalls to mind a part of reality that Daly and those feminists who follow her would have human beings either overlook or else go beyond: the desire of one sex for the other. For lesbian feminists, abortion is not a real problem since heterosexuality is not a real practice.

In her explanations of how patriarchy is all-embracing and goes far beyond Roman Catholicism,[69] Daly in *Pure Lust* finally makes a break with Simone de Beauvoir. So successful has patriarchy been in getting its death-dealing message across that even a thinker as astute as

---

[69]Cf. *Pure Lust*, p. 322, picking up on a theme first mentioned in *Beyond God the Father*, p. 5.

Beauvoir has fallen victim (cf. *Pure Lust*, pp. 136ff.) Apologizing for the matricide she is about to commit, Daly detects a Beauvoir profoundly patriarchal in her underlying assumptions. If there is a sin in Simone de Beauvoir, Daly believes she has uncovered it: it is masculinism.[70]

The depressing case Simone de Beauvoir weaves together in *The Second Sex* gives the impression that nothing can be done to change it, a conclusion that Daly understands but does not accept (p. 138). As a counter, Daly takes refuge in the work of those who have seen a matriarchy as predating the patriarchy currently in power.

What precisely are those elements in Simone de Beauvoir's thought which Daly has abandoned?

1. The animus against nature.
2. The total acceptance of the male as normative and masculine sexuality as the paradigm.

What has Daly *kept* from the thought of the French existentialist feminist?

1. Simone de Beauvoir's hostility toward motherhood and the family, if we can judge by one of Daly's most recent writings.[71]

---

[70]Cf. *Pure Lust*, p. 137. Daly is not alone in this discovery of *masculinism* in Simone de Beauvoir. There is a sustained feminist critique of Beauvoir's masculinism in Genevieve Lloyd, *The Man of Reason: 'Male' and 'Female' in Western Philosophy* (Minneapolis: University of Minnesota Press, 1984). Writes Lloyd: "What I am suggesting here is that the ideal of transcendence is, in a more fundamental way than de Beauvoir allows, a male ideal; that it feeds on the exclusion of the feminine" (p. 101). Note the comment made by Elaine Hoffman Baruch and Lucienne J. Serrano, *Women Analyse Women: In France, England and the United States* (New York and London: New York University Press, 1988), p. 9: "Simone de Beauvoir may be called the chief exemplar of liberal feminism, which holds that the male view of the world is the human view and that women should subscribe to it as much as possible."

[71]Mary Daly, "Be-Witching: Re-Calling the Archmagical Powers of Women," in Dorchen Leidholdt and Janice Raymond (eds.), *The Sexual Liberals and the Attack on Feminism* (New York: Pergamon Press, 1990), pp. 211–221, is, in effect, warning women to beware of any supposed need for babies and family. "Mother Nature" is proving to be quite resilient. Moral teaching based on natural law precepts proves to be a thorn in the feminists' side. One way of saying it is that of paragraph 15 of the 1974 *Declaration on Abortion* issued by the Sacred Congregation for the Doctrine of the Faith: "One cannot change nature. Nor can one exempt women, any more than men, from what nature demands of them. Furthermore, all publicly recognized

2. Abortion remains an essential component of women's liberation.[72] Even in a radical lesbian separatist feminism, the right to abortion is kept because it is, according to Mary Daly, a microcosm of women's oppression.

Commentary on Mary Daly:
Some Positive Points

Francis Mannion has described five varieties of feminist religious thought. He sees a dialogue possible with four of the five. The one sort of feminism that Mannion concludes cannot be talked with is Mary Daly's.[73] That is unfortunate in a way because some of what she writes has value.

1. Daly has shown herself willing to rethink positions that she formerly held but has come to regard as erroneous. She has come to see the ambivalent nature of technological progress. We noted her critical comments on a technology out of touch with humanity. On this point, some of what Daly is saying is reminiscent of the thought of Gabriel Marcel.

2. Daly takes language seriously, and she has always seen the importance of metaphysics in any serious discussion of feminism.

3. Of feminist theorists, Daly has had some success in breaking away from the culturalist thesis of Simone de Beauvoir. Nature makes a return in Mary Daly, even if somewhat tentatively.

4. Daly is right on target in saying that the sexual revolution is

---

freedom is always limited by the certain rights of others." Another way of putting it is that of John Gordon, *The Myth of the Monstrous Male*, p. 32: "The doctrine of natural law is just death for feminism."

[72]In all the radical spinning that Mary Daly has done as a feminist, she has been unable to get out of the position that abortion is somehow a great good for women, and this despite her insistence that women are biophilic and love life. In *Webster's First New Intergalactic Wickedary of the English Language*, Daly, as a weaver of words, plays on the word *webster*. There is a certain irony in the fact that a 1989 United States Supreme Court Decision limiting to some extent access to abortion was known as the the *Webster Decision*. A host of feminists sounded the call to arms in the aftermath of *Webster*.

[73]M. Francis Mannion, "The Church and the Voices of Feminism," *America* 165 no. 9 (1991), pp. 212–216f.

not the ultimate freedom for women that some have claimed it to be: "Women's liberation is profoundly antithetical to the 'sexual revolution,' and the second wave of feminism was energized into being largely because of the profound realization of betrayal that the 'sexual revolution' engendered" (*Beyond God the Father*, pp. 122–123). Even if Daly credits this insight to Herbert Marcuse, its validity is, to this observer at least, well-nigh incontestable.

5. Daly is honest in seeing that on the question of abortion her feminism and the teachings of the Catholic Church are irreconcilable. Believing what she does about abortion, she cannot in good conscience say she is a Catholic.[74]

Some Criticisms

Daly is open to the charge of being inconsistent. Let us grant for the sake of argument her ontological theory of a separate male and female nature. If women are biophilic by nature, as Daly says they are, if they love life while men love death, why is it that abortion remains a microcosm of female oppression? Why is biophilia, love of life, in favor of abortion and how is this different from necrophilia? How explain the killing that takes place in abortion as a biophilic solution? Simone de Beauvoir, as we have already seen, regards killing (or the lack of it) as the reason for the subjugation of the female sex. Mary Daly, able to think her way out of other Beauvoirian positions, notably on technology and the birth control pill, is unable to do so on the question of abortion. Is not this a trace and more than a trace of necrophilia in her biophilic world? After all, Daly herself has hurled the charge of necrophilia against the Right to Life movement (See *Outercourse*, p. 406).

Mary Daly's radical critique proves to be not radical enough. Able to work her positions away from Simone de Beauvoir's masculinist web in many other instances, she simply cannot get beyond the killing in practice (abortion) though she does so in theory (biophilia). We are brought back to the killing which was, in Simone de Beauvoir's vision, the key to the whole mystery of woman's subjugation.[75]

The film "Thelma and Louise" features two women who, after

---

[74] Why she continues to teach at a Catholic institution is, of course, another matter.

[75] Cf. *The Second Sex*, p. 58.

suffering indignities at the hands of men, learn to shoot, rob, and kill, just like men. Commenting on the film in response to a newspaper article, Daly says she likes the film because it contains figures of strong women who are fighting back: "Just as that ("Thelma and Louise") is an upper for women, the theology of a God the father is a downer for women. Whether you are talking about the movie or the church, the same phenomenon is taking place: the manipulation of minds to see the dominance of males as natural and unchallengable [sic]."[76] How does the theory of biophilia support Daly saying, in effect, that violence and killing are uppers for women?

In the final analysis, when Daly comes to view the question of abortion as an issue of power, she is espousing, by and large, Beauvoir's view. Though Daly works herself beyond the Church of her parents and the influence of Simone de Beauvoir in other areas of her thought, she is unable to get beyond the killing. When it comes to the matter of human abortion, Daly's biophilia kneels at the altar of Beauvoir's killing theory.

Daly can try to define away the fetus in terms of time or tissue. She can speak all she wants of male perfidy. In fact, Daly's constant recourse to a dualist metaphysics raises an important question: Have women *ever* been free, responsible agents, given Daly's metaphysics? If not, what leads Daly to think the situation will change now?[77] In the final analysis, the nature of the act of abortion cannot be erased from the mind or from the heart, Daly's dualist metaphysics notwithstanding.

Since Daly's feminist analysis—the abortion issue included—is at bottom a question of power, she ultimately finds herself sitting in a semicircle with a group of young women, chanting as the priests are entering the hall: "Our bodies, our lives, our right to decide." The chant is a way of getting the radical feminist slogan, "The personal is the political," to serve in the context of a bodyright argument for abortion. The translation of the slogan and the chant we have seen before: "There are words as murderous as gas chambers."[78] On this point at least, Mary

---

[76]Daly was interviewed for an article written by Kathryn Marchocki, "Issues of God's Gender Causes a Stir on Earth," *Boston Sunday Herald* (June 23, 1991), p. 16.

[77]The questions are posed to Daly by Moira Gatens, *Feminism and Philosophy: Perspectives on Difference and Equality*, pp. 79–84.

[78]Simone de Beauvoir, *Force of Circumstance*, p. 22.

Daly remains in the thrall of Simone de Beauvoir.

Beauvoir and Daly:
The Universal Patriarchy

Since Mary Daly is the only one of the three American feminists whom we shall study who openly acknowledges her debt to Simone de Beauvoir, it may prove opportune to summarize what we have uncovered thus far regarding the French feminist and her quondam American follower. Both Daly and Beauvoir were trained in philosophy. Both knew well enough the classic expression of the Sophist Protagoras: "Man is the measure of all things, of those that are, that they are, of those that are not, that they are not." When Daly finally makes her break with Beauvoir, she contends in effect that regarding *man*, Beauvoir has followed Protagoras literally, all too literally.[79]

Beauvoir opened the abortion floodgates, especially with her contention that no serious moral arguments remained against the practice. While human beings were attached to religious traditions for a time in the course of their evolutionary past, science and technology must be humanity's new guides. Having cast off the faith of her childhood, Simone de Beauvoir lived her life as if there were no God, there was only man; and man is the measure of all things, including attitudes toward human abortion.

As long as women still feel attached to the outmoded religious traditions, they will be unable to make their way out to see things as clearly as Simone de Beauvoir regarding human abortion. Along with this secular approach to the question of abortion, Simone de Beauvoir links the Church to the state as two instances of *patriarchy*. This is an amorphous term, to be sure, but basically it means that males possess all the real power in human society and females are subjected to this power in myriad ways.[80]

---

[79]From what we have seen on the abortion question, whether Daly herself is exempt from the charge of masculinism is open to question.

[80]Regarding the omnipresent *patriarchy* of which feminists are wont to speak, the entry under the apposite word in Lisa Tuttle, *Encyclopedia of Feminism*, is a good place to begin: "Patriarchy" is there defined as "the universal political structure which privileges men at the expense of women; the social system which feminism is determined to destroy. The term is frequently used by contemporary feminists, who

When Mary Daly, angry woman that she was, first read Simone de Beauvoir, it would appear that she still professed belief in Jesus Christ and his Church. Her initial approach to the abortion question, then, was a blend of Beauvoir's atheistic existentialism and her own Catholic faith.[81] Yet in accepting the claim of Simone de Beauvoir that male sadism was really behind the strictures of Church and state against abortion, Mary Daly buys so totally into Simone de Beauvoir's view of things that she forgets to check to see if Beauvoir's contention be canard or correct. Daly is satisfied to repeat the male sadism charge.

The Hypocritical Ethic

Beauvoir argued a case of sorts for the hypocrisy of the birth control teaching of the Catholic Church;[82] no such case is presented to show the hypocrisy of the Church in the matter of abortion, only an attack on Dr. Roy, an admirer of Marshal Pétain, a reference to French anti-abortion laws, and a reminder that the fetus is a parasite living off the mother's body.[83] The use of the language of parasite, it may be surmised, serves as Simone de Beauvoir's attempt to circumvent the question of the moral status of the fetus. Her earlier fictional treatments lead us to this conclusion, containing as we have already seen the language of "that thing in the womb," "that mysterious bit of rot."

That some churchmen (and perhaps some feminists too, for that matter) may be hypocrites is not in question nor is the fact that other Church teachings might be open to the charge of hypocrisy. But

---

are not always in agreement as to what they mean by it."

[81]The following text has the elements of Church teaching and Beauvoir working together in Daly's *The Church and the Second Sex*, p. 135: "In the United States, where the issue of legalized abortion has been hotly debated, not only the hierarchy but also most laymen of the liberal wing have strongly opposed its legalization. *They have rightly pointed out that this is a subject which must be kept distinct from that of birth control, since the life of an existing fetus is in question.* However, there has been an irrational refusal to recognize any moral ambiguity, the assumption being that the moral question has been completely answered in the past and need not be discussed" (my emphasis).

[82]Cf. *The Second Sex*, pp. 110–112.

[83]Cf. *The Second Sex*, p. 458.

the specific charge of hypocrisy, if it means anything at all in the question of Church teaching on abortion, ought to mean that the Church says one thing—"direct abortion is always and everywhere wrong"—and then goes ahead and does another—"but in this case it is all right to abort."[84] It is this very specific charge of Church teaching being hypocritical on abortion that is unsubstantiated in either Simone de Beauvoir or Mary Daly.[85] While Simone de Beauvoir and Mary Daly may be right in pointing up the hypocrisy of men who pass anti-abortion laws and then urge their women to abort their own children, their charge of hypocrisy against the Church in the same matter simply does not stand up as an explanation.[86]

The ability of the Church to help women through problem pregnancies by offering spiritual and material assistance is, of course, a part of the approach to the real-life human experience of pregnancy. If the Church were to fail in this regard, the charge of hypocrisy would have to be reconsidered, not on the level of moral teaching regarding the

---

[84]Cf. Vittorio Mathieu, "L'aborto e i fondamenti del diritto," in various authors, *Aborto No* (Milan: Edizioni Ares, 1975), pp. 71–95, who argues a case that it is the pro-choice side of the abortion question that is guilty of hypocrisy. Pro-choice author Faye Ginsburg, "The 'Word-Made' Flesh: The Disembodiment of Gender in the Abortion Debate," in Faye Ginsburg and Anna Lowenhaupt Tsing (eds.), *Uncertain Terms: Negotiating Gender in American Culture* (Boston: Beacon Press, 1990) pp. 59–75, explains why pro-life women regard pro-choicers as hypocritical: "A woman who endorses abortion denies the links between female reproduction and nurturant character and thus becomes culturally male" (p. 72).

[85]Hans Lotstra, *Abortion: The Catholic Debate in America* (New York: Irvington Publications, 1985), p. 298, is impressed with the way Roger Wertheimer presents the Catholic case against abortion in "Understanding the Abortion Argument," in Marshall Cohen, Thomas Nagel and Thomas Scanlon (eds.), *The Rights and Wrongs of Abortion* (A Philosophy and Public Affairs Reader) (Princeton: Princeton University Press, 1974), pp. 23–51.

[86]Daly, *Beyond God the Father*, pp. 100–102 in a section called "Hypocrisy of the Traditional Morality," treats hypocrisy largely in terms of Christianity's "obsession with obedience and respect for authority." Men make the morality, women live it. Since Christianity "fails to develop an understanding and respect for the aggressive and creative virtues, it offers no alternative to the hypocrisy-condoning situation fostered by its one-sided and unrealistic ethic." What seems to be a "feminine ethic" is in reality a "phallic ethic," as radical feminism will point out. The hypocrisy? "The traditional morality of our culture has been 'feminine' in the sense of hypocritically idealizing some of the qualities imposed upon the oppressed."

wrongfulness of direct abortion but rather that of pastoral practice toward women in difficult situations.

The Church forbids abortion both to the men whose patriarchal institution of the family the Church is supposedly a part of and to the women who abort for the sake of their men. The position is clear and consistent, far from hypocritical.[87] But neither Simone de Beauvoir nor Mary Daly makes her case on these grounds, preferring to make it instead on the rather amorphous grounds of a world-wide and wildly successful male conspiracy to keep women suffering. At the same time that Simone de Beauvoir was making her case for abortion in *The Second Sex*, Romano Guardini in *Das Recht des werdendes Menschenlebens* was making a strong case for *both* the pregnant woman *and* her unborn child. Abortion affects the whole woman in all her being and, thus, is a disaster both spiritually and physically. Guardini seems extraordinarily prescient.[88]

Male Sadism

Daly decided to forego her Church's teaching on the matter of abortion, preferring to side with Simone de Beauvoir's charge of male sadism against women, overlooking the fact that when men want their wives and lovers to abort, it is the Church, supposed male bastion of a patriarchal society, that goes against these desires. If the Church is an institution of a world-wide male patriarchal structure, then she certainly is so in her own fashion.[89] There has been a long and continous

---

[87]On the internal consistency of Roman Catholicism on the abortion question, see Barbara Katz Rothman, *Recreating Motherhood: Ideology and Technology in a Patriarchal Society* (New York: W. W. Norton and Co. 1989), p. 109.

[88]Can it be the case that the male Catholic priest and theologian speaks for the woman more eloquently than the French female philosopher and the American female philosopher-theologian?

[89]In her entry on "Saint Augustine," Mary Anne Warren, *The Nature of Woman: An Encyclopedia and Guide to the Literature*, p. 49, touches on an important point regarding the sexual double standard, one for men, one for women. While such a view may well be patriarchal, Warren notes that it is *not* the teaching of the Church. She regards as one of Augustine's few virtues for feminists his doing away with the double standard so prevalent in Old Testament morality and his insistence that women are to insist on strict fidelity from their husbands.

discussion of abortion in the Church, full of complexities and nuances. To level the charge of male sadism overlooks this effort of twenty centuries.

The Church's teaching on the complex matter of abortion is not due to the fact of a universal male sadistic conspiracy; Simone de Beauvoir came much closer to the truth with her observation that the Christian Church bequeathed the fetus a soul, the actual possession of which makes abortion the unspeakable crime of the Second Vatican Council's *Gaudium et Spes*, paragraph 51, and even the possible possession of which is so great and momentous that the taking of its life ought to be inconceivable, as stated in the 1974 *Declaration on Procured Abortion*.[90]

Is Nature Misogynist?

As an atheist, Beauvoir believed in no God; as an existentialist, she believed in no human nature, no female nature, and yet "Notre-dame de Sartre" did acknowledge the facts of biology. Daly at first followed Beauvoir on the matter of no fixed human nature before finding her own Nag-gnostic (sic) dualism of man bad, woman good. She also acknowledges the facts of biology. Since I do not know a better way of expressing their thought on the matter, I will phrase it in this way: are they not, in effect, asking: Is nature misogynistic? Even Daly concedes: "The Church is not to blame for this basic biological fact."[91]

The Surprises of Christian Ethics

Simone de Beauvoir is relentless in her attacks on the Church as an implacable foe of women. Given her starting point of atheism, this is not surprising: since there is no God, the Church can lay claim to no special divine prerogatives. Yet on occasion, Beauvoir admits, in a

---

[90]Cf. Paragraph 13 of that document: "From a moral point of view this is certain: even if a doubt existed concerning whether the fruit of conception is already a human person, it is objectively a grave sin to dare to risk murder. 'The one who will be a man is already one.'"

[91]Mary Daly, *The Church and the Second Sex*, p. 65. I am reminded of Marcuse's remark to the effect that the feminist revolution is a fight against the work of God.

roundabout way, that the Church has also done wonders and marvels. Not the least among them is that it is the Church which Beauvoir pillories pitilessly that acknowledges that women and their unborn children possess full membership in the human family.[92] The Church has recognized that these two traditionally suspect categories of humans possess (as a gift of the God in whom Simone de Beauvoir does not believe) that most precious of all spiritual qualities, the human soul. Even if grudgingly, Beauvoir testifies to the expansive, inclusivistic ethic of the Church she left in her childhood.[93]

The Sex that Kills

While on one level, the level of public consumption and the selling of abortion, as it were, Simone de Beauvoir seeks to establish a woman's abortion right as a safeguard against male hypocrisy and Church teaching, we must not overlook the importance she gives to killing in her existentialist analysis of women's status as the second sex. After all, she emphasizes that the key to the whole mystery of woman's subjugation is found precisely here.[94]

Mary Daly sees the abortion situation as a microcosm of women's oppression, revolving around the issue of power. By means of her dualist metaphysics and its attendant militant angry prose, Daly can speak of the right to dispose of unwanted fetuses as a way of atoning for past male atrocities, failing to ask how violence is the answer to violence

---

[92]Regarding women, Beauvoir observes in *The Second Sex*, p. 688: "Young and pretty, the slaves of the harem are always the same in the sultan's embrace; Christianity gave eroticism its savor of sin and legend when it endowed the human female with a soul." Regarding the fetus, cf. *The Second Sex*, p. 458: "As for the moral considerations, they amount in the end to the old Catholic argument: the unborn child has a soul, which is denied access to paradise, if its life is interrupted."

[93]Mary Anne Warren, "The Moral Significance of Birth," *Hypatia* 4 no. 3 (1989), pp. 59–61, argues to the effect that if the fetus is a person, the woman must be less than a person. Pregnancy is the only human relationship where the legal personhood of one human being is not compatible with that of another. To protect a fetus is to nullify woman's right to autonomy.

[94]Cf. Simone de Beauvoir, *The Second Sex*, p. 58. Her debt to Hegel on the fundamental hostility of each consciousness to every other consciousness was filtered through Sartre's "Hell is other people."

save in the context of taking refuge in seeing everything in terms of raw power and defining the fetus away as a part of this power approach. There can be no questions posed to her in her lesbian world, a world "beyond compromise."[95] Biophilia theory notwithstanding, Daly too is unable to get beyond the killing. Like Simone de Beauvoir, her quondam heroine, Mary Daly defines abortion into feminism.

Though Mary Daly does make the proper bows to the abortion issue as "the microcosm of female oppression," her lesbian separatist feminism means that abortion will not be quite the issue to her that it will be to heterosexual women.[96] Daly's fight for abortion is a fight against what she considers past patriarchal injustices. Hers is more an advocacy of abortion as might than as right. But that is coming, and it is not inconceivable that Daly has helped, in some way, to pave the road.[97]

Transition to Carol Gilligan

Beauvoir's epistemology of abortion tells women, in effect, that abortion makes them *know*. In unmasking the perfidies of patriarchy's alienating structures, Beauvoir believes that women learn the bitter truths regarding male irresponsibility, male hypocrisy, and male sadism. The abortion knowledge is a knowledge bought at a bitter price.

Daly's metaphysics of abortion is similarly bleak, a message telling women that it is in the very *nature* of males to humiliate women; such is the *metaphysical structure* of the male world. Indeed, as a

---

[95] *Gyn/Ecology*, p. 40: "As Harpies and Furies, Feminists in the tradition of the Great Hags are beyond compromise."

[96] An oft-cited representative of this heterosexual wing is Lucinda Cisler, "Unfinished Business: Birth Control and Women's Liberation," in Robin Morgan (ed.), *Sisterhood Is Powerful: An Anthology of Writings From the Women's Liberation Movement* (New York: Vintage Books, 1970), pp. 245–289.

[97] In *The Church and the Second Sex*, written in 1968, Daly notes that Catholics, from the hierarchy to even the most liberal of the laity, closed ranks when it came to the immorality of abortion. Twenty years later, Patricia Beattie Jung and Thomas Shannon (eds.), *Abortion and Catholicism: The Abortion Debate*, write: "Our basic point is that on both sides of the debate it is possible to develop reasonable arguments based on commonly held principles" (p. 4). And: "We recognize that our selection of articles implicitly validates the abortion debate" (p. 2).

microcosm of female oppression, abortion is a constant reminder to women that abortion humiliates them. Hence, her plea for a lesbian separatist world which avoids the humiliation of the procedure. In this sense, then, it is true to say that Beauvoir and Daly present a deeply pessimistic view of the nature of at least half the human beings on the face of the planet.

Carol Gilligan will try to furnish the abortion mentality with something lacking in both of her feminist forebears: for want of a better term, we may label it as an *optimism* of sorts in the procedure. As we shall see, Carol Gilligan's analysis will present women with the possibility that, all things considered, abortion—when done for the right reasons—can be an occasion of psychological growth.

CHAPTER THREE

CAROL GILLIGAN, 1936–

The Psychology of Abortion

The conflict precipitated by the pregnancy catches up issues that are critical to psychological development. These issues pertain to the worth of the self in relation to others, the claiming of the power to choose, and the acceptance of responsibility for choice. By provoking a confrontation with choice, the abortion crisis can become a "very auspicious time. You can use the pregnancy as sort of a learning, a teeing-off point, which makes it useful in a way." The same sense of a possibility for growth in this crisis is expressed by other women, who arrive through this encounter with choice at a new understanding of relationships and speak of their sense of "a new beginning," a chance "to take control of my life."[1]

Abortion in a Different Voice

In 1971 Mary Daly was invited to speak at Harvard as part of the continuing lecture series of the Harvard Divinity School. At the end of her talk she urged her followers to walk out of the Harvard Memorial

---

[1]Carol Gilligan, *In a Different Voice: Psychological Theory and Women's Development* (Cambridge: Harvard University Press, 1982), pp. 94–95. For the thirty-second printing, Gilligan has added a "Letter to Readers, 1993," but the text remains the same. *In a Different Voice* is the best-selling book in the history of Harvard University Press.

Church in protest that Christianity was not good enough for women.[2] At about the same time as Daly walked out of Harvard, Carol Gilligan walked in. Though she makes no mention of Mary Daly and cites Simone Weil rather than Simone de Beauvoir, Carol Gilligan will make the abortion issue a central piece of her feminism, as did the other two feminists whose thought on the matter we have already examined.

The power of words to shape the abortion debate is in evidence once again. While Beauvoir and Daly used the ponderous language of existentialist philosophy and theology,[3] Carol Gilligan writes about abortion in the cool and relatively clear discourse of contemporary developmental psychology. Even some feminist critics who take issue with other aspects of Gilligan's approach to women's morality confess that they are impressed by Gilligan's clear and relatively jargon-free literary style.[4] While she might approach the abortion decision in a different voice, the sound in the end is very much along the lines we have seen in Beauvoir and Daly: "Our bodies, our lives, our right to decide." But she will try to link the abortion question to the issue of rights and choice in a much more direct way than either Beauvoir or Daly. My contention on this point might seem strange because the feminine morality or, better, the different voice Gilligan is trying to describe, is often understood as a *morality of care* as opposed to a *morality of rights*, but in the course of this chapter I hope to illustrate how Gilligan accomplishes this task.

As an educational psychologist following in the footsteps of

---

[2]The incident is related in *Beyond God the Father*, p. 144, where Daly speaks of it somewhat biblically, labelling it the 1971 Exodus. One woman, explaining what the event meant to her, is quoted by Daly: "We were leaving to do whatever we had to do to become persons." See also Daly's comments on the incident in *Outercourse*, pp. 137ff.

[3]On the language of Beauvoir, see the comments by Marielouise Janssen-Jurreit, *Sexism: The Male Monopoly on History and Thought* (translated by Verne Moberg) (New York: Farrar, Straus and Giroux, 1982), esp. p. 166. Regarding Daly, Jean Bethke Elshtain, *Public Man, Private Woman*, speaks critically of what she calls "Mary Daly's metaphysical or 'metaethical' language of demonology" (p. 223).

[4]This is the opinion of Susan Faludi, *Backlash: The Undeclared War Against American Women* (New York: Crown, 1991), p. 327. See also Linda Kerber, Catherine Greeno, Eleanor Maccoby, Zella Luria, Carol B. Stack, and Carol Gilligan, "On 'In a Different Voice': an Interdisciplinary Forum," *Signs* 11 no. 2 (1986), pp. 304-333.

Lawrence Kohlberg, her colleague at Harvard, Gilligan, by means of her theory of woman's moral development, is attempting a psychological justification for the practice of abortion by purporting to demonstrate that abortion, when done for the right reasons, helps women take charge of their lives and fosters growth in the psychological sense. Through the decision to abort, women come to a maturity and grow in a feeling of taking charge of their own lives. While these themes are to be found *in nuce* in Beauvoir and Daly, Gilligan tries to give them birth in her writings.

The Importance of Psychology

One of the many issues upon which Mary Daly and Simone de Beauvoir agreed was their skepticism, if not downright antipathy, toward psychology in general and psychoanalysis in particular.[5] Simone de Beauvoir sees in Freud a determinism that clashes with her existentialist notion of absolute freedom; Daly is suspicious of psychoanalysis, regarding it a particularly insidious male plot to subjugate women. These misgivings notwithstanding, a portion of contemporary feminism has arrived at the point that psychology must be co-opted in the struggle against patriarchy.[6] If for no other reason,

---

[5]This hostility towards psychology and psychiatry is giving way to a cautious acceptance of Freud by the latest wave of feminist thinkers. Among them are Juliet Mitchell, *Psychoanalysis and Feminism: Freud, Reich, Laing and Women* (New York: Pantheon, 1974), and Dorothy Dinnerstein, *The Mermaid and the Minotaur: Sexual Arrangements and Human Malaise* (New York: Harper Colophon Books, 1976). See also the two books by Nancy Chodorow: *The Reproduction of Mothering: Psychoanalysis and the Sociology of Gender* (Berkeley: University of California Press, 1978) and *Feminism and Psychoanalytic Theory* (New Haven: Yale University Press, 1989). Also important is Elaine Hoffman Baruch and Lucienne J. Serrano, *Women Analyze Women in France, England, and the United States.*

[6]Cf. Naomi Goldenberg, *Changing of the Gods: Feminism and the End of Traditional Religions* (Boston: Beacon Press, 1979) predicts not only that feminism will destroy the God of Judaeo-Christianity but also that "feminist theology is on the way to becoming psychology" (p. 25). At the time she wrote this work, Goldenberg was a Jungian feminist theologian. In her most recent work she has become more attuned to Freud. See her *Returning Words to Flesh: Feminism, Psychoanalysis, and the Resurrection of the Body* (Boston: Beacon Press, 1990), pp. 83–95.

Gilligan's influence will be, on the whole, quite notable; developmental psychology is an easier sell than Beauvoir's existential philosophy or Daly's dualistic theology.

Gilligan's Critique of Kohlberg

Carol Gilligan has earned her place in the feminist sun by her criticism of her colleague at Harvard, the late Lawrence Kohlberg, whose theory of moral development *via* six stages was regarded by Gilligan as biased in favor of males and against females. Her 1982 book, *In a Different Voice*, is Gilligan's most sustained and well-known critique not only of Kohlberg but also of much of the male establishment in developmental psychology, including Freud and Piaget.[7] While Gilligan criticized Kohlberg, she worked with him on occasion and learned from him as well. Her views on autonomy, for example, are largely the legacy of Kohlberg who himself is a Kantian in this regard.[8] Gilligan continues

---

[7]Cf. *In a Different Voice*, p. 6: "The penchant of developmental theorists to project a masculine image, and one that appears frightening to women, goes back to at least Freud." On the next page Gilligan quotes Freud, who concluded that women "show less sense of justice than men, that they are less ready to submit to the great exigencies of life, that they are more often influenced in their judgments by feelings of affection or hostility." She notes that in Piaget's work "girls are an aside, a curiosity to whom he devotes four brief entries, in an index that omits 'boys' altogether because 'the child' is assumed to be male" (p. 18).

[8]See, for example, an article co-written by Gilligan and Kohlberg, "The Adolescent as Philosopher: The Discovery of the Self in a Post Conventional World," *Daedalus* 100 (1971), pp. 1051–1086. Gilligan also collaborated with other colleagues. See the article she wrote along with John Michael Murphy, "Moral Development in Late Adolescence and Adulthood: a Critique and Reconstruction of Kohlberg's Theory," *Human Development* 23 (1980), pp. 77–104. Kohlberg takes up Gilligan's critique of his theory, and along with co-authors Charles Levine and Alexandra Hewer, *Essays on Moral Development* Volume II: *The Psychology of Moral Development: The Nature and Validity of Moral Stages* (San Francisco: Harper and Row, 1984), pp. 342–343, lists the reasons why he does not agree with Gilligan's conclusions that there was a test bias in Kohlberg's studies on moral development. The same three authors try to respond to all of Kohlberg's critics, Gilligan included, in *Moral Stages: A Current Formulation and a Response to Critics* (Contributions to Human Development, vol. 10) (Basel and New York: Karger, 1983). Barbara Houston, "Gilligan and the Politics of a Distinctive Woman's Morality," in Lorraine Code, Sheila Mullett, and Christine Overall (eds.), *Feminist Perspectives: Philosophical Essays on Method and Morals*

her work and her writing, a sizeable portion of which is devoted to the task of explaining *In a Different Voice.*[9]

After noting Freud's criticism to the effect that women have a less well-developed sense of justice than men, Gilligan goes to the heart of the criticism she makes of her Harvard colleague:

> Kohlberg's six stages that describe the development of moral judgment from childhood to adulthood are based empirically on a study of eighty-four boys whose development Kohlberg has followed for a period of over twenty years. Although Kohlberg claims universality for his stage sequence, those groups not included in his original sample rarely reach his higher stages. *Prominent among those who thus appear to be deficient in moral development when measured by Kohlberg's scale are women, whose judgments seem to exemplify the third stage of his six-stage sequence* (*In a Different Voice*, p. 18: my emphasis).

In a Different Voice

The focal point of our understanding of the thought of Carol

(Toronto: University of Toronto Press, 1988), pp. 168–189, defends Gilligan and contends that Kohlberg in his "politics of dismissal" has not taken Gilligan's criticisms seriously.

[9]Among Gilligan's recent works are "Remapping the Moral Domain: New Images of the Self in Relationship," in Thomas Heller, Morton Sosna, and David Wellbery (eds.), *Reconstructing Individualism* (Palo Alto: Stanford University Press, 1986), pp. 237–252; "A Different Voice in Moral Decisions," in Diana Eck and Jain Devaki (eds.), *Speaking of Faith: Global Perspectives on Women, Religion and Social Change* (Philadelphia: New Society, 1987), pp. 19–33; Carol Gilligan, Jamie Ward, and Jill Taylor McLean (eds.), *Mapping the Moral Domain: A Contribution to Women's Thinking to Psychological Theory and Education* (Cambridge: Harvard Graduate School of Education, 1988). See also Carol Gilligan, Norma P. Lyons, and Trudy J. Hanmer (eds.), *Making Connections: The Relational Worlds of Adolescent Girls at Emma Willard School* (Cambridge, MA: Harvard University Press, 1990); and Carol Gilligan, "Women's Psychological Development: Implications for Psychotherapy," in Carol Gilligan, Annie G. Rogers, and Deborah L. Tolman (eds.), *Women, Girls and Psychotherapy: Reframing Resistance* (New York: Harrington Park Press, 1991), pp. 5–31.

Gilligan is her book, *In a Different Voice*. Interesting as her ruminations on the stages of moral development might be, our interest will focus especially on what Gilligan has to say about the abortion decision in the context of her own theory of moral development. Though Carol Gilligan, as we shall see, is a difficult author to pin down, I believe she is saying not only that women should have the right to control their reproductive lives, the point of Simone de Beauvoir and Mary Daly,[10] but also that abortion is, if not a positive good, then at least an occasion for moral growth, especially because, as one of her interviewees put it: "Abortion, if you do it for the right reasons, is helping yourself to start over and do different things" (*In a Different Voice*, p. 78). Gilligan attributes the words to a nameless adolescent; the sentiments—do they belong to Gilligan? One reason she is so hard to pin down is Gilligan's propensity for submerging herself in her interviewees' comments. At times it becomes quite a task to determine where the interviewees end and Gilligan begins.

In a Different Voice is a book of fewer than two hundred pages, replete with references to psychologists past and present, literary figures, mythological allusions as well as several scriptural citations. It puts together several of Gilligan's articles along with the findings she reached in the course of conducting several studies: the "Rights and Responsibilities" Study, the "College Student" Study, and the one most germane to our purposes, the "Abortion Decision" Study.[11] It is by

---

[10]Cf. the entry "Reproductive Rights" in Maggie Humm, *The Dictionary of Feminist Theory*, p. 191: "*Reproductive rights*. These include the right to become a mother and to contraception and abortion. Reproductive rights is a category often omitted in traditional, masculine politics. Feminist theory subverts this tradition by comparing public legality with private experience in its argument for reproductive freedom. The perception that control over the termination of pregnancy is central to the future of women and woman's place informs feminist struggles about abortion. . . . Adrienne Rich suggests that reproductive rights lie at the core of feminism."

[11]Cf. *In a Different Voice*, p. 72. Gilligan tells us that the "Abortion Study" upon which she bases her findings was conducted with a group composed of twenty-nine women. Of that number twenty-one had abortions, four gave birth, two had miscarriages; Gilligan was unable to contact the other two for the follow-up research. Critics, regardless of their own views on the matter of abortion, have been quick to note how small was Gilligan's sampling base. Among them are Linda Kerber et al., "On 'In a Different Voice': an Interdisciplinary Forum," *Signs* 11 no. 2 (1986), pp. 304–333.

means of these studies, interspersed with literary and biblical allusions, that Gilligan attempts to elaborate her view that women approach moral problems in a quite distinctive way that is not to be considered in any way inferior to the way men approach similar ethical situations.

In fact, while some critics insist that Gilligan is fostering what is termed a "female superiority" ethic,[12] Gilligan herself never claims that the different voice ethic is a female superiority ethic, though she does begin her discussion of women's rights (the fifth chapter of *In a Different Voice*) by citing the famous remark made to a reporter by nineteenth-century American feminist Elizabeth Cady Stanton (1815–1902): "'Put it down in capital letters: SELF-DEVELOPMENT IS A HIGHER DUTY THAN SELF-SACRIFICE'" (*In a Different Voice*, p. 129). Stanton, author of *The Woman's Bible* and harsh critic of organized religion, was herself a noted proponent of the female superiority view. Though Gilligan never mentions Mary Daly, both feminists are united in the respect they pay Stanton, and Daly must be classified as a proponent of a female superiority ethic. Gilligan—ever the psychologist—stresses Stanton's sentiments on the importance of self-development; Daly—ever the pioneer—emphasizes Stanton's views on the need for women to show self-reliance and courage.[13]

These two approaches to ethical decisionmaking are regarded by Gilligan in her 1982 book as *complementary*, a view she has since refined, speaking of the two moral ideologies along the lines of *Gestalt* psychology, though the argument developed in her *In a Different Voice* remains substantially the same.[14] While Gilligan is not regarded as an

---

[12]See, among others, Marcia C. Westkott, "On the New Psychology of Women: a Cautionary View," *Feminist Issues* 10 no. 2 (1990), pp. 3–18; and Judy Auerbach et al., "On Gilligan's 'In a Different Voice'" *Feminist Studies* 11 no. 1 (1985), pp. 149–161.

[13]Cf. *Pure Lust*, p. 281, after citing an 1851 text from Stanton, Daly observes: "Here Stanton Names the problem—the breeding out of courage from women under the guise of protection." And on p. 283, Daly speaks of Stanton as one of those "sturdy souls" who have cultivated "the Self-reliance" Daly so prizes.

[14]"Is it a rabbit or is it duck?"—along with its accompanying graphic—is usually associated with *Gestalt*. On Gilligan's use of the concept, cf. Owen Flanagan and Kathryn Jackson, "Justice, Care, and Gender: The Kohlberg-Gilligan Debate Revisited," *Ethics* 97 no. 3 (1987), pp. 622–637.

original thinker by some of her critics,[15] her influence has been notable nonetheless.[16] Interestingly enough, Gilligan is often cited favorably by those who would scarcely want to be identified with feminism while she is castigated by some who pride themselves on the label "feminist." Her work and its effects span gender differences too: men defend her, women take her to task.[17]

The Shadow of Simone de Beauvoir

Previous chapters have argued that Simone de Beauvoir elaborated an epistemology of abortion while Mary Daly provided some of the abortion mentality's metaphysical underpinnings with her notion of separate ontologies for men and women. Psychologist Carol Gilligan carries on their work without ever mentioning either of them by name. Of the two, Beauvoir by far exerts the most influence.

Abortion as a *rite de passage* from adolescence to maturity was never far from the minds of those who advocated abortion as a liberty for women; we need only recall Jean Blomart, the protagonist in Beauvoir's *The Blood of Others*, who speaks of Hélène's pregnancy and

---

[15]Cf. Michael Levin, *Feminism and Freedom*, p. 185: "Academic feminists have shown some interest in Carol Gilligan's work on sex differences in moral thinking—more as part of the case that society ignores women than for its possible implications about gender dimorphism—but Gilligan's work is hardly a Copernical [sic] Revolution."

[16]Gilligan's book was the topic of an entire issue of *Social Research* 50 no. 3 (1983). It also inspired several volumes: Eva Feder Kittay and Diana T. Meyers (eds.), *Women and Moral Theory* (Totowa: Rowman and Littlefield, 1987), Rita C. Manning, *Speaking from the Heart: A Feminist Perspective on Ethics* (Lanham, MD: Rowman and Littlefield Publishers, 1992), and Mary Jeanne Larrabee (ed.), *An Ethic of Care: Feminist and Interdisciplinary Perspectives* (New York and London: Routledge, 1993). Gilligan's influence extends to Europe. Cf. Ebe Quintavalla and Emanuela Raimondi (eds.), *Aborto, perchè?* (Milan: Feltrinelli "Saggi", 1989). It may be of some interest to note that the Italian translation of *In a Different Voice* comes close to giving the popular estimation of Gilligan's work: *Con voce di donna* (1987).

[17]One of her male defenders in the Gilligan-Kohlberg debate is Lawrence Blum, "Gilligan and Kohlberg: Implications for Moral Theory," *Ethics* 98 no. 3 (1988), pp. 472–491; one of her female critics in the debate is Debra Nails, "Social Scientific Sexism: Gilligan and the Mismeasure of Man," *Social Research* 50 no. 3 (1983), pp. 643–664.

subsequent abortion as a coming-of-age of sorts. Gilligan, through the women she interviews, endeavors to view the abortion decision not only as a rite of passage but also, and more importantly, as a progressive step from an infantile mode of being ethical to one that is fully mature. *Mirabile dictu*, we discover that this viewpoint as well had been elaborated by Simone de Beauvoir in *The Ethics of Ambiguity*.[18] It is in this sense, then, and despite the fact that Carol Gilligan does not cite Beauvoir, I think it safe to say that the Harvard educational psychologist does indeed continue to expound upon some of the themes found in the work of the French feminist. What Beauvoir says philosophically in *The Ethics of Ambiguity* Gilligan restates in psychological terms in *In a Different Voice*.[19] Simone de Beauvoir casts a long shadow.

As it was with Simone de Beauvoir and Mary Daly, so it is with Carol Gilligan: the new possibilities for women are owed in large part to technological advances, notably the birth control pill and the techniques of abortion. The following texts give evidence of Simone de Beauvoir's influence upon Gilligan:

> For centuries, women's sexuality anchored them in *passivity, in a receptive rather than an active stance*, where the event of conception and childbirth could be controlled only by a withholding in which their own sexual needs were either denied or sacrificed.[20]

---

[18]Cf. *The Ethics of Ambiguity*, p. 35: after relating with approval Descartes' claim that our misfortunes in this life are attributable to the fact that we were once infants, Beauvoir intimates that the essence of "bad faith" is choosing to remain in an infantile condition.

[19]William K. Kilpatrick, *Why Johnny Can't Tell Right from Wrong* (New York, Simon and Schuster, 1992), pp. 151–158, makes a strong case for the influence of Beauvoir upon Gilligan, and attempts to traces their views on morality to the nihilism of Friedrich Nietzsche.

[20]Carol Gilligan, *In a Different Voice*, p. 68: my emphasis. Simone de Beauvoir, *The Second Sex*, pp. 467–468, refuses to grant that childbirth is an *active* experience because the woman does not *control* the process: "Ordinarily life is but a condition of existence; in gestation it appears as creative; but that is a strange kind of creation which is accomplished in a contingent and passive manner. . . . She does not really make the baby, it makes itself within her."

And again:

> When *birth control and abortion provide women with*
> *effective means for controlling their fertility,* the dilemma
> of choice enters a central arena of women's lives. Then
> the relationships that have traditionally defined
> women's identities and framed their moral judgments
> no longer flow inevitably from their reproductive
> capacity *but become matters over which they have control.*
> *Released from the passivity and reticence of a sexuality that*
> *binds them in dependence,* women can question with
> Freud what it is that they want and assert their own
> answers to that question. However, while society may
> affirm publicly the woman's right to choose for herself,
> the exercise of such choice brings her privately into
> conflict with *the conventions of femininity,* particularly
> the moral equation of goodness with self-sacrifice.[21]

Gilligan's Moral Theory: Contextual Relativism

Basing herself in large part on what she acknowledges as the
pioneering work of Jean Baker Miller in the field of woman's
psychological development, Gilligan attempts to elaborate an ethical
theory true to the real-life experiences of women.[22] In real life, according
to Carol Gilligan, absolutes do not exist. The question of absolutes is, of
course, a theme that has obvious repercussions on a Judaeo-Christian
inspired ethical theory.

---

[21]*In a Different Voice,* p. 70: my emphasis. This is a standard argument made by
Simone de Beauvoir and repeated by Mary Daly, namely, that advances in
reproductive technology mean that women are now in a position to take control of
their reproductive lives. Gilligan continues to use concepts culled from Beauvoir
which by 1982 have become standard feminist fare as we see, for example, on p. 68
and again on p. 71. Beauvoir's epistemology of abortion was instrumental in getting
Daly to go deeper into the matter and come up with her dualistic metaphysics of
abortion, as it were.

[22]Gilligan acknowledges her debt to Miller's *Toward a New Psychology of Women,* the
second edition of which was published in Boston by Beacon Press in 1986.

The assault on moral absolutes is a leitmotif of Gilligan's book.[23] Why? The move away from moral absolutes and the accompanying awareness of the complexity of moral decision-making are indicators of moral growth, according to Gilligan, who draws on the work of William Perry to make her point:

> Perry describes the changes in thinking that mark the transition from a belief that knowledge is absolute and answers clearly right or wrong to an understanding of the contextual relativity of both truth and choice. . . . The awareness of multiple truths leads to a relativizing of equality in the direction of equity and gives rise to an ethic of generosity and care. For both sexes the existence of two contexts for moral decision makes judgment by definition contextually relative and leads to a new understanding of responsibility and choice (*In a Different Voice*, p. 166).

Here we see a bit of the difficulty alluded to earlier in noting that Gilligan is hard to pin down. Is this passage all the thought of Perry? Just how much is Gilligan appropriating to herself?

Early in the book, Gilligan describes her own ethical theory as "contextual relativism." Several passages are pertinent:

> When one begins with the study of women and derives developmental constructs from their lives, the outline of a moral conception different from that described by Freud, Piaget, or Kohlberg begins to emerge and informs a different description of development. *In this conception, the moral problem arises from conflicting responsibilities rather than from competing rights and requires for its resolution a mode of thinking that is contextual and narrative rather than formal and abstract* (p. 19: my emphasis).

A few pages later:

> Thus it becomes clear why a morality of rights and

---

[23]Cf. *In a Different Voice*, p. 22, p. 58, pp. 65–66, p. 87, p. 135, and pp. 165–166.

noninterference may appear frightening to women in its potential justification of indifference and unconcern. At the same time, it becomes clear why, from a male perspective, a morality of responsibility appears inconclusive and diffuse, given its *insistent contextual relativism* (p. 22, my emphasis).

The Return of Complementarity

Concluding that males and females approach ethical issues differently is an insight Gilligan reaches after studying Kohlberg's work with young children and seeing how they responded to different hypothetical moral situations, especially the "Heinz Dilemma."[24] Gilligan believes that a male morality hinges around the notion of rights; a female morality centers around the concept of care. In the context of her contextual relativism, Gilligan has this to say of the two moral approaches:

> In the transition from adolescence to adulthood, the dilemma itself is the same for both sexes, a conflict between integrity and care. But approached from different perspectives, this dilemma generates the recognition of opposite truths. The different perspectives are reflected in two different moral ideologies, since separation is justified by an ethic of rights while attachment is supported by an ethic of care (p. 164).

The mention of two different moral ideologies recalls our earlier statement in the Introduction regarding the worldviews approach to the abortion issue. While these two moral approaches are certainly different, Gilligan is reluctant to regard them as contrasting, preferring instead to view the two moralities as complementary. Many contemporary feminists, including feminist theologians, are deeply distressed by the

---

[24]Cf. *In a Different Voice*, p. 25: "In this particular dilemma, a man named Heinz considers whether or not to steal a drug which he cannot afford to buy in order to save the life of his wife." Gilligan treats the "Heinz dilemma" on pp. 25–31.

concept of *complementarity*.[25] Later on we shall see how Gilligan's two moral methodologies make up a key element of her approach to the abortion question.

The Danger in *Difference*

Many feminists who are uneasy with Gilligan are especially suspicious of her contention that she is able to detect a difference in the way men and women approach ethical issues.[26] Such feminist apprehension revolves around the very notion of *difference*;[27] they see in

---

[25]According to Mary T. Malone, *Women Christian: New Vision* (Dubuque: William C. Brown, 1985), pp. 4–5, the Catholic Church is wont to express its doctrine on men and women in the terms of complementarity. Feminist theologians are, generally speaking, distrustful of the notion, as we see, for example, in Catherine Mowry LaCugna, "Catholic Women as Ministers and Theologians," *America* 167 no. 10 (October 10, 1992), pp. 238–248. *Complementarity* is one of those words that gets the attention of feminists; Daly and Beauvoir would see in complementarity—in its several forms—the detested "Eternal Feminine" lurking in the background. Though some feminists will apparently continue to hold it against Gilligan that she makes use of the notion of *complementarity* in her book, Gilligan in my estimation is well aware that *complementarity* serves to shore up the argument she is attempting to make in *In a Different Voice*.

[26]Many scholars, feminist and otherwise, regard as a classic in the area of the differences between men and women, boys and girls, the study of Eleanor Maccoby and Carol Jacklin, *The Psychology of Sex Differences* (Stanford: Stanford University Press, 1974). There is quite a debate going on in feminist circles regarding the concept of differences, in no small part fueled by Gilligan's book. Luce Irigaray, *Éthique de la différence sexuelle* (Collection "Critique") (Les Éditions de Minuit, Paris 1984), p. 13, adverting to Heidegger's contention that each age has *one* question to think, insists that the question of *sex differences* will be ours.

[27]Critical of Gilligan, especially because of her use of difference, is Catherine MacKinnon, *Feminism Unmodified: Discourses on Life and Law*, pp. 38–39: "For women to affirm difference, when difference means dominance, as it does with gender, means to affirm the qualities and characteristics of powerlessness." We note here the *power* key in which much of contemporary feminism is accustomed to view things. MacKinnon herself has become a name, inspiring both admirers, as we see in Fred Strebeigh, "Defining Law on the Feminist Frontier," *The New York Times Magazine* (October 6, 1991), pp. 28–31ff, as well as critics such as Christina Sommers, "Hard-Line Feminists Guilty of Ms.-Representation," *The Wall Street Journal* 218 no. 92 (November 7, 1991), p. A14, who labels MacKinnon "a matron saint of gender feminism."

it the seeds of the *nature* which, according to the standard feminist interpretation perhaps best elaborated by Simone de Beauvoir, has spelled subjugation, subjection, subordination, and second-sex status for women since time immemorial. To the feminists who follow Beauvoir's lead on this matter and for whom culturalism reigns supreme, *difference* spells *death*.[28]

Beauvoir's strictures against nature—nativism, if you will[29]—and her attachment to the thesis of culturalism are threatened, in the minds of many feminists, by Gilligan's purported discovery of a different *voice* which, for all intents and purposes, is—at least in the popular imagination—a female way of thinking and doing things. Susan Okin, for example, is so fearful of any talk of *difference* that she warns that Gilligan's type of approach could be used against women by reactionaries such as John Paul II![30]

Easily dispatched by slogans such as "One is not born, but rather becomes, a woman," the reality of that *nature* which Simone de Beauvoir so much wanted to cast out from male-female discourse is

---

[28]To see the notion of gender feminism working its way into Church discussion, cf. Donna Singles, "La différence, destin ou projèt?" *Lumière et Vie* 38 no. 194 (1989), pp. 59–70. This entire issue of *Lumière et Vie* is devoted to the topic of sex differences. See also *Concilium* 218 no. 6 (1991), edited by Anne Carr and Elisabeth Schüssler Fiorenza, dealing with the theme: "The Special Nature of Women."

[29]"Nativism" is a term used by Michael Levin, *Feminism and Freedom*, p. 55. To it he contrasts what he considers the essential concept of contemporary feminist ideology: "Complete environmentalism—the denial that innate sex differences have anything to do with the broad structure of society—is central to feminism" (p. 3). He considers it scandalous that with all the scientific evidence available (including the book by Maccoby and Jacklin) feminism continues to have even a modicum of intellectual respectability (p. 70). Feminists as a rule regard Levin as a pariah; see, for example, the treatment he receives in Susan Faludi, *Backlash: the Undeclared War Against American Women*, pp. 296–300.

[30]Cf. Susan Moller Okin, *Justice, Gender and the Family* (New York: Basic Books, 1989), p. 15. Okin lists on p. 197, note 49, a number of feminists whose concept of a different morality, along the general lines traced out by Carol Gilligan, can spell doom for what Okin considers the real feminist revolution (which fairly well coincides with Simone de Beauvoir's vision). Among these "suspect" feminists, well-intentioned perhaps but not particularly in tune with "real" feminism, Okin lists, in addition to Gilligan, Jean Baker Miller, Nancy Chodorow, Dorothy Dinnerstein, Jane Flax, Sara Ruddick, and Nancy Hartsock.

proving to be quite formidable, stubborn, intractable, and persistent. Mary Daly reverts back to it in the context of an ancient dualism. Gilligan is not quite so blunt in championing Daly's extreme of radically different male and female natures, yet the effect is in some ways the same. To put it in other words, while Daly's dualistic metaphysics is the relatively uncomplicated one of male bad and female good, Gilligan's two moral ideologies of a *justice* perspective and a *caring* perspective, on the other hand, is somewhat more nuanced: one is good, the other is better; both are needed.

Nature remains an important feature of contemporary feminist debate; Simone de Beauvoir's famous feminist call to arms, "One is not born, but rather becomes, a woman," far from ending debate, has become itself a *punctum dolens*, serving to get the polemic started in earnest.[31] While the culturalist thesis à la Beauvoir continues to have its zealous adherents such as Delphy and Okin, other feminists continue to wrestle with the issue which Simone de Beauvoir brought to their attention, perhaps, but which *The Second Sex* in no wise ended.[32]

---

[31]While Beauvoir remained in theory at least a committed culturalist all her long existentialist and somewhat shorter feminist life, we remember the importance she gave to biological data in *The Second Sex*, pp. 1–33. As in so much else, Beauvoir went into biological detail, taking up a suggestion made by Jean-Paul Sartre. It is perhaps not without some interest to note that Sartre himself was not totally consistent in this matter of there being absolutely no human or female nature at all. To the question of the presence of female values, Sartre once remarked (in an interview he gave to Simone de Beauvoir) that there are indeed some values which involve feminine nature, though he was quick to add that these were minor. He also opined that women might well have better self-knowledge than men. Sartre noted that he always found men more comical than women. See "Simone de Beauvoir Interviews Jean-Paul Sartre," in Jean-Paul Sartre, *Life/Situations: Essays Written and Spoken* (translated by Paul Auster and Lydia Davis) (New York: Pantheon, 1977), p. 107.

[32]Cf. Evelyne Sullerot (ed.), *Le fait féminin*. In her introductory remarks, Sullerot offers a correction to Beauvoir's dictum and goes on to contend that it is easier to change *nature* than *culture* (p. 23). Agreeing with Sullerot on the matter is Yves Christen, *Sex Differences: Modern Biology and the Unisex Fallacy* (translated by Nicholas Davidson) (New Brunswick: Transaction Books, 1991), p. 111. He regards current feminist thought on the matter of *nature* as essentially contradictory, saying both *no* to it and *yes* to it at the same time (pp. 62–63).

Gilligan on Abortion

We have noted how difficult it can be to get a straight answer
from Gilligan. Her ability to blend into her interviewees and the
antiseptic psychological language she employs serve her well as a shield.
Hence, she can be understood as saying almost anything one wants to
have her saying in *In a Different Voice*. We remember Susan Moller Okin
imagining (as a sort of "worst case feminist scenario") that Gilligan
could be co-opted by the pope.

The very choice of *abortion* as a test-case of sorts for Gilligan's
theory of a different voice in morality ignites much of the controversy.
The gist of the controversy: since only women can become pregnant,
only women can know the full implications of the abortion decision.[33]
If Gilligan claimed Kohlberg was guilty of a male bias in the way he
conducted his research, is not the same skewering of results bound to
happen in choosing abortion as a moral test case? Is not 50% of
humanity left out of the discussion? How establish a "different voice" in
morality if an issue like abortion is chosen which excludes half of
humanity from the outset?[34]

That only women become pregnant seems to be a pacific claim,
one of the data of biology which Beauvoir and Daly both accepted.
While it is true that the effect of abortion on men has been the subject

---

[33]That males have an abstract view of abortion because they do not experience the
threat to personal autonomy which pregnancy and birth pose is the thought
expressed by Madonna Kolbenschlag, *Kiss Sleeping Beauty Good-bye: Breaking the Spell
of Feminine Myths and Models* (New York: Bantam New Age Books, 1981), p. 156.
I occasionally see bumper stickers with the feminist slogan: "If men got pregnant,
abortion would be a sacrament."

[34]This is one of the criticisms of Gilligan's use of the abortion issue as a test of moral
maturity made by Susan Faludi, *Backlash: The Undeclared War Against American
Women*, p. 330. Others who criticize Gilligan's choice of the abortion decision as a
test case for her supposed "different voice" in morality incude Lorraine B. Code,
"Responsibility and the Epistemic Community: Woman's Place," *Social Research* 50
no. 3 (1983), pp. 537–555, especially at p. 551, and Michele Moody-Adams, "Gender
and the Complexity of Moral Voices," in Claudia Card (ed.), *Feminist Ethics*
(Lawrence: University Press of Kansas, 1991), pp. 195–212.

of a recent study,[35] the major part of the abortion discussion has dealt with abortion's impact on women. An observation made by American sociologist Kristin Luker has always struck me as especially perspicacious in this matter: Men and women both become pregnant.[36]

We find the same widely disparate viewpoints on the abortion question in Gilligan and what her own position on the matter might be. Some will see Gilligan saying the exact opposite of what another sees her saying on the matter of the morality of abortion, for example.[37] Unless I am mistaken, the reason for this disparity of opinion is to be found in Gilligan's moral relativism, a point we see especially in her discussion of what it is that makes a decision a "moral" one: "The essence of moral decision is the exercise of choice and the willingness to accept responsibility for that choice."[38]

Several pages later we find a text in which Gilligan comes close to saying (or at least as close as gilliganese will allow) that abortion is, if done for the right reasons, a positive occasion for psychological growth. Characteristically enough for contemporary feminists, she will do so in language reminiscent of Simone de Beauvoir:

> When a woman considers whether to continue or abort
> a pregnancy, she contemplates a decision that affects
> both self and others and engages directly the critical

---

[35]Cf. Arthur B. Shostak and Gary McLouth with Lynn Seng, *Men and Abortion: Lessons, Losses, and Love* (New York: Praeger, 1984). There is a chapter in John Stoltenberg, *Refusing to Be a Man: Essays on Love and Justice* (New York: Penguin Books, 1989), entitled "The Fetus as Penis: Men's Self-interest and Abortion Rights," pp. 91–100.

[36]Cf. Kristin Luker, *Taking Chances: Abortion and the Decision Not to Contracept*, p. 136.

[37]As proof for my contention, one author, Mary Ann O'Loughlin, "Responsibility and Moral Maturity in the Control of Fertility-- Or, A Woman's Place Is In the Wrong," *Social Research* 50 no. 3 (1983), pp. 556–575 and especially on p. 562, concludes that Gilligan regards *every abortion as blameworthy*, while another, Janet E. Smith, "Abortion and Moral Development Theory: Listening With Different Ears," *International Philosophical Quarterly* 28 (1988), pp. 31–52, contends that Gilligan regards *no abortion as blameworthy*.

[38]*In a Different Voice*, p. 67. Cf. David Mall, *In Good Conscience: Abortion and Moral Necessity* (Libertyville: Kairos Books, 1982), p. 41. Citing this passage, Mall is "troubled" by Gilligan's contention.

moral issue of hurting. Since the choice is ultimately hers and therefore one for which she is responsible, it raises precisely those questions of judgment that have been most problematic for women. Now she is asked whether she wishes to interrupt that stream of life which for centuries has immersed her in *the passivity of dependence* while at the same time imposing on her the responsibility for care (p. 71: my emphasis).

Thus, in answering the question of Carol Gilligan's own position on the matter of abortion, we discover that for her the moral issue becomes secondary to the psychological growth potential possible in the abortion decision. It is a *rite de passage* into psychological maturity, or perhaps, better, it *can* be such if the abortion is done, as Gilligan's anonymous adolescent said, "for the right reasons." We would not be wrong in observing that the ethical theory she has chosen as her own in *In a Different Voice*, namely, contextual relativism, would prove helpful for those who would wish to "justify" a range of human actions which a Judaeo-Christian ethical theory would not allow.[39] It is on this precise point that we must insist: read *In a Different Voice* as one may, there simply are no *wrong* reasons ever given by Carol Gilligan for the abortion decision.

Opponents of abortion saw the importance of *In a Different Voice* from the very outset.[40] Their general critique of Gilligan's abortion study is the following: the very fact that the abortion decision is made by the woman herself seems to legitimate the abortion choice for Carol Gilligan. While it may be true that Gilligan never speaks of any abortion

---

[39]Is there originality in Gilligan's discovery of a "different voice" in ethics or is "the ethic of care" merely the latest way of expressing ethical situationism, pragmatism, and relativism? Cf. the comments of Rosemary Wittman Lamb in Mary Kenny, *Abortion: The Whole Story* (London and New York: Quartet Books, 1986), p. 225. As we remember, Gilligan does not hide her relativism.

[40]Wanda Franz did an early review of *In a Different Voice* in *National Right to Life News* 10 no. 21 (1983), p. 11. Gilligan's book then became the subject of several articles in a special section of *National Right to Life News* 11 no. 3 (1984). Franz had time to look at Gilligan in more depth and does so in "In an Immature Voice: the Case of Carol Gilligan," p. 6f. Also in this issue is Rosemary Bottcher, "Killing as Caring," p. 6f. Other reviewers include Nancy Koster and Dave Andrusko. All agree on what they consider Gilligan's pro-abortion message of *In a Different Voice*.

being the wrong decision, the difficulty in gauging her own position on the matter of abortion remains formidable, at least until we discover Gilligan saying in her "Letter to Readers, 1993" that *Roe v. Wade* was an instance of woman speaking for herself (p. ix). Other feminists *do* attempt to describe what they consider to be insufficient reasons, "wrong" reasons, if you like, for having an abortion.[41]

In the context of her developmental moral theory, and in the light of her professed contextual relativism, it would seem that Gilligan is saying something along these lines: abortion is legitimated by the very fact that it was a decision arrived at and acted upon by the woman herself.[42] If our supposition is correct, here too, it would appear, the moral issue of the act of abortion is circumvented,[43] not in the language of male sadism and hypocrisy of a Simone de Beauvoir or a Mary Daly but in the psychological growth vernacular of a Harvard educational psychologist. In a different voice, perhaps, but the results regarding abortion are the same.[44]

---

[41]Cf. Mary C. Segers, "Abortion and the Culture: Toward a Feminist Perspective," in Sidney and Daniel Callahan (eds.), *Abortion: Understanding Differences* (The Hastings Series in Ethics) (New York: Plenum Press, 1984), p. 249. Writes Segers: "A responsible feminist morality of abortion might begin by acknowledging the humanity of the fetus and accepting the burden of having to justify the decision to abort." Among those reasons Segers lists as "trivial": fear of a woman's losing her attractiveness, abortion as a rite of passage, and sex selection abortions.

[42]We have already noted that, for Gilligan, "the essence of moral decision is the exercise of choice and the willingness to accept responsibility for that choice" (*In a Different Voice*, p. 67).

[43]Gilligan certainly has the *subjective* aspect of morality covered by her view of who it is that is making the abortion decision; it it the *objective* aspect of morality that Gilligan is overlooking. *Choice* is indeed an important part of moral decision-making, but *what is being chosen* is also important. To choose either of these two poles of morality as the only one worth considering simplifies morality considerably, to be sure, but does so only at a great cost. But so powerful has *choice* become in American political and moral parlance that, in the words of Maggie Gallagher, *Enemies of Eros: How the Sexual Revolution Is Killing Family, Marriage, and Sex and What We Can Do About It*: "Choice is the opiate of the liberal" (p. 219).

[44]While the status of the fetus does not enter the formal argumentation of *In a Different Voice*, it is touched upon at least peripherally in the context of what some of Gilligan's interviewees have to say. Gilligan *has* dealt with the status of the fetus in "Justice and Responsibility: Thinking about Real Dilemmas of Moral Conflict and

What unites Simone de Beauvoir, Mary Daly, and Carol Gilligan is their view that technology is the great liberator, untapping women's sexuality from dependence and passivity (*In a Different Voice*, p. 68). In the end we can at least ask ourselves the question: does this mean that the state of technology has become the standard of right and wrong in the question of abortion in the three feminists we have seen so far?

Religion in Gilligan's *In A Different Voice*

We have witnessed in Simone de Beauvoir and Mary Daly the important role played by religion in their deconstruction of patriarchy and in their reconstruction of a new world for women, be it Simone de Beauvoir's androgynous or Mary Daly's lesbian separatist world.[45] Both are humanists of sorts, Simone de Beauvoir in the classical mold of a secular humanist, Mary Daly more along the lines of what one author calls "gynocentrism."[46] Simone de Beauvoir in *Memoirs of a Dutiful Daughter* did speak at length of her religious upbringing; Mary Daly sought her Church's highest *ecclesiastical* degrees. In her own way, Gilligan will likewise give witness to the importance of religion, both

---

Choice," her contribution to a volume entitled *Toward Moral and Religious Responsibility* which contains the 1980 Proceedings of the First International Conference on Moral and Religious Development. Gilligan's article is found on pp. 223–249.

[45]Elizabeth Badinter, *Mother Love: Myth and Reality: Motherhood in Modern History* (New York: Collier Books, 1981), an English translation of *L'amour en plus: histoire de l'amour maternel: XVIIe–XXe siècle*, continues Beauvoir's androgynous approach. On the possibility of feminism utilizing Whiteheadian thought along the lines of androgyny, cf. Valerie Saiving, "Androgynous Life: a Feminist Appropriation of Process Thought," in Sheila Davaney (ed.), *Feminism and Process Thought*, pp. 11–31. Martha Long Ice, *Clergy and Their Worldviews: Calling for a New Age* (New York: Praeger, 1987), in a study of seventeen clergywomen, concludes that androgyny is their dominant worldview.

[46]Cf. Iris Marion Young, "Humanism, Gynocentrism and Feminist Politics," *Women's Studies International Forum* 8 no. 3 (1985), pp. 173–183. What endears Daly to her followers, her radical lesbian separatism "beyond compromise," frightens many other feminists who see a "woman-centered" approach leading inevitably back to the old feminist devil—*nature*.

pagan and Judaeo-Christian.[47]

In a half-humorous, half-serious recall of the Adam and Eve Genesis story, Gilligan seems to poke some fun at her male colleagues in psychology and *possibly* at traditional religion.[48] But Gilligan is certainly not rabidly opposing religion along the lines of the invective of Mary Daly or the sarcasm of Simone de Beauvoir. Far from it. In fact, Gilligan acknowledges that Judaeo-Christianity will serve her aims of elaborating a different voice in morality extremely well, much better in fact than philosophical thought has heretofore been able to do:

> Among the most pressing items on the agenda for research on adult development is the need to delineate *in women's own terms* the experience of their adult life. My own work in that direction indicates that the inclusion of women's experience brings to developmental understanding a new perspective on relationships that changes the basic constructs of interpretation. The concept of identity expands to include the experience of interconnection. The moral domain is similarly enlarged by the inclusion of responsibility and care in relationships. And the

---

[47]Beauvoir, Daly, and Gilligan all show an interest in Greek mythology, especially the Demeter myth. Madonna Kolbenschlag, *Kiss Sleeping Beauty Good-Bye: Breaking the Spell of Feminine Myths and Models*, regards Demeter as a precursor of the Blessed Virgin Mary. One author who deals with the Demeter myth specifically in the context of abortion is Jean Shinoda Bolen, M.D., *Goddesses in Every Woman: A New Psychology of Women* (San Francisco: Harper Colophon Books, 1984), pp. 172–173. Demeter is the archetype who urges women to become pregnant. Non-Demeter women abort easily and feel relief; Demeter women feel grief if they abort, even if, as Bolen says, the abortion is in their best interests. Gilligan treats the Demeter and Persephone myth on pp. 22–23 of *In a Different Voice*.

[48]Speaking of male observational bias in what—on the surface at least—would appear to be a rather innocuous text such as Strunk and White's *Elements of Style*, Gilligan comments: "Implicitly adopting the male life as the norm, they have tried to fashion women out of a masculine cloth. It all goes back, of course, to Adam and Eve—a story which shows, among other things, that if you make a woman out of a man, you are bound to get into trouble. In the life cycle, as in the Garden of Eden, the woman has been the deviant" (*In a Different Voice*, p. 6).

underlying epistemology correspondingly shifts from
the Greek ideal of knowledge as a correspondence
between mind and form to the Biblical conception of
knowing as a process of human relationship.[49]

As a researcher, of course, Gilligan is interested in religion if for
no other reason than that some of the individuals she interviews have
religious concerns. If we scratch the surface, Gilligan's interest is not
hard to find, especially in those pages of *In a Different Voice* which
narrate the reactions of some of the women who took part in Gilligan's
abortion study.

Two Catholic Women Tell Their Stories

On occasion Gilligan tells her readers that one of her subjects is
Catholic.[50] Two that she thus names are Janet and Sandra. While
Gilligan's reason for the inclusion of the subject's religious affiliation is
not given in the text, we can surmise Gilligan includes mention of it
because knowlege of this fact will be important for the case that Gilligan
is trying to make in her book. Their Catholicism was an important
factor to be weighed by Janet and Sandra in reaching their decisions.[51] In
this regard, Gilligan tells us both Janet and Sandra go through with their
abortions, their Catholic faith notwithstanding. What Gilligan recounts,
in effect, is the reasoning process both women used to arrive at decisions

---

[49]*In a Different Voice*, p. 173: author's emphasis. Mary Daly, *Beyond God the Father*,
pp. 100–101, regards the presence of "female virtues" as evidence of the hypocrisy of
Christian morality: men make the theory extolling meekness and self-sacrifice, for
example, but it is only women who are forced in practice to live this "feminine ethic"
excogitated by guilty males. Gilligan, on the other hand, shows herself much more
sympathetic to biblically-based values. Some might regard this as odd in a way since
Daly is supposed to be the theologian, Gilligan the psychologist.

[50]While Gilligan, as a rule, does not give the religious affiliation of her other subjects,
she does report that Sarah, one of the women whom Gilligan feels has attained to the
highest level of ethical decision-making, has become a Quaker. Sarah is a recidivist in
abortion.

[51]An earlier observation bears repeating. According to Kristin Luker, *Taking Chances:
Abortion and the Decision Not to Contracept*, p. 45: the Church often plays the role of
"significant other" in abortion questions.

they know are opposed to the teachings of their Church.[52]

"Janet, a twenty-four-year-old married Catholic, pregnant again two months following the birth of her first child" (p. 83) knows what abortion is:

> "To me it is taking a life, and I am going to take that decision upon myself, and I have feelings about it, and talked to a priest. But he said it is there, and it will be from now on, and it is up to the person if they can live with the idea and still believe that they are good" (p. 84).

Janet resolves the issue by latching on to what Gilligan explains as a "good reasons" approach to abortion. Once again it is Janet speaking:

> "I still think abortion is wrong, and it will be unless the situation can justify what you are doing. . . . God can punish, but He can also forgive" (p. 85).

The next Catholic woman we meet is Sandra. Gilligan introduces her in striking fashion: "Sandra, a twenty-nine-year-old Catholic nurse who punctuates her arrival for an abortion with the statement, 'I have always thought abortion was a fancy word for murder'" (p. 85).

Guilty first of evading responsibility by trying to see her abortion as an act of sacrifice and hence "moral," Sandra is pressed (by Gilligan's questions, presumably) to see the inconsistency in her position.[53] Gilligan is speaking in her own voice regarding Sandra: "The

---

[52]Other authors desirous of establishing the legitimacy of abortion will utilize what amounts to a "Many Catholic Women Abort, You Know" argument. Some who do include Kristin Luker, *Taking Chances: Abortion and the Decision Not to Contracept*, p. 45, and even Catholic authors such as Pierre de Locht, *L'avortement: les enjeux d'un débat passioné* (Bruxelles: Vie Ouvrière, 1985), p. 65. If the point these authors are making is that believers at times do not live up to the teachings of their faith, that, of course, is undeniable.

[53]Cf. Patricia Elliot, *From Mastery to Analysis: Theories of Gender in Psychoanalytic Feminism* ("Reading Women Writing" Series) (Ithaca: Cornell University Press, 1991). Citing the work of Julia Kristeva, Elliot comments that the notion of "sacrifice" is regarded with scorn in much recent feminist discourse. In fact, she defines the third generation of feminism as "the antisacrificial current" (p. 224).

dishonesty in her plea of victimization creates a conflict that generates the need for a more inclusive understanding" (p. 86). Sandra phrases it in this fashion:

> "I am saying that abortion is morally wrong, but the situation is right, and I am going to do it. But the thing is that eventually they are going to have to go together, and I am going to have to put them together somehow."

Sandra then elaborates:

> "I would have to change morally wrong to morally right. (*How?*) I have no idea. I don't think you can take something that you feel is morally wrong because the situation makes it right and put the two together. They are not together, they are opposite. They don't go together. Something is wrong, but all of a sudden, because you are doing it, it is right."[54]

Gilligan speaks in her own voice regarding Sandra's tergiversations:

> In discovering the gray and questioning the moral judgments that formerly she considered absolute, she confronts the moral crisis of the second transition. Now the conventions which in the past guided her moral judgment become subject to a new criticism, as she questions not only the justification for hurting others in the name of morality but also the 'rightness' of hurting herself. However, to sustain such criticism in the face of conventions that equate goodness with self-sacrifice, Sandra must verify her capacity for independent judgment and the legitimacy of her own

---

[54]*In a Different Voice*, p. 86. The similarities in the way both Janet and Sandra worked their way toward the decision to abort are striking: they both show an awareness of the demands of their faith, they both are aware of what an abortion is, and they both choose *situationism*, an offshoot of utilitarianism, to justify abortion. Mary Daly once made a perspicacious observation when speaking of Joseph Fletcher's "Christian situation ethics": "One may well ask why the label 'Christian' is necessary. What does it add to 'situation ethics'?" (*Beyond God the Father*, p. 105).

point of view (p. 87).

The passage alludes to a central concern of Kantian ethics, *autonomy*, a major feature of Kohlberg's theory of moral development, and one that forms a fundamental concern for feminist ethics, Gilligan's included. That the *woman* makes the decision and not the *decision* the woman makes is behind Gilligan's comments here. We note also how subtly Gilligan's own ethical theory of contextual relativism is being presented. We remember her theory has as one of its essential components the refusal to admit moral absolutes.

Though we have focused our attention on the two subjects, Janet and Sandra, whose Catholic faith is mentioned as such in the book, all the others who took part in Gilligan's research have stories to tell as well. Since we are dealing with the abortion situation, each case is a matter of life and death. It is not only the stories of Janet and Sandra that are important. But to see how Gilligan presents the stories of these Catholic women can perchance give us an appreciation that each of the women is presenting her own intensely personal story.[55]

The Violence in Abortion

We have already noted the importance of killing for Simone de Beauvoir's existential analysis of the human situation. We also observed Beauvoir attesting to the fact that abortion does violence upon a woman. Daly is not unaware of this. In fact, this is precisely the nature of the abortion situation. Daly is fond of quoting the lines to the song: "Every way you look at it, you lose."[56] This is especially the case with abortion. This too is part of the abortion situation; the women who speak in their own voices in Gilligan's book likewise are aware of the

---

[55]Janet E. Smith, "Abortion and Moral Development," treats the stories of Denise, Sarah, and Betty in some detail. A study somewhat similar to Gilligan's and published the same year is Judith G. Smetana, *Concepts of Self and Morality: Women's Reasoning About Abortion* (New York: Praeger, 1982). Smetana does not regard the moral dimension of the abortion question as of central importance, at least for many of the women who took part in her study. She is aware of Gilligan's accent on the moral aspect of abortion but considers such a view an overgeneralization.

[56]Mary Daly, *Beyond God the Father*, p. 109.

nature of abortion.[57]

American feminist Adrienne Rich once wrote of the violence that is abortion.[58] The women in Gilligan's study are certainly witnesses to this aspect of the abortion dilemma. We see it especially when Gilligan allows her interviewees to tell their abortion stories in their own words, in their sometimes rambling, sometimes pertinent, sometimes frightening comments.[59]

Abortion is presented in all its tragic complexity with many of the women observing that they know full well that they are taking a life but somehow the situation in which they find themselves seems to them to make it somehow right. Sandra as a nurse certainly knows what takes place in an abortion; Sarah wonders if her contemplated second abortion would not make her feel, as she herself puts it, "like a walking

---

[57]On the question of the women knowing what the abortion decision entails, cf. Mary Kenny, *Abortion: The Whole Story*, especially pp. 225–252. In chapter nine, "What the Female Philosophers Say," Kenny relates the views of nine women philosophers, including Carol McMillan, on the matter of abortion. The Catholic Church has no need to argue for the humanity of the fetus, avers McMillan, since everybody knows this. If anything, the position of the Church is criticized for being overly rationalistic and legalistic regarding abortion. The evil of abortion is so great that even the talk about a fetus's right to life is odious to McMillan. Kenny herself notes: "All the women philosophers that I consulted considered abortion to be inherently evil, even when they accepted that it was sometimes a necessary one" (p. 231). For her book, Kenny interviewed Mary Warnock, Mary Midgley, Judith Hughes, Philippa Foot, Janet Radcliffe Richards, Anne Kelleher, Sissela Bok, and Onora O'Neill. Carol McMillan is the only Catholic in the group.

[58]Cf. Adrienne Rich, *Of Woman Born: Motherhood as Experience and Institution*, p. 274: "Abortion is violence; a deep, desperate violence inflicted by a woman upon, first of all, herself."

[59]Ruth is rambling, p. 103, and Denise is pertinent, p. 92. What Sarah says is frightening. Gilligan begins with a comment in her own voice before letting Sarah speak: "Although Sarah does not 'feel good' about having a second abortion, she concludes: 'I would not be doing myself or the child or the world any kind of favor having this child. I don't need to pay off my imaginary debts to the world through this child, and I don't think that it is right to bring a child into the world and use it for that purpose.'" Gilligan, if we recall, rates Sarah very high on the level of moral development (pp. 90ff).

slaughter-house."[60]

After listening to nineteen-year-old Judy tell of her boyfriend's directness in situations in contrast to her own reluctance to hurt anyone, Gilligan adds a commentary of her own:

> At this point of development, conflict arises specifically over the issue of hurting. When no option exists that can be construed as being in the best interest of everybody, when responsibilities conflict and decision entails the sacrifice of somebody's needs, *then the woman confronts the seemingly impossible task of choosing the victim.*[61]

"Choosing the victim," "a deep, dark violence," "the sex that kills is the one that is honored": maybe on this point the words of the song that Mary Daly is fond of quoting hit the nail right on the head: "Every way you look at it, you lose."

Commentary on Carol Gilligan

Simone de Beauvoir once observed: "The fact that we are human beings is infinitely more important than all the peculiarities that distinguish human beings from one another" (*The Second Sex*, p. 685). What may pass for an obvious platitude becomes much debated when Beauvoir tries to link it to her thoroughgoing culturalist hypothesis. Though she owes a debt to the mother of contemporary feminism on other matters, including abortion, as we have seen, it is to her credit that Carol Gilligan reminds contemporary feminists that there are indeed two sexes and that gender is not something incidental to the human

---

[60]Cf. *In a Different Voice*, p. 91. Janet E. Smith, "Abortion and Moral Theory," p. 46, comments on recidivism: "Many of those assessed by Gilligan had more than one abortion: none were evaluated as backsliding in their moral development because of their second abortion."

[61]*In a Different Voice*, p. 80: my emphasis. Barbara Katz Rothman, *The Tentative Pregnancy: Prenatal Diagnosis and the Future of Motherhood* (New York: Viking Press, 1986), uses Gilligan's work to show that the most important thing for women is not to hurt anyone (p. 243). Rothman cites the passage on "choosing the victim" in the context of the film, "Sophie's Choice" (pp. 179–180).

person.[62] If for no other reason, the thought of Carol Gilligan and her "Difference Feminism" has proven to be a necessary and welcome corrective to the extremes of some feminist discourse.

It is at this point that we can begin putting together the strands of thought we find in Carol Gilligan's approach to the abortion question. Gilligan's feminist forebears make their case for abortion on a strategy that is more political and rhetorical than it is moral. Though both Simone de Beauvoir and Mary Daly speak of abortion in the language of ethics, their ultimate strategy is to use the language of power politics to attain their aims: Beauvoir marching through the streets of Paris at the head of a phalanx of French feminists, Daly urging women to see abortion as a "microcosm of female oppression."

Gilligan, by means of the women who tell their confusing, heart-rending, at times tortured tales, is much more subtle and, in my opinion, much more effective. If she has learnt the epistemological and metaphysical lessons of Beauvoir and Daly on the abortion question, Gilligan is trying to turn this knowledge into an occasion for psychological growth, if done for the right reasons.[63]

Gilligan makes what appears to me to be a quite well-thought-out use of *complementarity* to buttress her case for abortion. A glance at her two moral ideologies will be illuminating.[64]

---

[62]Jean Bethke Elshtain, "Antigone's Daughters," *Democracy* 2 no. 2 (1982), pp. 46–59, is appreciative of Gilligan's "difference feminism."

[63]It appears to me that Gilligan's approach makes her more formidable on the abortion question than either Simone de Beauvoir or Mary Daly. They were making the most of a bad situation. Gilligan is trying to turn the necessary evil into a good. What the Second Vatican Council regards as "the unspeakable evil" of abortion is on its way to becoming what radical feminism considers "the essential feminist message."

[64]On the notion of "two different moral ideologies," see Gilligan's remarks on p. 164 of *In a Different Voice*. Gilligan herself has no such diagram. I have put together this section on "Gilligan's Two Moral Ideologies" after reading *In a Different Voice*. Helpful to me in this regard were the introductory remarks made by Eva Feder Kittay and Diana T. Meyers to a volume they edited, *Women and Moral Theory* (Totowa: Rowman and Littlefield, 1987).

Gilligan's Two Moral Ideologies

THE MORALITY OF RIGHTS	THE MORALITY OF CARE
MALE	FEMALE
FORMAL REASONING	CARE AND RESPONSIBILITY
AUTONOMY	RELATIONSHIP
HIERARCHY	WEB, NETWORK
PERFECTION	CARE
VIOLENCE	CARE AND PROTECTION
DANGER IN CLOSE AFFILIATION	DANGER IN IMPERSONAL
POWER	VIRTUE
UNIVERSAL ABSTRACT REASONING	CONTEXTUAL AND CONCRETE
NONINTERFERENCE	GIVE CARE
SEPARATISM	CONNECTION
ABSTRACT	CONCRETE
RIGHTS	RESPONSIBILITIES
AWARENESS OF DUTY	CARE
IMPERSONAL	PERSONAL
UNIVERSAL RULES	PRESENCE OF THE PERSON

Women are caring, aware of the need not to hurt, interested in keeping relationships going, not burning bridges, continually building webs of relationships, trying to see the connections among human beings, and intensely interested in the human person. At this point, however, Gilligan is in a quandary; whatever else abortion might be, it is a violence, and it seems to show that women are, at least to the fetus they are carrying, uncaring, capable of inflicting harm, hurt, and death, and willing to sever that first and most fragile of all human connections, the umbilical cord linking a mother to her child.

If I may risk an oversimplification: it would seem that the reasons to have the child are found in the morality of care, the reasons to have an abortion are found in the morality of rights. Why Gilligan wants *both* approaches in her morality should be apparent: she can have her cake and eat it too. Women are caring and loving, to be sure, but abortion is sometimes necessary in this harsh world, and women are to be judged none the less caring and loving for it.[65] Gilligan states the dilemma, first in the words of Cathy:

> "I don't know what choices are open to me. It is either to have it or the abortion; these are the choices open to me. I think what confuses me is it is a choice of either hurting myself or hurting other people around me. What is more important? If there could be a happy medium, it would be fine, but there isn't. It is either hurting someone on this side or hurting myself" (*In a Different Voice*, p. 80.)

Gilligan adds in her own voice:

> Although the feminine identification of goodness with self-sacrifice clearly dictates the 'right' resolution of this dilemma, the stakes may be high for the woman herself, and in any event the sacrifice of the fetus compromises the altruism of an abortion motivated by concern for others. Since femininity itself is in conflict in an abortion intended as an expression of love and care, this resolution readily explodes in its own contradiction.[66]

---

[65]One author who believes that there is much of what she calls "feminist doublethink" on the abortion issue, and Gilligan's version of it in particular, is Martha Bayles, "Feminism and Abortion," *The Atlantic* 265 no. 4 (1990), pp. 84–88, and reprinted in *Human Life Review* 16 (Summer 1990), pp. 37–46. One example of this feminist doublethink is that women have the power to *end* potential life but have no responsibility for *conceiving* life in the first place. Bayles believes she finds this doublethink in the author of *In a Different Voice* whose approach to abortion is so "tortured" because Gilligan *always* interprets her subjects' abortions as responsible decisions. Bayles sees such a view as endemic to those who espouse the theory of female moral superiority: by the very fact that a *woman* chose an action, it *must* be moral.

[66]*In a Different Voice*, p. 80. Gilligan's words cause us to reflect: "an abortion intended as an expression of love and care." Abortion is an act of violence. And it is. "Every way you look at it, you lose" indeed. On occasion, some will try to present abortion as a sign of love and attachment. Cf. Ginette Paris, *The Sacrament of Abortion* (translated by Joanna Mott: original title: *L'enfant, l'amour, la mort*) (Dallas: Spring Publications, 1992), p. 93: "Most women who choose abortion love children and are tempted, often unconsciously in an animal way, to keep the fetus. But it is through consciousness, a feminine consciousness, that they choose not to give birth." Jean

It seems to me Gilligan is aware of being at an impasse. She would want to understand care, of course, in such a way that it ideally includes all the parties concerned.[67] But the nature of abortion is what it is, a "deep, dark violence." How to turn it into an occasion for growth, "an expression of love and concern"? How to bridge the gulf? A caring ethic, an ethic which seeks to hurt no one would seem to preclude such a move.[68] Gilligan puts it this way:

> A progressively more adequate understanding of the psychology of human relationships. . . informs the development of an ethic of care. This ethic, which reflects a cumulative knowledge of human relationships, evolves around a central insight, that self and other are interdependent. . . . The fact of interconnection informs the central, recurring recognition that just as the incidence of violence is in the end destructive to all, so the activity of care enhances both others and self.[69]

Toulat, *La droit de naître* (Paris: Pygmalion: Gérard Watelet, 1979), reports that at a birth control conference a certain Mme. Iff of Planned Parenthood received a standing ovation for her statement: "Abortion is an act of love and of life" (p. 61).

[67]Cf. J. Theodore Klein, "Transforming Moral Theory," *The American Philosophical Association Newsletter on Feminism and Philosophy* 90 no. 2 (1991), pp. 92–96. The author clarifies how feminists use *care*: "Caring does not involve sacrificing oneself or accepting oppression. Caring, being relational, involves self as well as others, and as inclusive caring includes self as well as others." In the words of Rita C. Manning, *Speaking from the Heart: A Feminist Perspective on Ethics*, p. 71: "I don't think that we are obligated to be like Mother Teresa, who cares for continuously."

[68]That an ethic of care need not preclude violence is the thought of Victoria Davion, "Pacifism and Care," *Hypatia* 5 (1990), pp. 90–100.

[69]Cf. *In a Different Voice*, p. 74. As Letty Cottin Pogrebin, *Family Politics: Love and Power on an Intimate Frontier* (New York: McGraw-Hill Paperbacks, 1983), p. 191, views the matter: "I see abortion as an expression of respect for motherhood. Almost any biological female *can* reproduce. Only human females have the brainpower to decide whether they *should* reproduce. To deny women that decision-making power is to reduce us to animals. And to deny children mothers who have consciously and willfully chosen to have them is to reduce motherhood to breeding."

But an ethic fashioned on a more impersonal basis might allow such actions "if done for the right reasons." Gilligan herself comments on the essential features of the masculine morality:

> The morality of rights differs from the morality of responsibility in its emphasis on separation rather than connection, in its consideration of the individual rather than the relationship as primary.[70]

If I am not mistaken, it is precisely here that we find the formidable nature of Gilligan's abortion position. It is based on the precise point in her book so many feminists criticize: the Harvard educational psychologist's use of *complementarity* to describe the two moral ideologies Gilligan believes she has uncovered in the course of her several studies.[71] Where many of her feminist critics think they see in the use of complementarity the seeds of the dreaded *nature* slinking in to

---

[70]*In a Different Voice*, p. 19. Cf. Christine Keller, "Feminism and the Ethics of Inseparability," p. 261. The *masculine* voice of the fundamental hostility of each consciousness to every other consciousness (Beauvoir's ethics) does not fare well when compared to the *feminine* voice which Gilligan is elaborating. Celia Wolf-Devine, "Abortion and the 'Feminine Voice,'" *Public Affairs Quarterly* 3 no. 3 (1989), pp. 81–97, argues a case *against* abortion along the lines of Gilligan's ethic of care. Does not abortion seem a rather violent response to a human relational problem? "If, as Gilligan says, 'an ethic of care rests on the premise of non-violence—that no one should be hurt,' then surely the feminine response to an unwanted pregnancy would be to try to find a solution which does not involve injury to anyone, including the unborn" (Wolf-Devine, p. 87; the quote within the text is from *In a Different Voice*, p. 174).

[71]Gilligan has been so involved in elaborating the "different voice" for women in ethics that at times it may appear she overlooks the role men play (or, perhaps better, *ought to play*) in the abortion decision. Mary Ann Glendon, *Abortion and Divorce in Western Law: American Failures, European Challenges* (Cambridge: Harvard University Press, 1987), p. 52, comments: "It is striking how many of Carol Gilligan's subjects in her chapter on the abortion decision stated that one of the reasons they were seeking abortions was because the men in their lives were unwilling to give them moral and material support in continuing with pregnancy and childbirth. This fact surely must have been central to their moral dilemma, but Gilligan, surprisingly, never picks up on this aspect of her data."

wreak havoc upon hard-won feminist gains,[72] it seems to me that they fail to appreciate that Gilligan's use of complementarity has gone a long way in giving abortion the one thing that neither Simone de Beauvoir nor Mary Daly could give the violent procedure: a veneer of ethical respectability. Abortion shifts perceptibly from the *killing and the power* perspective of Beauvoir and Daly into the *choice and rights* perspective of Carol Gilligan.

Summary and Conclusions

The violence of abortion is acknowledged, without a doubt, but along with it comes the knowledge stemming from Simone de Beauvoir that sometimes we have to do violent things in this world.[73] Such actions, as Mary Daly points out, are humiliating to women. Suppose someone—perhaps a psychologist—were to come along and show that from this violent, humbling knowledge can come an opportunity for personal growth. Abortion is acknowledged for what it is, a violent procedure, but, all things considered, an acceptable one since, in the final analysis, it may be the harbinger of personal moral development: "Although inclusion is the goal of moral consciousness, exclusion may be a necessity of life."[74] Here would seem to be a formidable feature of Gilligan's position on abortion. If she can show how the violence is really "an expression of love and care," then perhaps abortion can be envisioned, despite its attendant ambiguity and ambivalence, as a means of psychological maturity, if undertaken "for the right reasons."[75]

---

[72]Madonna Kolbenschlag, *Kiss Sleeping Beauty Good-Bye: Breaking the Spell of Feminine Myths and Models*, p. 113, defines *complementarity* as "a disguised neurotic symbiosis that perpetuates immaturity."

[73]We remember Simone de Beauvoir, *The Second Sex*, p. 58, stressing killing as the key to the whole mystery of woman's subjugation. While Gilligan, to the best of my knowledge, does not cite texts from Beauvoir, she certainly seems to be utilizing the ideas of the French feminist. By the time Gilligan wrote *In a Different Voice*, many of Beauvoir's ideas had come to be associated with feminism, period.

[74]*In a Different Voice*, p. 148. Is this Kate or is it Gilligan?

[75]On the theme of abortion as a sign of concern and care, cf. Marge Piercy, Foreword to Ellen Messer and Kathryn E. May, Psy. D., *Back Rooms: Voices From the Illegal Abortion Era* (New York: Touchstone Books, 1988), p. xiii: "Abortion is a necessary activity for our species, until and unless we can absolutely control our fertility,

Is Gilligan providing "good reasons" for abortion,[76] or is she engaging in rationalization?[77] This is a difficult question to answer. Part of the difficulty is found in the way the Harvard psychologist submerges herself and her opinions in her interviewees. Since Gilligan allows women to speak in their different voices, we are left wondering at times if Gilligan herself accepts the reasons given for abortion by the women she is interviewing. Is Gilligan herself for or against abortion?[78] Whatever answer we give to this question, it is probably true to say that it is not as important as what people *think* they hear Gilligan saying.[79]

It also appears that Gilligan is taking a calculated gamble on the abortion issue. She is honest enough to acknowledge the profound upheaval abortion often causes in the lives of women and lets these women speak in their own voice. These women know what they are doing: it is killing; and somehow they are trying to turn what they

---

because we are bonded to our young for such a long time before they can carry out an independent existence."

[76]Ellen Herman, "Introduction" to Kathleen McDonnell, *Not an Easy Choice: A Feminist Re-examines Abortion* (Boston: South End Press, 1984), pp. i-xv, especially at p. viii, opines that feminist ethics will eschew talk of right and wrong on the abortion question and instead employ Gilligan's categories of responsibilities and relationships to justify the practice.

[77]Dave Andrusko, "Choosing the Victim," *National Right to Life News* 11 no. 3 (1984), pp. 7-8f, is troubled that a scholar like Gilligan is so bent on discovering a basis for the injustice of abortion that she subverts her own intellect. Andrusko laments the loss of a fine mind ruined by ideology.

[78]Cf. Barbara Milbauer with Bert Obrentz, *The Law Giveth: Legal Aspects of the Abortion Controversy* (New York: Atheneum, 1983), p. 180, who contends that Gilligan does *not* approve of abortion. On the other hand, David C. Reardon, *Aborted Women: Silent No More* (Foreword by Nancyjo Mann) (Chicago: Loyola University Press, 1987), believes that she *does*. What is my position on the matter? In the light of her contextual relativism which entails a rejection of ethical absolutes, and aware that she never says that any of her subjects who chose abortion made the *wrong* decision, we conclude that Gilligan herself holds a pro-choice position which says, in effect, that abortion, when done "for the right reasons," can be an occasion for psychological growth.

[79]We have already observed what appeared to be the eagerness on the part of some to welcome Gilligan's thesis of *In a Different Voice* despite some very serious questions about drawing conclusions based on a sampling of twenty-nine women from one relatively affluent area of the country.

know is wrong in their hearts to what is right by their words.[80] Gilligan gambles that she can describe abortion in the words of these women, with all the talk of killing and anguish and babies and slaughterhouses, and somehow be able to pull it all together in such a way that the unspeakable crime becomes an understandable decision, nay, what is more, a good one if "done for the right reasons."

Gilligan finds a *powerful* ally in the notion of *rights*. Here she draws on a long tradition of feminist thought in America, and here, it seems to me, is the proper place to situate the several other studies she makes a part of her book, notably the "Rights and Responsibilities" Study. Pilloried by some feminists for what they feel is Gilligan's eschewing a morality of rights for a morality of care, Carol Gilligan has—in my estimation— taken out an insurance policy of sorts on the abortion question; if she cannot make her case for *abortion as an expression of love and concern*, then perhaps she can make out a case for *abortion as a right*.[81] Here we find the right to abortion. This helps explain the apparent anomaly of Gilligan espousing, at the heart of a feminine ethic, the ethic of care, one of the central elements of the masculine ethic, the notion of rights.

Transition to Beverly Wildung Harrison

Carol Gilligan approaches the abortion issue from the standpoint of developmental psychology. By her contextual relativism and its ability to make it appear that abortion, if undertaken for the right reasons, can be an occasion of psychological growth, it seems that the Harvard psychologist has gone part of the way toward trying to find some sort of a moral grounding for the "deep dark violence" that is abortion. Even for women with religious sensibilities, abortion—when

---

[80]Is it possible that women have a special gift for detecting the presence of the person in situations often seen as impersonal? While such a view would be anathema to the culturalist feminism of Simone de Beauvoir (who might see in it the seeds of the return of the myth of the eternal feminine), the thesis is developed by Edmée Mottini-Coulon, *De l'ontologie à l'éthique par la maternité* ("Problèmes et controverses") (Paris: Vrin, 1981). It is hinted at in Juliana Casey, *Where Is God Now? Nuclear Terror, Feminism and the Search for God* (Kansas City: Sheed and Ward, 1987).

[81]Gilligan's approach, then, is twofold: first, try to establish abortion as *good* ("if done for the right reasons"), and second, try to establish abortion as a *right*.

done for the right reasons (Gilligan's psychology)—can allow women to *know* (Beauvoir's epistemology) what it means to *be* female (Daly's metaphysics).

Liberal Protestant feminist theologian Beverly Wildung Harrison constantly stresses the need for feminism to take the high moral ground on the question of abortion, and not to leave this to those whom she calls the "'so-called pro-life' zealots." In *Our Right to Choose*, Harrison attempts to go even further than Gilligan and will endeavor to show that the right to abortion is—despite certain problematic aspects—a great good for women.[82] It is to this professor of Christian Ethics that we now turn.

As we do so, we would do well to bear in mind that in the first three feminist thinkers whose thought on abortion we have investigated, we have discovered an indebtedness to what we may term, for lack of a better word, *masculine* values, "tools," if you will,[83] as their solution to *male* perfidy (see Beauvoir and Daly) or to *male* irresponsibility (see Gilligan). To spell this out, we remember that in their analyses of abortion, Beauvoir relies heavily on *killing*, Daly on *power*, and Gilligan on *choice* and *rights*.

On the abortion issue can it be that the words of the Sylvia Plath poem ring true: "From that pale mist/ Ghost swore to priest:/There sits no higher court/ Than man's red heart"? The words of another feminist poet come hauntingly to mind: "The Master's tools/ Can never dismantle the Master's house."[84]

---

[82]If Gilligan tried to show *either* that abortion is right *or* that abortion is a right, Harrison will attempt to establish that abortion is *both* right *and* a right.

[83]Cf. Carol McMillan, *Women, Reason and Nature: Some Philosophical Problems with Feminism*: "Here again we have a clue to why the right to control their bodies through contraception and abortion is such a crucial demand for feminists. It might be said that contraception and abortion are to woman what the tool was to man" (pp. 127–128).

[84]Audre Lorde, *Sister Outsider: Essays and Speeches* (The Crossing Press Feminist Series) (Freedom, CA: The Crossing Press, 1984), pp. 110–113.

CHAPTER FOUR

BEVERLY WILDUNG HARRISON, 1932–

The Theology of Abortion

> From a feminist theological point of view, prohibition
> of legal abortion involves the effort to deny full
> freedom or centered moral agency, and hence full
> humanity, to over half the population.[1]

T he last of the four feminist thinkers to be treated is Beverly
Wildung Harrison. Born in 1932, she is a professor of Christian
Ethics at the Protestant Union Theological Seminary in New York,
serves on the editorial board of *Concilium*, and is past president of the
Society of Christian Ethics. Her influence has been notable in the
United States, especially in social ethics. At least two books have been
dedicated to her,[2] and other authors writing in the field of Christian
ethics often cite her.[3] One author regards Harrison's work on the ethics

---

[1]Beverly Wildung Harrison, *Our Right to Choose: Toward a New Ethic of Abortion*
(Boston: Beacon Press, 1983), p. 116.

[2]One of them is Barbara Hilkert Andolsen, Christine Gudorf, and Mary Pellauer
(eds.), *Women's Consciousness, Women's Conscience: A Reader in Feminist Ethics*. As
the editors dedicate the volume to Harrison, they do so by noting that it was she who
taught them what a passion for justice was. The other is Isabel Carter Heyward, *The
Redemption of God: A Theology of Mutual Relation* (Lanham, MD: University Press of
America, 1982).

[3]A good place to observe Harrison's influence in American religious ethics is James
F. Childress and John Macquarrie (eds.), *The Westminster Dictionary of Christian
Ethics* (Philadelphia: Westminster Press, 1986). One finds not only several entries
written by Harrison herself but also mention made of her in a host of other entries,
especially in the bibliographies.

of abortion as one of the two most important pro-choice feminist treatments of the subject.[4]

Carol Robb, editor of Harrison's collection of essays entitled *Making the Connections*,[5] finds five central ideas animating the feminist social ethics of the Protestant theologian. It is an ethics which is

1. justice centered;
2. concerned with objectivity;
3. focussed on autonomy as the goal of ethics;[6]
4. continuous with the sources of religious norms;[7] and
5. one in which embodied reason is the way to test norms.[8]

The three authors whose ideas we have examined treated the question of abortion in the context of their views on woman's condition. While each treats the abortion question at least once in some detail, none of the three presents an exhaustive treatment of the issue *per se*, and none writes a monograph on the subject as does Harrison who attempts to remedy any deficiencies she finds in earlier treatments. If Beauvoir, Daly, and Gilligan appropriate the linguistic resources of epistemology, metaphysics, and psychology to make their cases for abortion, Harrison will attempt to construct a pro-abortion argument

---

[4]Cf. Sidney Callahan, "Abortion and the Sexual Agenda," *Commonweal* 113 no. 8 (1986), pp. 232-238. In the abortion books of Beverly Harrison and Rosalind Petchesky, Callahan finds "complex arguments, which draw on diverse strands of philosophy and social theory and are often interwoven in pro-choice feminists' own version of a 'seamless garment'" (p. 232).

[5]Cf. Carol Robb, "Introduction," *Making the Connections* (Boston: Beacon Press, 1985), pp. xi-xxii.

[6]Robb expounds on autonomy and sees it as the enhancement of personhood "defined as capacity for responsible self-direction." Religious definitions for sex roles, especially those using concepts based on "natural law" categories, are particularly pernicious. Feminists are to be on their guard against words such as *complementarity* and expressions such as *according to the design of the Creator*.

[7]Robb lists these as sacred scripture, tradition, other human sciences, experience, and rational reflection.

[8]Robb means by this that all dualism is to be avoided.

based on the words and in the language of Christian theology.[9]

While *Our Right to Choose* is the focal point of our study, containing as it does her most sustained argument on the matter, Harrison has dealt with the issues of abortion and reproductive rights in the context of Christian theology on other occasions as well.[10] At times she writes an article reacting to the pronouncements of others on the topic of abortion; at other times we find her endeavoring to put the long argument of *Our Right to Choose* into a shorter format.[11]

Harrison and the Catholic Ethical Tradition

Our investigation into the writings of Simone de Beauvoir, Mary Daly, and Carol Gilligan has unearthed the important role played by religion in general and by Roman Catholicism in particular in contemporary feminist discourse.[12] Beverly Harrison follows their lead in this matter. On several occasions she speaks of the respect she has for the Roman Catholic tradition in moral theology. She believes that it is

---

[9]Harrison is certainly not the stylist that the others are, acknowledging as she does in *Our Right to Choose*, p. vii, the book's "unwieldy text" and her "complex, Germanic prose."

[10]Since Harrison is quite insistent on linking the two issues of abortion and reproductive rights, I am following her lead and doing the same. Thus, the expression, "abortion and reproductive rights," has been chosen purposely.

[11]Cf. Beverly Wildung Harrison, "Theology of Pro-choice: A Feminist Perspective," in Edward Batchelor, Jr. (ed.), *Abortion: The Moral Issues* (New York: Pilgrim Press, 1982), pp. 210–226; and the chapter Harrison wrote with the help of Shirley Cloyes entitled "Theology and the Morality of Procreative Choice," in Beverly Wildung Harrison, *Making the Connections*. See also "A Feminist Perspective on Moral Responsibility," *Conscience* (special double issue) vol. 5, no. 6 and vol. 6, no. 1 (Winter 1984/1985), pp. 1–3; and "Situating the Dilemma of Abortion Historically," *Conscience* 112 (March/April 1990), pp. 15–20. Harrison also contributed to a Pro-choice Forum on the topic: "Abortion: How Should Women Decide," with the article "Feminist Realism," *Christiantiy and Crisis* 46 no. 10 (July 14, 1986), pp. 233–236.

[12]Cf. Marilyn Falik, *Ideology and Abortion Policy Politics*, p. 89: "Catholicism is generally regarded as the finest example of a holistic and comprehensive system of explanation."

superior to her own Protestant tradition in many areas of moral evaluation, notably on social justice.[13] While she clearly disagrees with the teaching of Roman Catholicism on reproductive issues,[14] she makes the same observation that Simone de Beauvoir had made in this regard: in the matter of abortion, the one serious moral argument made against it is that of the Roman Catholic Church.[15]

Beverly Harrison's respect for the Roman Catholic tradition is clearly seen in these words: "It is also worth noting that a feminist theological ethic has more in common with a Roman Catholic moral approach than with Protestant biblicism."[16] Since Harrison has influenced many, it is not surprising therefore to find other feminist authors treating this same possibility, namely, the appropriateness of elements of Roman Catholicism for the construction of a feminist ethic.[17]

Misogyny in the Christian Tradition

In a sense, of course, we *expect* Beverly Harrison to be interested

---

[13]Cf. *Making the Connections*, pp. 115–116.

[14]See her comments in *Making the Connections*, p. 116. To add the proper nuance, we should note that Harrison herself makes it clear that her disagreement is with issues of *natural law* and of the authority of the Roman Catholic *hierarchy* on the abortion issue.

[15]Cf. Simone de Beauvoir, *The Second Sex*, p. 458, and Beverly Wildung Harrison, *Making the Connections*, p. 116. While *Our Right to Choose* goes into some detail regarding Catholic teaching on abortion, Harrison by no means overlooks her own Protestant tradition. Mary Daly likewise treats both Catholic and Protestant ethicists on abortion in *Beyond God the Father*.

[16]*Our Right to Choose*, p. 115. From the context it appears Harrison prefers the Catholic teaching based on a biblicism nourished by a living tradition to a Protestantism too exclusively dependent on biblicism.

[17]The regnant feminist thinking, namely, that Catholicism is one of the major obstacles to women's liberation, is reported by Maria Teresa Bellenzier, "Panorama bibliografico sulla 'questione femminile: I," *Rassegna di Teologia* 16 (1975), pp. 552–565, especially at p. 565. The author notes that to many feminists, religion is the culprit and Roman Catholicism the chief villain in keeping women relegated to subordinate status.

in religion (she *is* a Christian theologian after all), but hers is a rather critical investigation as she attempts to rework her own Christian religious tradition in order to make it more just in the way it treats women. She makes a rather serious accusation against opponents of abortion: misogyny.[18] Not surprisingly, Simone de Beauvoir argued a similar case of misogyny, levelling the charge against males in society in general.[19] Harrison will try to make hers against the entire Christian theological tradition: "Unfortunately, the growing impact of feminist scholarship on many academic disciplines is almost absent in *Christian Theology which remains perhaps the most misogynist of disciplines.*"[20] What is more, Harrison believes she knows precisely where to go to find the evidence of misogyny in the Christian tradition: the teaching on abortion (pp. 6–10). Yet she also makes an observation that is of pivotal importance for her argument:

> One cannot easily or readily spot this misogyny simply by going directly to explicit abortion teaching. Basically, one must scrutinize carefully what a given theological stream teaches or assumes about women, sexuality, procreation, and the family and observe how these assumptions shape abortion teaching (*Our Right to Choose*, p. 63).

Thus, *Our Right to Choose* can be viewed in one sense as an attempt to document the serious charge of misogyny. Harrison will attempt to show connections between misogyny, the hatred of women,

---

[18]Cf. *Our Right to Choose*, p. 8. She does grant that at times these patterns of misogyny are transmitted by males "unawares." Cf. the entry "Misogyny" in Maggie Humm, *The Dictionary of Feminist Theory*, p. 139: "Adrienne Rich has characterized misogyny as organised, institutionalised, normalised hostility and violence against women."

[19]Simone de Beauvoir treats misogyny in the context of abortion in the central section of her exposition of abortion iin *The Second Sex*, pp. 463–464.

[20]*Our Right to Choose*, p. 7: my emphasis. The usual meaning of the word *misogyny* is "hatred of women." Harrison herself uses the word in this strong sense. Cf. her article, "Theology of Pro-choice: A Feminist Perspective," p. 210: "Much discussion of abortion betrays the heavy hand of misogyny or the hatred of women."

and strictures against abortion. She hopes to force this well-hidden misogyny out into the open.

A Search for the High Moral Ground

Harrison does not think that the Christian moral tradition has been fair to women in its teachings on abortion and reproductive rights. As a result she sets out her task in *Our Right to Choose*: "A formulation of the ethics of abortion which is fair to women's reality is a moral necessity" (p. x).

Seeing the way the abortion discussion was being conducted in the United States, Harrison agrees with an observation made by Stanley Hauerwas that the abortion debate is becoming "ritualistic."[21] One aspect of the debate in the American context that especially troubles Harrison is a point she noted as early as 1977, namely, that the foes of abortion have taken the high moral ground on the matter.[22] Harrison returns to this theme of "the high moral ground" many times in *Our Right to Choose*:

> Pro-choice women have entered the political struggle valiantly and the political debate eloquently. But the impression is left that 'the ethics' of the issue are 'owned' by anti-abortion proponents (p. 6).

> In spite of some good reasons to be cautious about moral entanglements, moral legitimacy needs to be wrested from those who oppose procreative choice (p. 41).

> Furthermore, even if crass utilitarian arguments prove effective in the short run, we need to remember that at the moment the other side controls the moral

---

[21]Cf. *Our Right to Choose*, p. 6. Here Harrison speaks of Hauerwas as a well-respected Christian ethicist. Later, she notes that he is one of those critical of the linchpin of her argument for the right to abortion, the bodily integrity argument. Cf. *Our Right to Choose*, p. 307, note 26.

[22]Cf. Beverly Wildung Harrison, "Continuing the Discussion: How to Argue About Abortion: II," *Christianity and Crisis* 37 no. 21 (1977), pp. 311–313. Harrison warns abortion advocates of the danger in leaving the high moral ground to the absolutists.

momentum on the issue (p. 49).

My reading of *Our Right to Choose*, leads me to conclude that Beverly Harrison has written this work on the ethics of abortion as an attempt to reclaim that high moral ground for the pro-choice forces. She puts it this way:

> Dispelling the myth of moral superiority on the so-called pro-life side of the abortion debate commits us to develop our moral arguments more compellingly and also to evaluate critically existing moral theory and moral theology as they bear on the abortion controversy.[23]

In her desire to reclaim the high moral ground for the pro-choice side in the abortion debate, Beverly Harrison contends that if feminism is anything at all, it is a plea for justice. In her words: "Feminism is fundamentally a moral claim" (p. 7).

By the time she came to write *Our Right to Choose*, Beverly Wildung Harrison was aware that, the contributions of her feminist predecessors notwithstanding, there simply existed no sustained argument to establish abortion as a fundamental right of women and as an essential aspect of what it is that constitutes a good society. Aware of this lacuna, she attempts to fill it by means of *Our Right to Choose*.

The Influence of Beauvoir

Of the three feminist authors we have already examined, Beverly Harrison makes explicit mention of Mary Daly and Carol Gilligan in *Our Right to Choose*. While Simone de Beauvoir is not cited, I believe it is true to say that her influence upon Harrison is quite notable nonetheless. At the very least we can talk about a possible debt

---

[23]*Our Right to Choose*, p. 41. That opponents of abortion *do* possess the high moral ground on some major aspects of the abortion issue is the contention of Brigitte and Peter Berger, *The War Over the Family: Capturing the Middle Ground* (Garden City, NY: Anchor Press/ Doubleday, 1983), p. 79. That pro-choice advocates lack a high moral ground is the contention of Bernard Nathanson, *The Abortion Papers: Inside the Abortion Mentality* (New York: Frederick Fell Publishers, 1983), p. 208.

the Christian feminist owes the French thinker.[24] While Beauvoir's *words* may not be quoted directly, I would contend that her *ideas* are certainly present in *Our Right to Choose*. Indeed, as our study of Daly and Gilligan has shown, Beauvoir's ideas have become commonplace, an accepted part of the discourse of contemporary feminism. We see Beauvoir's influence upon Harrison especially in two areas: first, in the way Harrison treats the question of nature, and second, in the carefully-chosen title of her book on abortion.

The Control over Nature

As did Simone de Beauvoir with her espousal of culturalism, Beverly Harrison takes aim at any mention of a special women's nature, noting how vital it is for feminists to break the concept of a fixed nature.[25] Wherever we see such an approach, we are in the heartland of Simone de Beauvoir's vision of feminism: "One is not born, but rather becomes, a woman" (*The Second Sex*, p. 249). Allied with this is another Beauvoirian theme appropriated by Beverly Wildung Harrison, namely, that women are finally taking charge and control over the forces of nature: "For the first time in history, large numbers of women are free from the total conditioning of our lives by a power we do not control" (p. 173).

At times, even the language in *Our Right to Choose* is fairly redolent of that of Simone de Beauvoir. For example: "The quality of our lives depends not on blindly embracing an automatic organic process" (p. 228). Harrison speaks of "the sometimes unbearable problem of fertility" (p. 183). In a text that has echoes of our question, Is Nature Misogynist? we read in Harrison: "For a number of women, *nature's sometimes vicious profligacy* often has presented a life-threatening situation" (p. 156: my emphasis). Of the United States Supreme Court decision in *Roe v. Wade*, Harrison says that it has "given women a measure of negative control over pregnancy which has released many

---

[24]Cf. *Our Right to Choose*, p. 109. In her emphasis on the *historical* and in her downplaying the importance of the *natural* dimensions of human existence, Harrison gives clear evidence of being influenced by existentialism.

[25]Cf. Beverly Wildung Harrison, "The New Consciousness of Women: a Socio-Political Response," *Cross Currents* 24 (Winter 1975), pp. 445–462, especially at p. 451.

from a fatalistic connection to 'natural process.'"[26] In these and other texts, the influence of Beauvoir upon Harrison's abortion discussion is, I believe, quite notable.

The linking of the issues of birth control and abortion which we find in Simone de Beauvoir as part of the reproductive rights package offered women by modern technology is likewise an important motif in the thought of Beverly Harrison.[27] If Simone de Beauvoir believes that foes of women's liberation are guilty of hypocrisy, especially regarding abortion, so too does Beverly Harrison, taking to task those so-called pro-lifers who utter "empty rhetoric, the hypocrisy of those whose moral ideals do not engage reality."[28]

Following the lines of Simone de Beauvoir's argumentation, Harrison contends that the purported link between nature and destiny is nothing more than a part of the male mythology dominating our world.[29] She invokes another important Beauvoirian theme when she employs on occasion the language of *desacralization* (p. 89, p. 181, and p. 213).

The Well-Chosen Title: *Our Right to Choose*

Simone de Beauvoir spent the better part of her life writing; words were her stock-in-trade. She was also well aware of the importance of language in the whole problematic of abortion. Thus, in the very careful choice of a title for her major work on abortion, Harrison is utilizing language in a way that appears to be decidedly

---

[26]Cf. *Our Right to Choose*, p. 249. Beauvoir's comments on artificial insemination come to mind as we read these words of Beverly Harrison.

[27]Cf. *Our Right to Choose*, p. 84: "It is time to acknowledge that church teaching on the subject of contraception and abortion is implicated in a system of control over women's power to reproduce the species." Harrison is aware of the abortifacient nature of the birth control pill; hence her linking of the issues of birth control and abortion. See for example p. 303, note 68.

[28]*Our Right to Choose*, p. 258. We have seen the charge of male hypocrisy made both by Beauvoir and Daly.

[29]The aphorism often attributed to Freud, "Anatomy is destiny," is a famous illustration. Beauvoir records it in *The Second Sex*, p. 42, after observing that "Freud never showed much concern with the destiny of woman" (p. 34).

Beauvoirian: Why *Our Right to Choose*? Each word is well-chosen:

OUR helps to situate her work in the context of women's solidarity because Harrison stresses the community dimensions as she presents her case for abortion.[30] She dedicates her abortion book to her sisters' collective judgment (Cf. *Our Right to Choose*, p. 10).

RIGHT is a word especially appropriate in the context of political life in the United States of America. On this point Harrison is quite insistent: talk of rights forms what she calls the "wider moral framework for the act of abortion" (pp. 196–201).

TO is effective as an action word, to denote what it is that is our right. Harrison continually notes that she is fighting for women's moral agency.

CHOOSE shows how well Beverly Harrison understood the dynamics of the abortion debate. If the word *abortion* is loaded with connotations that still have to be overcome, it would be unwise to use it at this delicate point in the title. Far less combative and much more acceptable is the word *choice*.[31] In another work, Harrison, in fact, explains the decision to frame her argument in the wider context of reproductive rights and control.[32]

---

[30]Cf. *Our Right to Choose*, p. 49. Harrison warns feminism to steer clear of the atomism and individualism which are endemic to political discourse in the United States. She considers the approach of Italian feminism to be a good guide since it argues for abortion on the grounds of foundational social justice. On this point, Italian feminists are "learning from the wisdom of their Catholic heritage" (p. 44).

[31]Cf. James R. Kelly, "Abortion: What Americans *Really* Think and the Catholic Challenge," *America* 165 no. 13 (1991), pp. 310–316. This sociologist gives an indirect confirmation of how rhetorically astute is Harrison's selection of words. Kelly observes the power of the word *choice*—when used in polls and questionnaires—to sway opinion regarding abortion: when the word is employed to frame the abortion debate, 47% of American Catholics say they are pro-choice.

[32]She writes in *Making the Connections*: "The right in question is body-right, or freedom from coercion in childbearing. *It is careless to say that the right in question is the right to an abortion. Morally, the right is bodily self-determination*, a fundamental condition for personhood and a foundational moral right" (p. 288, note 2: my emphasis). The remark is reminiscent of the approach of Simone de Beauvoir. Cf.

ABORTION When Harrison finally does use the word *abortion*, it is relegated to the subtitle, "Toward a New Ethic of Abortion." She has prepared her case for abortion with extreme care.[33] While Beauvoir is never mentioned in *Our Right to Choose*, it seems that her influence upon Harrison is nevertheless present and palpable, even in the careful choice of a title. On one of the most important points, Harrison endeavors to ground the right to abortion on the keystone of her feminist edifice, the bodyright argument.

As we see Harrison's argument for abortion taking shape in *Our Right to Choose*, we should keep in mind these linguistic precisions. Rather than see her arguing exclusively for the right to abortion, it is more precise to say that the right Harrison is seeking is the right to what she calls "bodily self-determination," which has as one of its major components the right to safe, legal abortion.[34]

The Influence of Daly and Gilligan

When Beverly Harrison refers to Mary Daly, she does so in a way that is perhaps indicative of the way most mainstream feminists treat the lesbian feminist professor from Boston College: she thanks

---

Force of Circumstance, p. 500. I recounted the issue *Supra*, p. 55

[33]The chant, "Our bodies, our lives, our right to decide," is another example of an attempt to control the rhetorical landscape in the abortion controversy. For a work by a pro-life feminist who adds what she feels is a needed corrective to the slogan, cf. Juli Loesch, "Our Bodies, Their Lives," in Jeannine Parvati Baker et al., *Conscious Conception: Elemental Journey Through the Labyrinth of Sexuality* (Berkeley: North Atlantic Books, 1986), pp. 202–203.

[34]Other feminists will follow Beauvoir's lead and use the bodyright argument as their chief argument for abortion. Among them is Christine Gudorf, "To Make a Seamless Garment, Use a Single Piece of Cloth," *Cross Currents* 34 no. 4 (1984), pp. 473–491, especially at p. 484: "Bodily integrity is a rather basic human right." Cf. David A. J. Richards, "Constitutional Privacy, Religious Disestablishment, and the Abortion Decisions," in Jay L. Garfield and Patricia Hennessey (eds.), *Abortion: Moral and Legal Perspectives* (Amherst: The University of Massachusetts Press, 1984), pp. 148–174, especially footnote 89, who acknowledges that his pro-choice bodyright argument is based on the work of Beverly Harrison.

Daly for all she has meant to feminism, especially with her insights into the importance of religion for feminism (Cf. *Our Right to Choose*, p. 96). Daly has taught contemporary feminism this valuable truth: "The hold of patriarchal idolatry on Christianity goes to the heart of its story and its sense of mission" (p. 58). This credit having been given, Harrison also goes on to observe that Daly is somewhat removed from the feminist mainstream.[35] Especially does Harrison take pains to distance herself from any tendency toward a female superiority viewpoint.[36]

In light of Harrison's continuing criticisms of any female superiority position,[37] I believe we would be justified in concluding that she would be opposed to it wherever she happened to find it. Interestingly enough, when Harrison in *Our Right to Choose* speaks of the work of Carol Gilligan it is with approval; apparently at this time she detected no traces of the female superiority viewpoint. In fact, Harrison in *Our Right to Choose* speaks well of the work of Carol Gilligan in general and also of Gilligan's use of the abortion study as a test case of sorts for women's ethics.[38] After having had time to ponder the import of Gilligan's work, Harrison does voice some caution in regard to it. As Harrison sees it, justice is at the heart of her vision of feminist ethics. She is apprehensive that the work of Gilligan may be

---

[35]Cf. *Our Right to Choose*, p. 101. Harrison insists that any version of a "female superiority" view of things is to be eschewed as going against the mainstream feminist insight that *relationality* lies at the heart of all reality. Mary Daly's error in perpetuating "reverse dualisms," Harrison goes on to say in effect, is at least understandable in light of patriarchal, male-superiority traditional theology.

[36]That Harrison avoids the female superiority view is at least debatable. A trace of it may be detected, for example, when Harrison writes: "It is to my sisters' collective judgment that I submit my work in this book" (p. 10).

[37]*Our Right to Choose* is not the first time Harrison takes issue with the female superiority view. Cf. "The New Consciousness of Women: A Socio-Political Response," especially at p. 460, note 1. Harrison makes a distinction between "hard" and "soft" feminism: "hard" feminism refuses to grant any special nature to women while "soft" feminism does allow such a move. She herself comes down on the side of the former.

[38]In *Our Right to Choose*, p. 15, Harrison uses Gilligan's work to establish "that many women share a historically shaped gift of moral sensibility such that they do not find it easy to prescribe morality for others, especially when life-shaping questions are at issue."

used in such a way that a morality of care is seen as a rival to a morality of justice.[39]

Harrison's Case for Abortion in *Our Right to Choose*

Beverly Harrison sets before herself a two-fold task in *Our Right to Choose* (pp. 6–7):

1. To criticize the misogynist bias of traditional Christian moral teachings on abortion; and,
2. To elaborate the elements necessary for an ethic of procreative choice.[40]

Since Harrison is seeking to establish the right to abortion as a foundational claim to justice, she is saying in effect: with abortion as a legal right, women at long last will be able to take their rightful place in society. At times she even speaks of abortion as a positive moral good: "The act of abortion is sometimes, even frequently, a positive moral good for women" (p. 16).

Her argument to this end, however, is no slogan; she attempts to support her case by means of a long and somewhat complicated argument. She avails herself of some of the critical tools of Simone de Beauvoir, Mary Daly, and Carol Gilligan in her elaboration of the right to abortion; in other instances, she attempts to blaze her own trail.

The Power to Control the Species

Harrison's argument is contained in the book's eight chapters. Chapter 1 places the abortion controversy in the context of who shall control the power to reproduce the species. Her methodology is an important, integral part of her presentation; on this point she is insistent: *women* in their actual historical situation are to be treated first;

---

[39]Harrison discusses Gilligan's view of justice in *Making the Connections*, p. 300, note 21.

[40]In *Our Right to Choose*, p. 42, Harrison lists some of elements she would include under the rubric of "procreative choice." In addition to birth control and abortion, she notes "sterilization abuse, too-ready resort to unnecessary hysterectomies, and broader issues of women's health care and social well being."

the *fetus* is to be treated only later. Why wait until Chapter 7 to treat the status of the fetus and to argue against the traditional view of abortion as an intrinsically wrong act? Harrison explains:

> Some readers may be surprised, perhaps even offended, by my decision to delay a full discussion of this key issue. I would not defer this question if I agreed with the premise most moralists assume—that the status of fetal life is *the* determining issue in the moral debate about abortion. In fact, I believe that whenever we encounter this view we should be aware that the line of moral reasoning sustaining it is intrinsically sexist (*Our Right to Choose*, p. 16).

In a best possible world, Harrison grants in another work, abortions would be kept to a minimum.[41] Ours, unfortunately, is not such a world and women have to cope with present realities. In this context, Harrison gives a one-sentence précis of her book's argument: "The existence of a safe, surgical, legal abortion is often a genuine moral blessing, despite a degree of moral ambiguity that needs to be acknowledged."[42]

Reproductive Rights: A Matter of Justice

As we see Harrison's argument unfolding in the second chapter of *Our Right to Choose*, we once again find clear evidence that it is Simone de Beauvoir's culturalist interpretation of women's existential situation that is informing Beverly Wildung Harrison's vision. Indeed, the language and the ideas expressed are quintessential Beauvoir. Lamenting what she styles the "harsh capriciousness of most women's fertility" (p. 36), Harrison notes that women are *ambivalent* regarding

---

[41]Cf. Beverly Wildung Harrison, "Theology of Pro-Choice," p. 225, where she entertains the possibility of a a pro-life feminist position, provided that abortion remains available as a last resort.

[42]Cf. *Our Right to Choose*, p. 18. We note the cautious phrasing.

childbearing whatever decision they reach.[43]

The right to an abortion is a moral necessity if women are to attain full equality with men. Abortion is part of a more inclusive range of issues which Harrison calls by the umbrella term of "procreative choice." It is important to see how she frames her argument:

> Unless procreative choice is understood as a desirable historical possibility substantively conducive to every woman's well being, all debate regarding abortion is morally skewed from the outset (p. 41).

Sexual self-determination is likewise regarded as a right, "and sexual pleasure is a foundational value that enhances human well-being and self-respect."[44] Since birth control is not perfect, abortion is a

---

[43]A lengthy citation may help make Harrison's debt to Beauvoir clear: "Women, despite their strong identification with motherhood, always reveal some ambivalence in studies that give them an opportunity to confidentially disclose their real feelings about childbearing. A considerable number of women acknowledge some regret about *whatever* choices they make. And because the formidable social construction of women's lives beckons us to 'celebrate motherhood,' only later in life do myriad women recognize that childbearing was not chosen, that it was the result of pervasive social pressure that, they see in retrospect, they had no ability to refuse at the time. No one can deny that traditional female socialization tends to undermine woman's capacity to know clearly what she wants for herself. Women frequently drift into motherhood only to discover after the fact the high social cost of mothering. This does not mean that such women regret having borne their children. Most live into their ambivalence and overcome it. Many young women also experience their very first, life-changing coming of age when they find themselves unexpectedly pregnant; for many, pregnancy is their first genuine and realistic encounter with adult reality. That some women's first real awareness of the need to take charge of their lives, in the face of very limited social options, comes from unwanted pregnancy is sad. Such psychological innocence is rooted both in female socialization and in young women's social powerlessness" (*Our Right to Choose*, p. 37). This text, it seems to me, is a fairly accurate précis of *The Second Sex*, pp. 456–497.

[44]*Our Right to Choose*, p. 39. On the theme of sex as salvation as a characteristic feature of certain forms of religion in the United States, cf. Peter Gardella, *Innocent Ecstasy: How Christianity Gave America an Ethic of Sexual Pleasure* (New York: Oxford University Press, 1985). Harrison may be utilizing the theme.

necessity as a backup method when birth control fails.[45] Harrison is quite clear on the matter, noting that Catholic moralist Germain Grisez is quite correct in contending that abortion *is* being used as a birth control method. This is true, avers Harrison, and given the present state of contraceptive technology, it will probably remain so for some time.[46]

If feminism is to succeed, Harrison urges it to steer clear of individualism and atomism, pillars of early liberalism.[47] She is well aware that abortion is most assuredly *not* a private matter: "From a moral point of view the idea that abortion is and should be a strictly 'private' matter does not deserve standing" (*Our Right to Choose*, p. 52). On this point, at least, Harrison agrees with John T. Noonan, Jr.[48] Aware of how the abortion issue is handled by women in other countries, she exhorts American feminists to follow the lead of their Italian counterparts in arguing for abortion on the grounds of foundational social justice.[49] A socially conscious feminism must place community at

---

[45]We recall that the use of abortion as a birth control backup is looked upon favorably by Germaine Greer, *Sex and Destiny: The Politics of Human Fertility*, p. 231: "Abortion is an extension of contraceptive technology, and the most promising extension of it at that."

[46]Cf. *Our Right to Choose*, p. 42. Later on, Harrison criticizes John T. Noonan, Jr. for his insistence that the questions of birth control and abortion be treated separately; she maintains that they must be taken together (p. 125). She cites several Protestant theologians—Karl Barth and Helmut Thielicke, among them—who will accept birth control but draw the line at abortion (p. 75).

[47]Cf. *Our Right to Choose*, pp. 50–51. Others sounding the same alarm regarding individualism and atomism as inimical to the aims of feminism include Mary Ann Glendon, *Abortion and Divorce in Western Law: American Failures, European Challenges*. John Hardwig, "Should Women Think in Terms of Rights?" *Ethics* 94 (1984), pp. 441–455, contends that "rights thinking" is associated with enterprises that are egoistic, asocial, atomistic, and individualistic, pitting "I against You" rather than fostering a "We" mentality.

[48]Cf. John T. Noonan, Jr., *A Private Choice: Abortion in America in the Seventies* (New York: Free Press, 1979). Harrison often treats Noonan's views on abortion as a foil to her own. See the section in *Our Right to Choose*, pp. 125–129.

[49]Cf. *Our Right to Choose*, pp. 43–44. On the harmful effects of atomism and individualism, see Philip J. Rossi, "Rights Are Not Enough: Prospects for a New Approach to the Morality of Abortion," *Linacre Quarterly* 46 (1979), pp. 109–117; Larry R. Churchill and José Jorge Gracia, "Abortion and the Rhetoric of Individual

the center of its moral vision:

> The effect of liberal rhetoric on some mainstream
> feminist argument is noticeable in the implication that
> individualism is a more basic value than genuine
> community. This is simply untrue; when the
> conditions of community collapse, "individual"
> centeredness is also threatened.[50]

As a tactical point Harrison urges feminism to be wary of utilitarian arguments for abortion such as cost-benefit or race. Such arguments risk leaving the high moral ground to opponents of abortion.

Cognizant of the fierce debates sparked by abortion in the United States, Harrison tries to put her finger on the source: "It is obvious that much of the hysteria generated by the abortion controversy stems from the fear of some people that women cannot be competent historical agents."[51]

Rights," *Hastings Center Report* 12 no. 1 (1982), pp. 9–12; and Lisa Sowle Cahill, "Abortion, Autonomy and Community," in Patricia Beattie Jung and Thomas Shannon (eds.), *Abortion and Catholicism: the American Debate*, pp. 85–97; Cf. also Sidney and Daniel Callahan (eds.), *Abortion: Understanding Differences*, p. xxi. The editors regard the critiques of atomism and individualism to be one of the outstanding features of most of the articles in the book.

[50]*Our Right to Choose*, p. 52. A comment made by Elizabeth Fox-Genovese, *Feminism Without Illusions: A Critique of Individualism* (Chapel Hill: University of North Carolina Press, 1991), seems most germane: "It is not easy to reconcile the feminist metaphors of motherhood and community with the feminist defense of abortion on the grounds of absolute individual right" (p. 83). Later, Fox-Genovese observes: "Feminism is the daughter of that male individualism which so many feminists attack" (p. 243). Harrison herself attempts to embrace both the *community* metaphors as well as the *individual* bodyright argument. In this sense, then, Fox-Genovese's critique may be said to apply to her.

[51]*Our Right to Choose*, p. 56. The question of woman's moral agency is a major topic in the articles found in Barbara Hilkert Andolsen, Christine Gudorf, and Mary Pellauer (eds.), *Women's Consciousness, Women's Conscience: a Reader in Feminist Ethics*. Cf. H. Tristram Engelhardt, Jr.,"Medicine and the Concept of Person," in Tom L. Beauchamp and Seymour Perlin (eds.), *Ethical Issues in Death and Dying* (Englewood Cliffs: Prentice-Hall, 1978), pp. 271–284, especially at p. 276: early abortions are necessary to give respect to women as moral agents, an argument not unlike the one Harrison is presenting. Lisa Sowle Cahill, "Abortion, Autonomy and

Four Masculinist Theologies

It is in the third chapter of *Our Right to Choose* that Harrison tries to explain more in detail what I have called the "high moral ground position" of some theologians in the abortion debate. Here she critically examines four varieties of theological thought: fundamentalism, biblical conservatism, neo-orthodoxy and theological liberalism. The first three are plagued, according to Harrison, by a lack of historical consciousness; the fourth is better on this point, yet it too is not immune to criticism.

Fundamentalism, "masculinist spirituality writ large," is infected with dualism and with a tendency to stress a fixed female nature. Biblical conservatism suffers, according to Harrison, from a lack of historical thinking about procreative matters as well as from the uncritical use made of the pronatalist tales such as the Annunciation and the Visitation.[52] To invoke Psalm 139, for example, as a biblical proof for the full personhood of fetuses is— in Harrison's eyes—to confuse poetry with science (p. 77). She criticizes neo-orthodoxy mainly for its largely unhistorical character.[53]

On some points, Harrison finds liberal theology an improvement over the others. Especially valid in liberal theological analysis is its historical consciousness:

> Nothing is more characteristic of modern liberal
> Christian theological conviction than the generative
> idea that concrete world-historical human existence is

Community," in *Abortion and Catholicism*, pp. 85–97, especially at p. 87: women are indeed responsible moral agents, and this is good; what is bad is that in an overly individualistic age, the fetus is forgotten.

[52]Cf. *Our Right to Choose*, p. 64: "The ecumenical consensus about the biblical story in the Church's life probably has benefited Christian theology overall. Without a critical historical perspective on women's lives, however, which feminist biblical and historical scholarship only now is beginning to provide, biblical theologians have been guilty of using biblical stories, especially pronatalist ones, in uncritical ways."

[53]The Catholic moralist Bernard Häring comes in for some criticism and so does the Protestant Karl Barth, the latter unable to escape from what Harrison calls "ahistorical universalism" (p. 72).

the major expression of God's blessing on humanity.[54]

Yet Harrison points out that theological liberalism also has its flaws: its tendencies toward individualism, romanticism, and the pedestalization of women. Indeed, complementarity is also present in this theology. As better ways of approaching the complex historical and cultural factors behind the reproductive situation, she suggests an approach based on three central factors:

1. *Relationality*
2. *Liberation theology*
3. *Process theology*

She is confident that an approach which utilizes these three valuable tools will not only be able to avoid moral relativism but can also enable Christian theology to circumvent the pitfalls she has pointed out.

As Harrison ends chapter three, she quotes at length from Sister Marie Augusta Neal, and then goes on to add that the Catholic sociologist is talking of historical relativity, to be sure, but that this is to be confused neither with subjectivism nor moral relativism.[55]

Relationality

Harrison immediately applies these hermeneutical principles in Chapter 4. *Relationality* is the key element in Harrison's attempt to rework the Christian tradition in order to allow women to make

---

[54]Cf. *Our Right to Choose*, p. 77. It would appear that Harrison is trying to use historical consciousness in such a way as to serve as a substitute for natural law thinking, a point she makes clear in her book review of Sheila Davaney (ed.), 'Feminism and Process Thought,' *Signs* 7 no. 3 (1982), pp. 704–710. We note in passing that the worldviews thesis seems to be in the background here.

[55]*Our Right to Choose*, p. 90. Marie Augusta Neal, "Sociology and Sexuality: a Feminist Perspective," *Christianity and Crisis* 39 no. 8 (1979), pp. 118–122, may be drawing upon the worldview thesis elaborated by Bernard Lonergan, S.J., "The Transition from a Classicist World View to Historical Mindedness," in James E. Biechler (ed.), *Law for Liberty: The Role of Law in the Church Today* (Baltimore: Helicon, 1967), pp. 126–133. It is also found in Lonergan's *A Second Collection* (edited by William F. J. Ryan, S.J. and Bernard J. Tyrrell, S.J.) (Philadelphia: Westminster, 1974).

decisions regarding childbearing in a humanly inclusive way (p. 91). She
reiterates the contention of feminist spirituality that human lives are
intrinsically culture-creating.[56] At the same time, she takes pains to avoid
falling into the trap of subjectivism: "The moral world, although the
coconstruction of subjects, is never merely subjectivist" (p. 109). *Process
thinking* animates Harrison's elucidation of some major ideas of her
feminist ethics, notably mutuality, reciprocity in relation, and utopic
envisagement.

The use of relationality and process thought leads to a liberation
theology perspective. It is in this light that Harrison re-envisions, in a
feminist liberationist key, some themes of Christian ethics, among them
passivity, *agapé*, self-sacrifice, and the necessity of justice.[57] Our
knowledge of human freedom has been expanding, notes Harrison. She
warns against a turning back of the clock in regard to abortion:

> The current theological crusade against safe, legal
> abortion is predicated on a well-meaning, but
> disastrously misguided, conviction that the
> termination of freedom of choice in an area of human
> life that intricately and irrevocably affects women's
> experience will put our culture back on a
> "God-fearing" track. An adequate theological
> perspective helps us to see that, in fact, we would be
> taking a step backward both historically and
> morally.[58]

---

[56]Cf. *Our Right to Choose*, p. 97. She draws on the work of Mary Daly and Starhawk.

[57]As did Beauvoir and Daly, Harrison, *Our Right to Choose*, p. 113, uses the example
of Mary the Mother of Jesus as a paradigm of the passive woman in front of God. Cf.
the discussion of *agapé* by Barbara Hilkert Andolsen, "*Agapé* in Feminist Ethics,"
Journal of Religious Ethics 9 (Spring 1981), pp. 69–83. Many themes treated by
Harrison are also present in the writings of Margaret Farley. See for example the
entry, "Feminist Ethics," in *The Westminster Dictionary of Christian Ethics*, pp.
229–231.

[58]*Our Right to Choose*, p. 116. Compare Harrison's claim that the Church is on a
crusade against abortion with Daly's comment in *Beyond God the Father*, p. 3: "In the
early 1970s the Roman church launched all-out warfare against the international
movement to repeal anti-abortion laws."

A Feminist Reading of Christian Moral Teaching

Harrison's earlier remarks on the importance given by liberal Protestantism to historical consciousness bear fruit when she presents, in the fifth chapter, a case for the "The History of Christian Teaching on Abortion Reconceived." In it she attempts to demonstrate that the teaching of the Christian churches on abortion has been, at least until rather recently, of relatively minor and marginal importance (p. 118). While sounding a note of caution that male supremacy patterns might well be present in the historical record, she also ackowledges that "there was considerable tradition of pastoral concern for women, which is often suppressed in the current debate" (p. 124).

Harrison considers it significant that canonists and moralists rather than professional church historians have done the work on the historical reconstruction of Christian teaching on abortion. Critical of the way John Noonan and Germain Grisez handle the historical record, she prefers the analysis of Jesuit John Connery. Better still is the work of Susan Teft Nicholson to correct some of the deficiencies found especially in Noonan. Yet Harrison contends that on one important point, *all* the above have erred: namely, in overestimating the value early Christianity gave to fetal life.[59]

As Harrison rereads the historical record, she appropriates some of Nicholson's thesis,[60] describing it in these words:

> The *moral reason* for opposition (to abortion) was condemnation of women's sexuality, aimed at censuring wicked, "wanton" women—that is, those who expressed their sexuality apart from procreative intent. In the texts she [Nicholson] cites, abortion is a special evil because it signifies female wickedness and a refusal of women's divinely decreed lot. . . .

---

[59]On this point, might it not be the case that the question of the value of the fetus was not raised precisely because it was never in doubt? Perhaps early Christians saw no need to argue for such an obvious truth. Perhaps the same holds true for thinkers such as Nicholson and Noonan.

[60]Cf. Susan Teft Nicholson, *Abortion and the Roman Catholic Church* (Nashville: Religious Ethics, Inc., 1978).

> No premodern, specific Christian anti-abortion
> teaching is unsullied by procreative functionalism and
> the antisexual bias Nicholson rightly acknowledges.[61]

Past Church teaching on abortion has been more allied with what Harrison calls an "antisexual ethic" than with an ethic devoted to the defense of fetal life.[62]

Reading the historical record with the help of Samuel Laeuchli, Harrison examines the tradition, both Catholic and Protestant, in light of the "procreative functionalism" and sex-negativity she believes she has discovered in the Christian past.[63] She urges the adoption of a sexual morality attuned to the needs of the present.[64]

---

[61]*Our Right to Choose*, p. 129. In her rereading of the Christian historical record, Harrison sees "procreative functionalism" as a constant, at least until our present era. A word may be in order on "procreative functionalism": by it Harrison seems to mean the view that identifies women exclusively or almost so with maternity. Such a view, according to her, may have been somewhat understandable in the past but is no longer so today, especially in the light of our historical consciousness. For a theology of sexuality filtered through lesbian feminist lenses, see the book written by Harrison's friend, Carter Heyward, *Touching Our Strength: The Erotic as Power and the Love of God* (San Francisco: Harper and Row, 1989). One of Heyward's major contentions: "Sex is a process of godding "(p. 150).

[62]Cf. *Our Right to Choose*, p. 129. This theme of the sex-negativity of Christianity is found in Aline Rousselle, *Porneia: On Desire and the Body in Antiquity* (translated by Felicia Pheasant) (Oxford: Basil Blackwell, 1988; original edition 1983), and Uta Ranke-Heinemann, *Eunuchs for the Kingdom of Heaven: Women, Sexuality and the Catholic Church* (translated by Peter Heinegg) (New York: Doubleday, 1990).

[63]Cf. Samuel Laeuchli, *Power and Sexuality: The Emergence of Canon Law at the Synod of Elvira* (Philadelphia: Temple University Press, 1972). The book leads Harrison to observe: "He [Laeuchli] suggests that the loss of identity following Roman imperial persecutions may have led some church leaders to shape Christian identity in terms of sexual conformity. This minor council (Elvira) was, in fact, a generating source of increasing Christian sex-negativity" (*Our Right to Choose*, p. 139).

[64]Compare Harrison's views with those found in a document drafted by Lester Kirkendall and then edited by the American Humanist Association, "A New Bill of Sexual Rights and Responsibilities," *The Humanist* 36 no. 1 (January/February 1976), pp. 4–6. What both seem to be saying, in effect, is what I would label the "P.L.E.A.S.U.R.E. Principle:" to wit, the Practically Limitless Expression of Any Sexual Urge is a Right of Everyone. Regarding the question of sexual mores, we should keep in mind that there are many feminisms. Secular feminism accepts

A Feminist Perspective on Abortion

Harrison in chapter 6 places the question of abortion in the context of the question she posed in the first chapter: Who shall control the power to reproduce the species?[65] Technology has at long last allowed women to gain a semblance of control over what Harrison considers the capriciousness of nature. Modern society makes childrearing difficult because of the atomistic setting in which it must be conducted; childrearing is much less onerous in extended rural settings. Until recently, abortion was a risky medical procedure; new advances in technology have changed the situation: "The development in the last decade of the suction methods of uterine extraction represents a particular breakthrough" (p. 169).

Returning once again to the link between birth control and abortion, Harrison is insistent:

> In women's lives the two issues (birth control and abortion) are never, ever separable. The major reformist strategy in mainstream Christian ethics—to separate fertility control, or contra-ception, from abortion—is the worst sort of casuistry. Abortion is and always has been a means of birth control, as its all but universal practice attests. And I believe we must continue to assert that, given the limits of birth control technology, it will remain the birth control method of last resort for many women, whether or not it is legal and/or safe. In fact, for many women it

---

abortion as an integral part of the sexual revolution and does so without any reference to religion. Christian feminism will view the matter somewhat differently. Then again, there are several Christian feminisms.

[65]On this issue, Harrison acknowledges her debt to Mary O'Brien, *The Politics of Reproduction* (Boston: Routledge and Kegan Paul, 1981), who deals with the sasme question: who shall control the power to reproduce the species? In another work, Mary O'Brien, *Reproducing the World: Essays in Feminist Theory*, p. 28, has claimed that the debate on abortion is a smokescreen to hide the *real* issue: reproductive technology. On p. 10, O'Brien opined that the invention of the birth control pill atoned in a way for what Engels had termed "the world-historical defeat of the female sex." O'Brien writes from a dialectical materialist point of view.

is the most reliable, and, at least when used infrequently, it is safe.[66]

Harrison uses a text from pro-choice advocate Ellen Willis to illustrate the pivotal role control over reproduction plays in defining women's well-being:

> To oppose legal abortion is to define women as child-bearers rather than autonomous human beings, and to endorse a sexually repressive morality enforced by the state (p. 185).

As Harrison views the matter, what Willis is saying may well sound irrational and excessive "to those who have not grasped the centrality of procreative choice to women's well-being and the importance of procreative choice as a foundational element in a good society that includes women" (p. 186).

The Status of the Fetus

It is in chapter 7 that Harrison treats the question of the status of the fetus. Bringing into her discussion deontological and teleological points of view,[67] she opens by noting areas of broad agreement: both sides of the abortion debate accept the intrinsic value of human life as well as the evil of unjustified killing. But Harrison adds that the evaluation of fetal life is complex (p. 193). To begin the discussion, she gives a definition of abortion currently in use: "An act undertaken by the pregnant woman, with medical assistance, to terminate an unwanted pregnancy at any stage in the process of gestation prior to birth" (p. 194). *Therapeutic* abortions are those controlled by the medical profession; *elective* abortions are those controlled by women. Harrison is quite clear that the moral agency of women demands that the moral debate about

---

[66]*Our Right to Choose*, p. 162. Later in the chapter, Harrison restates her position, once again in terms of the limits of birth control technology and in terms of women's health and medical safety: "The *safest* long-term means of fertility control are the barrier methods, combined with abortion as a backup" (*Our Right to Choose*, p. 180: Harrison's emphasis).

[67]Harrison, p. 191, characterizes herself as a mixed theorist.

abortion be conducted in terms of *elective* rather than *therapeutic* abortion:

> To argue, as I do here, that women are properly *the* moral agents of accountability in the decision about abortion is to claim that *elective* abortion is the proper context for assessing the morality of abortion.[68]

A large part of the case Harrison is trying to make rests on what she calls "the wider framework for the act of abortion."[69] She frankly acknowledges that few moralists go as far as she does in linking the case for abortion to the argument for bodily integrity:

> Women's capacity for full moral agency is only one of several moral presumptions that require recognition prior to an evaluation of the act of abortion itself. We need also to acknowledge the bodily integrity of any moral agent as a foundational condition of human well-being and dignity. Freedom from bodily invasion, a right increasingly recognized as having some precedents in our common law traditions, at least when coercion in medical treatments is at issue, is no minor or marginal issue morally; rather it is central to our conception of the dignity of the person (p. 196).

The right to bodily integrity, popularly known as the bodyright argument, is also central to the case Harrison is making for women's right to choose abortion:

> I argue that a society which would deny the conditions of procreative choice to women, or which

---

[68]*Our Right to Choose*, p. 195: author's emphasis. She is by no means arguing that all elective abortions are morally justified. In a later article, Harrison, "Feminist Realism," *Christianity and Crisis* 46 10 (July 14, 1986), pp. 233–236, considers sex selection abortions to be an unqualified moral wrong.

[69]"The Wider Framework for the Act of Abortion" is the title of this section of *Our Right to Choose*, pp. 196–210.

treats women merely or chiefly as reproductive means to some purported end of that society's own self-perpetuation, is one that mandates women's inferior status as less than full, rational beings, denying women full claim to intrinsic value in the process (p. 197).

Harrison is aware of the contested nature of the feminist argument.[70] Criticisms notwithstanding, she holds her ground:

I claim that the fact of women's biological fertility and capacity for childbearing in no way overrides our moral claim to the "right" of bodily integrity, because this claim is inherent to human well-being. . . . Reproductive choice for women is requisite to any adequate notion of what constitutes a good society (pp. 198–199).

When the discussion turns to the question of the status of the fetus, Harrison utilizes the culturalist feminist view of the role of nature and human mastery over it. Attempting to argue the case on scientific grounds as she does, she has recourse to several key ideas of Simone de Beauvoir in this matter to aid her case: first and foremost, "nature" must be understood as a cultural construct.[71] Second, science itself must be seen as a cultural construct: "Biological science itself is a complex, cultural construct" (p. 200). Harrison's indebtedness to process thought is apparent in chapter 7. Relationality, one of her three keys to seeing abortion in a wider framework, is an important feature of process thinking and Harrison finds it helpful for her argument: "A process view of nature automatically rejects the conclusion that all potentiality in

---

[70]In *Our Right to Choose*, p. 307, note 26, Harrison speaks of two critics, Richard A. McCormick and Stanley Hauerwas, who evince an "almost incredulous disbelief" of feminist attempts to elucidate an argument for bodily integrity.

[71]Harrison prefers the newer explanation of natural law given by Daniel Maguire and Anthony Battaglia to the older view elaborated by Germain Grisez and Joseph T. Mangan, S.J. She rejects the older view because of what she perceives as its inability to account for freedom in biological reproduction. She concludes: "This theory is permeated by misogyny" (*Our Right to Choose*, p. 202).

nature must be realized."[72]

> To imply that no conscientious person could entertain distinctions between "a form of human life," "a human life," "an individual human life," and a "person" simply flies in the face of our whole philosophical and theological heritage (p. 207).

To Beverly Harrison the proper question to ask regarding the fetus is not: "When does human life begin?" but rather: "At what point is it morally wise to assess fetal life as human life?"[73] Too much emphasis on the fetus can lead to an abstracting from the decisive role the woman's body plays in the process of fetal development.[74] She warns against "reification" which can mask our own interpretive power and cautions against any "sacralization" of the human genetic code.[75]

Arguing as she does against the position that human life deserves protection from the moment of conception, Harrison does so fully aware of the implications following from her oft-repeated contention that abortion is a birth control method:

> We may call it "*the* fetus," but it is not yet in any sense *an actually alive organism* with human complexity. . . . I believe it is inadmissible to predicate to a fetus at any given point in its development

---

[72]*Our Right to Choose*, p. 204. Harrison, pp. 215–216, avails herself of the thought of American process philosopher Charles Hartshorne, "Concerning Abortion: An Attempt at a Rational View," *Christian Century* 98 no. 2 (January 2, 1981) to aid her case.

[73]*Our Right to Choose*, pp. 208–209. If we recall, Mary Daly, *Beyond God the Father*, p. 111, also declines to approach the abortion issue by means of the question, "When does human life begin?" She categorizes it an instance of "the unanswerable argument."

[74]Harrison's espousal of the categories of process thought enables her to accept a developmental view of the fetus: "We are seeking developmental criteria for stipulating the degree of similarity to existing human beings required for counting fetal life as *a* human life" (*Our Right to Choose*, p. 209).

[75]*Ibid*. The talk about the danger of "sacralization" is reminiscent of Beauvoir's "demystification" of motherhood.

existent human functions that its actual degree of
structural complexity cannot sustain (*Our Right to
Choose*, p. 214: Harrison's emphasis).

What is Harrison's own position as to when it is morally wise
to assess fetal life as human life? "I hold that the most plausible early
biological criteria for justifiably imputing to a fetus the status of an
individuated human life form comes with the development of fetal
viability" (p. 216). Aware as she is of the myriad views on this matter,
Harrison does acknowledge that other positions are also possible: one is
birth,[76] another is drawing a first breath. These two, in her estimation,
are not unserious moral positions. We note the late character of these
two positions; they fit in well with Harrison's process-based position in
this chapter. Her own choice of viability meets the same criterion.

The choice of viability and the mention of even later points at
which it would be wise to assess fetal life as worthy of protection[77] are
used by Harrison to comment on our era's crisis of the personal and our
age's tendency to overlook the social context of all human moral
relations:

A biologically reductionist understanding of our
species, which fully conflates the biologically human
and the "person," threatens to intensify this crisis in
our human moral relations. Ironically, the "fetishizing

---

[76]On birth as the criterion of humanity, cf. Mary Anne Warren, "The Moral
Significance of Birth," *Hypatia* 4 no. 3 (1989), pp. 46–65, and Joan C. Callahan, "The
Fetus and Fundamental Rights," in Patricia Beattie Jung and Thomas Shannon (eds.),
Abortion and Catholicism: The American Debate, pp. 217–230. According to an
obstetrician and gynecologist, Bernard Nathanson, *Aborting America*, p. 210, from
a medical point of view, birth is insignificant, a mythology. Cf. Richard Stith, "The
World as Reality, as Resource, and as Pretense," *American Journal of Jurisprudence* 20
(1975), p. 148: "If we say life begins at birth, only self-interested arguments remain to
prevent infanticide." According to John Connery, S.J., *Abortion: The Development of
the Roman Catholic Perspective* (Chicago: Loyola University Press, 1977), p. 308, the
only view of ensoulment condemned by the Church is that of animation at birth.

[77]Cf. *Our Right to Choose*, p. 225: While granting that the fetus in the later stages of
development can properly be assessed as human life, Harrison nevertheless believes
it would be unwise to bestow legal rights upon fetuses because of the long-standing
misogyny she believes she has detected in society.

of fetuses" in the abortion debate may well exacerbate our already overdeveloped tendency to consider ourselves "normatively human" quite apart from the world of social relations our moral action creates.[78]

As she nears the end of her treatment of the status of the fetus, once again her words bespeak the continuing presence of Simone de Beauvoir in the whole evolution of the right to abortion:

> If a pregnancy is unwanted, a woman's moral obligation is best expressed by early recognition and termination of fetal life. That many women have yet to deliberate these matters seriously or to recognize that there is an obligation to intentionality in childbearing has much to do with female socialization and the objective disadvantage females incur in any society. The condemnatory ethos prevailing around the abortion debate in the United States is itself a force in delaying this "coming of age" for many women.[79]

The Politics of Abortion, American-Style

The American political landscape frames the eighth and last chapter of *Our Right to Choose*. By the 1960s, notes Harrison, American feminism was beginning to see two allied issues quite clearly: 1. *abortion reform* was a women's rights issue, and 2. *legal abortion* was "a basic

---

[78] *Our Right to Choose*, p. 222. Regarding what Harrison labels the "fetishizing of fetuses," a comment may be in order. We see how much Harrison tries to stake out the high moral ground for a pro-choice position in the pages of *Our Right to Choose*. While she may contend that the status of the humanity of the fetus is tenuous enough to allow abortion up until viability, not all reach such a latitudinarian position when confronting the unborn child and his or her humanity. Indeed, an atheist has observed: "Even if God does not exist, the foetus does." The text, attributed to Bernard Nathanson, is quoted in Mary Kenny, *Abortion: The Whole Story*, p. 199.

[79] Cf. *Our Right to Choose*, p. 229. Harrison credits the "coming of age" phrase to Dietrich Bonhoeffer.

condition of women's historical struggle for liberation."[80]

Central to understanding Harrison's argument is her contention that *Roe v. Wade*, the 1973 United States Supreme Court Decision, was only partially a victory for women, only partially a feminist decision.[81] It is in terms of her bodily integrity argument that Harrison explains the weaknesses of the 1973 abortion decision: *Roe* "gave very provisional and extremely limited support for a woman's reproductive rights and explicitly denied any absolute right to control one's own body."[82] This is why Harrison is wary of any calls for compromise in the wake of *Roe*; the decision itself is already a compromise.[83] Women at least and at last

---

[80]Cf. *Our Right to Choose*, p. 233. An author who approaches the politics of abortion along the same general lines as Harrison is Eva R. Rubin, *Abortion, Politics and the Courts: Roe v. Wade and Its Aftermath* (Westport CT: Greenwood Press, 1982).

[81]The theme that *Roe* is, at best, only a partial feminist victory is sounded by Kristen Booth Glen, "Abortion in the Courts: A Laywoman's Historical Guide to the New Disaster Area," *Feminist Studies* 4 no. 1 (1978), pp. 1–26; Lucinda Cisler, "Abortion Law Repeal (Sort of): A Warning to Women," in Anne Koedt, Ellen Levine, and Anita Rapone (eds.), *Radical Feminism* (New York: Quadrangle Books, 1973), pp. 151–164; and Catherine MacKinnon, "*Roe v. Wade*: a Study in Male Ideology," in Jay Garfield and Patricia Hennessey (eds.), *Abortion: Moral and Legal Perspectives*, pp. 45–54.

[82]Cf. *Our Right to Choose*, p. 235. One author who *does* attempt a defense of the legal reasoning in *Roe* is Laurence H. Tribe, *Abortion: The Clash of Absolutes*, pp. 135–136: "Calmly assessed, *Roe v. Wade* does not seem to represent a blatant power grab by the Supreme Court, an exercise in fiat rather than in constitutional interpretation. A difficult decision, yes; an indefensible decision, no." See also Ronald Dworkin, "Feminism and Abortion," *New York Review of Books* 40 11 (June 10. 1993), pp. 27–29.

[83]Cf. *Our Right to Choose*, p. 232. According to Janet Radcliffe Richards, *The Skeptical Feminist: A Philosophical Inquiry*, p. 213: "Abortion is an all-or-nothing matter, with no possibility of compromise." Some authors do not feel *Roe* was *enough* of a compromise. One of them is Guido Calabresi, Ideals, Beliefs, Attitudes and the Law: Private Law Perspectives on a Public Law Problem, p. 95, who observes that *Roe* said, in effect, to a large number of American citizens: "*Your* metaphysics are not a part of *our* Constitution." Another is Mary Ann Glendon, *Abortion and Divorce in Western Law: American Failures, European Challenges*, p. 18. Following up on Calabresi's ideas regarding *Roe v. Wade*, Glendon contends that compromise *is* possible on the abortion issue. The same approach is taken by Elizabeth Mensch and Alan Freeman, *The Politics of Virtue: Is Abortion Debatable?* (Durham and London: Duke University

have some measure of control over what had long been, in Harrison's words, "a fatalistic connection to 'natural process.'"[84]

Noting the existence of two extremes in the American abortion context, the absolute prohibition of all abortion and absolutely no state prohibitions against any abortion, Harrison comments that for "feminists who regard control of procreation as the institutional linchpin in women's historical subjugation," any talk of *compromise* with respect to procreative choice" would be seen as nothing else than "a tactic to forestall women's liberation."[85] She then gives her own position:

> Women like myself who believe that the feminist "extreme" is correct, being soberly realistic about the efforts of male-dominated institutions to control procreation historically, already have consented to a genuine balancing of legitimate interests. From our perspective, Roe v. Wade is such a decision.[86]

She urges both sides to work to diminish the number of abortions: "Our goal, and the goal of all persons of irenic spirit, should be to support those policies that actually will minimize the need for abortion by furthering procreative choice" (p. 250). Once more she returns to the theme of the high moral ground and urges pro-life

---

Press, 1993).

[84]Cf. *Our Right to Choose*, p. 249. The language is fairly evocative of Simone de Beauvoir.

[85]*Our Right to Choose*, p. 237. Harrison herself would seem to concur with the standard feminist interpretation that "control of procreation is the institutional linchpin in women's historical subjugation." See her comments on p. 315, note 21. This is the same theme with which she began the book: Who shall control the power to reproduce the species?

[86]*Our Right to Choose*, p. 237. Since *Roe* is already a compromise and since feminists have granted "the salience of the moral debate about the value of fetuses in the later stages of gestation," Harrison is saying, in effect, that the next concession is to be made by the other side: "We await some sign that those who would foreclose nearly all legal abortion are prepared to extend the same concrete recognition of moral claims regarding women's well-being. This, we insist, is a requirement of 'compromise'" (p. 237).

advocates to show adequate social concern for the well-being of women with problem pregnancies who choose to have their babies but also to have "genuine respect for those who choose not to do so" (p. 252). To create a good climate for compromise, pro-life advocates ought to admit that those on the pro-choice side "also hold a principled moral stance."[87]

Harrison concludes with an evocation of the biblical theme of *covenant* which can serve as a common bond in a theological sense as both sides grapple with the complexities of the abortion question.[88] *Covenant* fits in well with her earlier evocation of *relationality* and *community* as the proper framework for discussing procreative choice and abortion. It is the notion of the common good that must take center stage in the discussion.[89]

For a woman to enter into a covenant of love with the child and with the society is not easy to do, given present societal inequities and the harsh realities in the experiences of pregnancy, birth, and childrearing: "We must never imagine that the conditions for such deeply humane covenant exist" (p. 255). It is often easier to say *no* to the

---

[87]*Our Right to Choose*, p. 253. A similar approach to the abortion question is that of Gregory Baum, O.S.A., "Abortion: an Ecumenical Dilemma," *Commonweal* 99 (1973), pp. 231–235; reprinted in Edward Batchelor, Jr., (ed.), *Abortion: The Moral Issues*, pp. 38–47. Catholics are to avoid a "holier than thou" attitude and are not to characterize those on the pro-choice side of the abortion issue as selfish and cruel. Interestingly, Baum goes on to use a worldview approach to back up his contention.

[88]Cf. Mary Segers, "Abortion: a Feminist Perspective. Review of Beverly Wildung Harrison, 'Our Right to Choose,'" *Christianity and Crisis* 43 no. 17 (1983), pp. 410–413. After noting that Harrison employs some standard existentialist themes, including voluntarism and historicity, Segers adds: "The novel element that Harrison adds to this is an appropriation of covenant theology to justify feminists' use of the distinction between wanted and unwanted children" (p. 411). While Harrison's use of *covenant* may be original, Segers feels "impelled to question whether such a voluntaristic emphasis can adequately capture the complex issues of pregnancy and childbearing. In Harrison's world of rational choice and volitional affirmation, there seems to be little room for events or happenings, for accident or serendipity, for mystery or ambivalence" (p. 412). Segers goes on to intimate that Harrison's approach may well be masculinist.

[89]We remember that this social dimension of ethics was regarded by Harrison as being especially prominent in Roman Catholic moral reflection.

covenant of life by abortion than to say *yes* to the covenant of life by birth (p. 256). We as a human community must work to correct this. Stressing the relationality of all human existence once again, Harrison concludes:

> Our acknowledgement of each other in relation is not an optional addition to life, an afterthought; it is constitutive of life itself. For a vital human life to be born, a woman must say yes in a strong and active way and enter positively into a life-bearing, demanding, and, at times, extremely painful process. Freedom to say yes, which, of course, also means the freedom to say no, is constitutive of the sacred covenant of life itself. Failure to see this is also failure to see how good, how strong and real, embodied existence is in this world we are making together (p. 256).

Harrison's Personal Postscript

It is in a brief "postscript" to *Our Right to Choose* that we find one of the book's few personal touches. When Harrison goes on the lecture circuit as a pro-choice activist, she is sometimes asked if she would have wanted abortion legal at the time she was born:

> The question, when it has been pressed on me, has always caused me to smile; for I almost was a medically dictated abortion, and I have lived much of my life with that knowledge. But I also know, as anyone who comprehends the development of self-awareness will understand, that if I *had* been aborted, there would have been no "I" to experience it (p. 257).

After citing American process philosopher Charles Hartshorne who made a similar observation, the Protestant feminist theologian continues:

> My mother's love and courage, like all women's, were no mere biologically induced responses but the expression of her moral commitment to us. In the absence of such tenderness and care, born not of instinct but of moral freedom, it would have been

better for me, or anyone else, not to have been born.[90]

Whatever else we think of Harrison's reasoning, it does serve to bring into sharp relief the obvious fact that abortion confronts all of us with our own mortality and humanity. It poses to us questions about human finitude and limitations, about who we are as human beings. Whatever else it is, abortion is a life and death matter in which all human beings, mother and child especially but certainly not exclusively, have a stake.[91]

Commentary on Beverly Wildung Harrison: Some Positive Elements

Simone de Beauvoir approaches the abortion question as an essayist using the language of existential philosophy. Mary Daly does so in terms largely taken not only from Beauvoir but also from scholastic philosophy and theology. Carol Gilligan treats the abortion decision with the tools of developmental psychology. While Harrison does base her argument to an extent on the work of Beauvoir, Daly, and Gilligan, she does so in the language of liberal Protestant theology and with an acknowledgement of her debt to Roman Catholic tradition in moral theology. In point of fact, Harrison at times employs the language of moral absolutes and as a mixed theorist utilizes deontological principles in addition to teleological ones. Hers is by far the most elaborate and sustained argument we have seen for the right to an abortion.[92]

Harrison's thesis is nothing if not bold (our *right* to choose) and her approach is nothing if not fearless: she is willing, in effect, to take on

---

[90]*Our Right to Choose*, p. 257. A Kantian argument against abortion, based on the principles of universalizability, prescriptivity, and the Golden Rule, has been elaborated by Harry J. Gensler, "A Kantian Argument Against Abortion," *Philosophical Studies* 49 (1986), pp. 83–96. We should keep in mind that some pro-choice arguments are based on the Kantian principle of autonomy.

[91]Harrison brings up the fact that ours is not a perfect world and, at times, tenderness and care are indeed lacking. Is abortion the solution in such instances?

[92]Harrison's book is praised by some as the high-point of the feminist case for choice. Cf. Madonna Kolbenschlag, "Abortion and Moral Consensus: Beyond Solomon's Choice," *Christian Century* 102 (1985), pp. 179–183; reprinted in Patricia Beattie Jung and Thomas Shannon (eds.), *Abortion and Catholicism*, pp. 121–127.

the entire moral tradition of the Christian churches. As we have seen, she is quite candid in pointing out the complexity inherent in the question of reproductive choice and abortion.[93] To situate the abortion issue in these terms, as Harrison has certainly attempted to do, gives witness to the intractable difficulties so characteristic of the abortion problematic. In a word, Beverly Harrison has gone to great lengths to respect the ambiguity, ambivalence, and the societal implications involved in the question of human abortion.[94]

She grants that the pro-life position is a principled moral stance; all she asks is that pro-life advocates concede the morality behind the pro-choice view:

> Relevant to creating an ethos on compromise is the need for greater acknowledgement among anti-abortionists that pro-choice adherents, now so readily labeled "extremists," also hold a principled moral stance (p. 254).

While she will make a case for abortion as a social good for women in any definition of a humane society, she refuses to do so at the cost of oversimplifying the abortion issue. To her credit, Harrison does not seek to claim that hers is the *only* truly moral position; but she does seek to have her view regarded as *one* truly moral position. In her search for the high moral ground, Harrison grants that the pro-life side does have, at the very least, a sound *prima facie* case for its position. In a sense, then, *Our Right to Choose* attempts to establish a similar respectability for the pro-choice side in the abortion debate.

Her study is wide-ranging, and Harrison is not slow to

---

[93]We have already pointed out Harrison's one-sentence synopsis of *Our Right to Choose*, p. 18: "The existence of safe, surgical, legal abortion is often a geniune moral blessing, despite a degree of moral ambiguity that needs to be acknowledged."

[94]True, there *are* feminist defenses of abortion as a privacy decision. One of them is Nitza Shapiro-Libai, "The Right to Abortion," *Israel Yearbook on Human Rights* 5 (1975), pp. 120–140. Yet others approach the abortion issue in the way Harrison does, tying their case for abortion to the wider social issue of how to construct a society which is truly mindful of women's well-being. Among them are Rosalind Pollack Petchesky, *Abortion and Woman's Choice* (revised edition) (Boston: Northeastern University Press, 1990).

appropriate elements of other approaches when these elements will help in elaborating her own position. The riches of the Christian thought of the past, process thought, liberation theology, as well as themes sounded by existential philosophy are all utilized. As part of this eclectic approach, Harrison has duly noted and recognized the profound debt she owes to the Catholic ethical tradition, especially strong in the area of social ethics. That she has learned this lesson well is indicated by her approaching the question of abortion not as an *individual* right but rather in the wider framework of an ethic of *social* concern. The role Harrison gives *relationality* is another instance of how well the Protestant feminist theologian has understood what it is that animates Catholic ethics.[95]

Equally fine is Harrison's emphasis on woman's dignity as a child of God and with it her accentuation of the dignity of woman as a moral agent. Unlike other feminists, she refuses to skirt the status of the fetus;[96] but as a sign of her commitment to women's well-being, she makes it an important part of her methodology in *Our Right to Choose* to discuss the status of the fetus only after she has properly situated women in their actual historical conditions.

What is more, Harrison does not shrink from the implications of her position. She tries to be consistent on the matter of procreative choice and reproductive rights. She believes that abortion is demanded by her views of human sexuality and birth control and is not afraid to come out and say in effect: abortion *is* a form of birth control, so let's

---

[95]Bernard Nathanson's *The Abortion Papers: Inside the Abortion Mentality*, contains a chapter in which the author, an abortionist turned pro-life advocate, speaks of what he calls "the Catholic Card" in the American abortion debate: it consists in abortion rights advocates attempting to drive a wedge between the Catholic *hierarchy* and the *rank-and-file faithful* on the abortion issue. Nathanson notes that the National Abortion Rights Action League (NARAL), an organization he helped found, played this card very successfully in its drive for abortion reform. It is possible that there are whiffs of such an approach in *Our Right to Choose*, especially pp. 238–239.

[96]Our study of chapters two through five leads us to conclude that, all things considered, the status of the fetus is simply not an important issue for Beauvoir, Daly, or Gilligan. On this point, Harrison sees an obvious lacuna which her book addresses. She returns to the status of the fetus several years after she writes *Our Right to Choose*. See her "Feminist Realism," *Christianity and Crisis* 45 no. 10 (July 14, 1986), pp. 233–236.

be honest about it.[97] We know exactly where Beverly Harrison stands on the abortion question. On this point she stands in contrast to Carol Gilligan.

Arguing the case as she does in the context of the American political landscape, Harrison endeavors to avoid making hers a mere theoretical exercise. *Roe v. Wade* touches real people, one way or the other. For this decision to be overturned would have serious repercussions on the fabric of society. Since feminism is a serious moral claim for justice, Harrison shows herself fully cognizant of the seriousness of the moral claims she is making. She pulls no punches: while she claims the right to abortion as a matter of justice for women, she is also aware that abortion is a matter of life and death.

Some Criticisms

The abortion issue has a way of bringing out the passions in people and Beverly Harrison is no exception. Though she tries to be clear and dispassionate in her approach, she does at times slip into personal attacks on some of her adversaries. Attempting to defend her choice of the relatively late point of viability as the time when it would be wise to assess fetal life as human life, she tries to make a case that such is in reality the view of L. W. Sumner, who has articulated a "sentience" position which Harrison finds "neither clear nor consistent." She goes on to add:

> His actual position seems to approximate my own, namely, that third-trimester gestating fetuses deserve our respect from a moral point of view. I would be less critical of Sumner's views if he were not so

---

[97]Cf. *Our Right to Choose*, p. 42: "Unbelievable as it may seem, many Christian ethicists, *including* proponents of legal abortion, would prefer to ignore or even suppress the fact that abortion is a birth control method." Compare Harrison on this point with another author: "For if it is not true that abortion is murder, it still cannot be considered in the same light as a mere contraceptive technique; an event has taken place that is a definite beginning, the progress of which is to be stopped." The words are those of Simone de Beauvoir, *The Second Sex*, p. 462.

contemptuous toward others' positions.[98]

At times Harrison characterizes opponents of a liberal abortion policy in rather harsh terms:

> Matters relating to women's health and well-being are *never* urgent in this society. Only if we keep these facts in view as the genuine historical dimension of the problem will we recognize the depth of moral hypocrisy involved in a so-called pro-life movement that proclaims even a zygote, at the moment of conception, is a "person" and should be viewed as a citizen but still denies full social and political rights to women (p. 185).

It is true that on occasion Harrison has had to defend herself from the charge of "virulent anti-Catholicism." Speaking of the political incursions of American Catholic bishops into the abortion controversy, Harrison observes:

> The primary reason for my opposition to the bishops' initiatives in "pro-life" politics concerns their professed moral position, which is from many perspectives debatable and, in my considered opinion, palpably wrong. Many have ducked the normative issue in criticizing the bishops' stance, but I have no desire to do so. They, along with leaders of other Christian groups, have tried to foist upon society as "rationally justified" a position about abortion whose "traditional" roots do not rest in concern for the unborn and whose contemporary rationales for deciding when a human life begins are

---

[98]Cf. *Our Right to Choose*, p. 313 note 58. If we remember, while Harrison herself opted for "viability" as the time when she thought it wise to accord moral status to the fetus, she did also speak of "birth" as a not unserious moral position (p. 217). Cf. L. W. Sumner, *Abortion and Moral Theory*, pp. 53–54. In his opinion, the choice of "birth" as the time when the fetus acquires a right to life is shallow and arbitrary and goes on to add that, in general, feminists disregard the fetus in their writings. This might explain Harrison's rather blunt remark.

simply not adequate.[99]

As we have observed on several occasions, John Noonan comes in for rather severe criticism from Harrison. Nothing so unusual in this, of course, especially among scholars. Seeking as she does the high moral ground on the abortion issue, Harrison is especially annoyed at what she considers Noonan's penchant to define the position of his opponents as unworthy of serious moral consideration.[100]

Harrison makes the same observation of another of her critics, Richard McCormick, who writes à propos of the feminist abortion linchpin, the bodyright argument:

> Nothing in femaleness as such makes women more or less vulnerable to error or bias in moral discourse than men, yet when all is shrieked and done, the basic point remains valid: The abortion discussion proceeds at its own peril if it ignores women's perspectives.[101]

Harrison comments:

> The problem, of course, is that if the "shriekers" insist on the bodily integrity argument, his own way of formulating the issues already precludes his hearing of it (p. 307, note 26).

---

[99]Our Right to Choose, p. 239. Cf. the remark found in John Tracy Ellis, American Catholicism (second edition, revised) (Chicago: University of Chicago Press, 1969). Historian Arthur M. Schlesinger, Sr., once told Ellis: "I regard the prejudice against your Church as the deepest bias in the history of the American people" (p. 151).

[100]Cf. Our Right to Choose, p. 128: "Over time, Noonan has escalated his claim that, almost without exception in Christianity, a fetus has been viewed as a fully human person and abortion unequivocally denounced. In his most recent work, a diatribe against present social policy on abortion, he has even inveighed with a special rancor against those, like myself, who claim that official Roman Catholic teaching on sexuality, especially its teaching against contraception, constitutes a reason why the Roman Catholic tradition is so adamantly opposed to abortion. Noonan insists, even though in some of his work he has actually cited data to the contrary, that it always has been maintained among Christians that abortion is without exception the killing of human life."

[101]The text from McCormick is reported in Our Right to Choose, p. 307, note 26.

If the charge be true of Noonan and McCormick, namely, that they define their opposition as unworthy of serious moral consideration in the very way they frame their arguments, we might also want to consider if this charge does not apply as well to Harrison herself. On occasion she herself seems to define the abortion issue in such a way that the only *possible* reasons for such opposition must be either sexism or else misogyny. Several texts may help illustrate:

> It is far too late for anyone to deny the truthfulness of protests against antiwoman bias in established religious and moral traditions, especially as these traditions have shaped views of sexuality, procreation, and abortion (p. 41).

In speaking of the view of certain moralists that the status of the fetus is *the* most important issue to resolve in the abortion controversy, Harrison notes of such an approach: "I believe that whenever we encounter this view we should be aware that the line of moral reasoning sustaining it is intrinsically sexist" (p. 16). Opposition to abortion is characterized in this fashion:

> From a feminist theological point of view, prohibition of legal abortion involves the effort to deny freedom or centered moral agency, and hence full humanity, to over half the population (p. 116).

Misogyny once again seems to be the *real* reason behind the position of anyone who refuses to see the unwanted pregnancy situation as Harrison depicts it:

> All participants in the abortion conflict need to actively renounce the dubious assumptions holding sway about women and a procreative functionalist view of woman's sexuality. To value and respect human life must mean, at the very least, that one recognizes the possibility of genuine conflict between the life and well-being of a pregnant woman and the fetus she carries. If one cannot envision such potential conflict, it will surely be because for that individual, women do not yet count as full, valuable persons *in their own right*, apart from their social utility as

procreative beings.[102]

It appears that Harrison is engaging in some circular reasoning. Much of the case in *Our Right to Choose* is predicated on two elements which Harrison believes she has found present in her rereading of the Christian moral tradition: sex-negativity and misogyny. As we have seen, *any* opposition to abortion found in the historical past is handled in terms of one of these two mechanisms. Sex-negativity is Harrison's way of handling the early period of Christianity; misogyny is the way she handles the more recent record.

It is the sex-negativity element which accounts for the early Church's opposition to abortion, not any respect for the value of fetal life. How do we know if a doctrine is misogynist? Go to the teaching on abortion. How do we know if a doctrine is sex-negative? Go to the teaching on abortion. And if we go to the doctrine on abortion, what will we find? Sex-negativity and misogyny.[103]

The charge of misogyny levelled at the Christian tradition by Beverly Harrison is a serious accusation. We remember that Harrison is not making it only against certain churchmen; she is trying to make it against the entire tradition of Christian theology. While she tries to make a case of sorts for the charge that *misogyny* (in its usual and strong sense of "hatred of women") permeates the historical Christian record,[104]

---

[102]*Our Right to Choose*, p. 152: Harrison's emphasis. Perhaps what is at issue here is Harrison's exasperation with those who refuse to see what she obviously believes is the reasonableness of her position: how can one *really* be pro-woman and anti-abortion at the same time? Can one be opposed to abortion and still be committed to women's well-being? The answer to this question is the theme of our concluding chapter. We have often spoken of the abortion controversy in the context of worldviews, one pro-choice, the other pro-life.

[103]"Misogyny" covers a wide range of views with which Harrison disagrees and would apply to those who define women by their procreative functions, thus belittling and demeaning the agency of women. It seems to me that the expression "procreative functionalism" used by Harrison to characterize much of the Christian tradition serves as another way of bringing in the charge of misogyny. I would contend that our question, "Is nature misogynist?" is not far from the surface.

[104]Mary Daly thinks the case she made in *The Church and the Second Sex* is irrefutable. She writes in *Beyond God the Father*, p. 5: "The history of antifeminism in the Judeo-Christian heritage has already been exposed." In the note accompanying the

she understands *misogyny* in such a way that for all practical purposes, it can come to mean any view with which she disagrees.

Writing of the natural law views of Germain Grisez, for example, Harrison reasons as follows:

> The radicality and distinctiveness of human moral freedom and creativity, with all of the moral responsibility this freedom entails, is not only minimized but condemned by this theory. Because this assumption operates most clearly when gender relations are at issue, "freedom" in "biological reproduction" is understood as particularly inappropriate. *Neither, then, is it an overstatement to say that this theory is permeated by misogyny* (p. 202: my emphasis).

As she begins her argument in *Our Right to Choose*, Harrison notes how difficult it was to detect the misogyny embedded in the Christian tradition regarding abortion (p. 63); at the end, misogyny is everywhere. Indeed, Harrison makes a case that says, in effect, that *any* opposition to abortion is misogynist. Harrison, in a word, simply defines feminism in such a way that it cannot be conceived without abortion.[105] In my estimation, this is far from being the case.[106]

Along with most feminists, Harrison takes pride in her ability to detect the hidden connections between apparently unconnected ideas. Her criticism of Church teaching on the meaning of human sexuality

---

passage, she cites herself. Not all would agree. Cf. Frances Quere-Jaulmes (ed.), *La femme: Les grandes textes des pères de l'église* (Préface de Françoise Mallet-Joris) (Paris: Éditions du centurion, 1968).

[105]It is true, as we noted earlier, that Harrison *does* speak about abortions being kept to a minimum in a best of all possible worlds scenario. But at this point, we must remember her views on sexuality. She constantly stresses the fact that there is to be no distinction between birth control and abortion since they are part of the total fabric of a woman's life. Hence, I believe it is in this sense that we can safely say that Harrison defines abortion into the very heart of her feminist vision.

[106]Cf. Daniel Callahan, "The Abortion Debate: Is Progress Possible?" in Sidney and Daniel Callahan (eds.), *Abortion: Understanding Differences*, p. 314: "I know too many feminists, including my wife, who are antiabortion to see any necessary or inevitable identity at all between the abortion issue and the more general rights of women."

finds fault with the Church for doing precisely the same thing. To include procreation among the important meanings of human sexual expression is certainly not to denigrate the other meanings.[107] What Harrison calls the Church's "sex-negativity" may well be explained in other ways.[108]

In emphasizing as it does the relational, communitarian aspects of human existence, on the one hand, while linking the right to abortion to the absolute right of an individual to control her own body (the feminist bodyright argument) on the other, Harrison's thought is in constant tension with itself. Thus, while cautioning against individualism, for example, Harrison herself can be seen as fostering it.[109]

In the final analysis, it appears that Beverly Harrison is saying in effect: abortion is indeed the linchpin of the entire edifice I am constructing. I know it is morally ambiguous, and complex, and ambivalent. But I also know that I can not practice "utopic envisagement" without this morally ambiguous procedure. Her professed willingness to live with moral ambiguity is belied, it would seem, by her willingness to act on the matter. On this point Beverly

---

[107]Christopher Derrick, *Sex and Sacredness: A Catholic Homage to Venus* (San Francisco: Ignatius Press, 1982) makes some relevant observations regarding *sex-negativity* and *sexual realism*. Recent Catholic writings on human sexuality which attempt to avoid the pitfalls of the former include Karol Wojtyla, *Love and Responsibility* (translated by H. T. Willetts) (New York: Farrar, Strauss, and Giroux, 1981; original Polish edition, 1960); James V. Schall, S.J., *Christianity and Life* (San Francisco: Ignatius Press, 1981); Raymond Dennehy (ed.), *Christian Married Love* (San Francisco: Ignatius Press, 1981); Donald DeMarco, *The Anesthetic Society* (Front Royal, VA: Christendom Publications, 1982); and Kevin Thomas McMahon, *Sexuality: Theological Voices* (Braintree: The Pope John Center, 1987).

[108]Other useful treatments include Carol McMillan, *Women, Reason and Nature: Some Philosophical Problems With Feminism*; Jo Durden-Smith and Diane DeSimone, *Sex and the Brain* (New York: Arbor House, 1983); Mary Pride, *The Way Home: Beyond Feminism, Back to Reality* (Westchester IL: Crossway Books, 1985); Roger Scruton, *Sexual Desire: a Moral Philosophy of the Erotic* (New York: Free Press, 1986); and Maggie Gallagher, *Enemies of Eros: How the Sexual Revolution Is Killing Family, Marriage, and Sex and What We Can Do About It*.

[109]Cf. M. Cathleen Kaveny, "Toward a Thomistic Perspective on Abortion and Law in Contemporary America," *The Thomist* 55 no. 3 (1991), pp. 343–396.

Harrison and the Roman Catholic tradition from which she professes to have learned so much have come to a parting of the ways.

Beverly Harrison's work on the abortion question fills an obvious void in the pro-abortion literature: a long and detailed assault on the one tradition that has held firm against abortion, namely, the Christian. While it is true that Harrison undertakes to make her case for abortion based on her feminist re-interpretation of the principles that animate the Christian tradition, in the final analysis she has not succeeded. The reason goes to the heart of the matter: Where abortion is the practice, atheism is the theory.[110] Abortion is at home in Beauvoir's thought, but it is alien to Harrison's Christian tradition.

Transition to the Final Chapters

The abortion views of Simone de Beauvoir, Mary Daly, Carol Gilligan, and Beverly Wildung Harrison have exerted a great influence upon other feminists. We encounter nuances, to be sure, as each makes her case for abortion. It is serious, a matter of life and death, and none treat abortion in a cavalier fashion. Yet at the end of our journey from atheist philosopher Simone de Beauvoir to Christian theologian Beverly Harrison, we witness a veritable sea-change in societal attitudes toward human abortion: the "power to kill" has become "our right to choose."

If some who call themselves Christian feminists can agree with atheist feminists on abortion, it must be that the right to abortion and the aims of feminism are intertwined. Right? Our final two chapters will endeavor to provide the answer. Chapter five will summarize what we have unearthed in the course of this study of four feminist theoreticians of abortion and see what some of those who follow in their footsteps are saying in defense of pro-choice feminism. Our final chapter shall present what I consider the only viable alternative: Pro-life feminism.

---

[110]Cf. John T. Noonan, Jr., *Abortion in Our Culture*, p. 5: "Abortion is atheism put into practice."

CHAPTER FIVE

PRO-CHOICE FEMINISM

Can a woman be both a feminist and anti-choice on abortion? . . . The question cannot be answered, of course, without asking another, more fundamental question: what is feminism? This is not the place to digress into such a theoretical discussion, but it is worth pointing out that feminism is growing more diverse, is developing more "schools" of thought, than ever before. It would have been much easier to come up with a comprehensive definition of feminism in the early seventies than it is now. Still, to the vast majority of feminists, abortion is a bedrock issue. By some indeed, it is viewed as the foundation of feminism itself. No less a feminist than Simone de Beauvoir recently affirmed her belief that freedom for women "began with the womb:" "I have not stopped fighting for the essential feminist message—the right of abortion."[1]

---

[1] Kathleen McDonnell, *Not an Easy Choice: A Feminist Re-examines Abortion* (Boston: South End Press, 1984), p. 88. McDonnell tells her readers that the quote from Beauvoir appears in Paul Webster, "De Beauvoir Reveals Sartre's Macho Ways Sparked Her Crusade," *Globe and Mail*, May 19, 1984, p. E 12. See also Beauvoir's comment in Alice Schwarzer, *After 'The Second Sex': Conversations With Simone de Beauvoir*," p. 47: "We hope to convince the public that women must be assured of the right to procreate freely, of public support for the burdens of motherhood—especially crèches—and of the right to refuse unwanted pregnancies through contraceptive measures and abortion. We are demanding that these be free and that women have the right to choose." The last words of this quote call to mind the title of Beverly Harrison's book on abortion.

W e have seen the practice of human abortion go from what the Roman Catholic Church considers an unspeakable crime to what many contemporary feminists regard as an absolute right. The atheist Beauvoir sees the right to abortion as "the essential feminist message." The Christian Harrison prefers to speak of the right to abortion as a right to bodily self-determination, "our right to choose." In whatever way many feminists go about expressing it, abortion is absolutely essential to the better world for women that they envision. In this chapter we examine pro-choice feminism, a feminism with abortion as its linchpin.

Abortion and Autonomy

Ours is an age that desires autonomy.[2] The existentialism of Jean-Paul Sartre and Simone de Beauvoir is an attempt to construct a philosophy of total freedom, independent of all norms of nature and Church. Much of contemporary feminist ethics is an undertaking that seeks to deal with autonomy;[3] abortion is an important part of this

---

[2]On the general theme of our age being characterized by its search for autonomy, cf. Jeffrey Stout, *The Flight from Authority: Religion, Morality, and the Quest for Autonomy* (Notre Dame: University of Notre Dame Press, 1981), and Thomas E. Hill, Jr., *Autonomy and Self-respect* (New York: Cambridge University Press, 1991).

[3]Cf. Monique Dumais, *Les droits des femmes* (Collection "Interpellations") (Montréal: Éditions Paulines Médiaspaul, 1992). She speaks of the three "A"'s of feminism as accomplishment, affirmation, and autonomy. The theme of autonomy and its importance for feminism is treated in many of the articles in Anneliese Lissner, Rita Süssmuth, and Walter Karin (eds.), *Frauen Lexicon: Traditionen, Fakten, Perspektiven* (Freiburg: Herder, 1988), as well as in Barbara Hilkert Andolsen, Christine Gudorf, and Mary Pellauer (eds.), *Women's Consciousness, Women's Conscience: A Reader in Feminist Ethics.* See also Ruth Smith, "Feminism and the Moral Subject," pp. 235–250. Cf. Eva Feder Kittay and Diana T. Meyers (eds.), *Women and Moral Theory;* Carole Pateman and Elizabeth Gross (eds.), *Feminist Challenges: Social and Political Theory*, especially p. 8, where Gross contends that women ought to be more interested in autonomy than in equality. Cf. Louise Hardin Bray, "Body-Decisions as Sacred," in Elizabeth Dodson Gray, *Sacred Dimension of Women's Experience* (Wellesley: Roundtable, 1988), pp. 228–231. The author gives witness that some Christians (she and her husband are Methodists) attempt to argue a case for abortion on the basis of autonomy.

desire. As pro-choice champion Laurence Tribe sees it, abortion is "a basic source of personal autonomy and self-respect."[4] Perhaps a foe of abortion has stated it most succinctly: "Abortion is the epitome of autonomy."[5]

Following in the lines traced out by the four feminist theoreticians whose thought on abortion we have investigated, some of their disciples have come to deem the right to abortion as the center of their feminist vision. Beauvoir herself is a good index. In 1949 she speaks of the ambivalence and heartbreak that abortion can bring about in the lives of women. In 1984, two years before her death, the French feminist foregoes all nuances and sets abortion at the very center of her vision of feminism, as we see in the quote with which we have begun this chapter.

A summary of the abortion ideas of the four authors we have studied may prove helpful in seeing how abortion as the linchpin of much of contemporary feminism came to pass. The first four chapters have established that each of the four has added an element to the abortion edifice: Beauvoir the killing, Daly the power, Gilligan the choice, and Harrison the right. Their legacy? *The right to choose is the rhetoric, the power to kill is the reality.* As we re-examine each one in turn, we shall once again encounter some of the major abortion texts of the four feminist thinkers.

Simone de Beauvoir: Epistemology and Killing

In her major work on the abortion issue, Simone de Beauvoir speaks of abortion as a moment of feminist epistemological insight:

> The one thing they [women] are sure of is this rifled and bleeding and womb, these shreds of crimson life, this child that is not there. It is at her first abortion that woman begins to "know." For many women the world

---

[4]Laurence Tribe, *Abortion: The Clash of Absolutes*, p. 75. Joel Feinberg, "Abortion," in Tom Regan (ed.), *Matters of Life and Death: New Introductory Essays in Moral Philosophy* (New York: Random House, 1980), pp. 183–217, says substantially the same.

[5]Susan T. Foh, "Abortion and Women's Lib," in Richard Ganz (ed.), *Thou Shalt Not Kill: The Christian Case Against Abortion* (New Rochelle: Arlington House, 1978), p. 179.

will never be the same (*The Second Sex*, p. 464).

What was it that abortion had taught Simone de Beauvoir thirty-five years later? By 1984, she had come to regard the right to abortion as "the essential feminist message." How did she arrive at this lesson? If our analysis is substantially correct, the male as model is her teacher:

> It is not in giving life but in risking life that man is raised above the animal; that is why superiority has been accorded in humanity not to the sex that brings forth but to that which kills. . . . Here we have the key to the whole mystery [of woman's subjugation] (*The Second Sex*, p. 58).

Some will frankly acknowledge the killing that takes place in abortion and do so from a purely secular standpoint:"The starting point for a discussion about abortion ought to be the frank recognition that the issue is life or death. To abort a fetus is to kill, to prevent the realization of a human life."[6]

Janet Radcliffe Richards puts it this way: "We can, for instance, accept that the killing of an unborn child is an intrinsically bad thing, but still be committed to the campaign for abortion on demand because we think other things are more important than saving foetal life."[7] It is worth noting that Richards makes this comment only after observing that it was Simone de Beauvoir who said it is acceptable to sacrifice things which cost more than they are worth. As we have seen, in Beauvoir's analysis of woman's condition, killing—or the lack of it—is the key.

Of all the feminists writing of the killing that place in abortion, none is more terse and terrifying than Ellen Willis. She minces no words and goes right to the heart of matter when she speaks as clearly as she does of "women's moral right to autonomy and sexual love, and

---

[6]Elizabeth Mensch and Alan Freeman, *The Politics of Virtue: Is Abortion Debatable?*, p. 157.

[7]Janet Radcliffe Richards, *The Sceptical Feminist: A Philosophical Inquiry*, p. 206.

therefore *their moral right to kill an unwanted fetus.*"[8]

When Beauvoir's hostility toward the God of Christianity is coupled with her interest in religion, some of her feminist followers will explain the killing in abortion in terms of Eastern and pagan religions: "Every woman has a Kali side; every mother has a secret devourer, a baby killer in her soul."[9]

> The majority of women who abort do so because they know that the unwelcome child, born of constraint or misfortune, will be wounded in some unacceptable way. As Artemis might kill a wounded animal rather than allow it to limp along miserably, so a mother wishes to spare the child a painful destiny.[10]

Beauvoir's abortion legacy is continued especially in the work of Daly, Gilligan, and Harrison, themselves a blend of the secular and the religious. If Beauvoir stresses the killing, Daly emphasizes the power.

Mary Daly: Metaphysics and Power

Mary Daly picks up on several key Beauvoirian themes. Beauvoir had spoken of the symbolic meaning in the sexual language of males and females.[11] For the French feminist, the usual position for intercourse attests to the humiliating nature of heterosexual intercourse;

---

[8]Cf. Ellen Willis, "Betty Friedan's 'Second Stage': a Step Backward," *The Nation* 233 no. 16 (November 14, 1981), pp. 494–496: my emphasis. Is it a coincidence that we find in Willis a linking of three ideas, to wit, that woman's moral rights of autonomy and sexual freedom lead to the conclusion of a further moral right, the moral right to kill? Beauvoir could not have it expressed it any more clearly.

[9]Naomi Ruth Lowinsky, Ph.D., *The Motherline: Every Woman's Journey to Find Her Female Roots* (New York: Jeremy P. Tarcher/ Perigee Books, 1992), p. 195.

[10]Ginette Paris, *The Sacrament of Abortion*, p. 56. Paris had said substantially the same in *Pagan Meditations: The Worlds of Aphrodite, Artemis and Hestia* (translated by Gwendolyn Moore), (Dallas: Spring Publications, 1986), esp. pp. 146–147.

[11]Cf. the first chapter of *The Second Sex*, "The Data of Biology." Among Beauvoir's other findings: It is through the *sperm* that the male transcends; the female egg possesses no such transcendent principle. See *The Second Sex*, p. 19.

it bespeaks subjugation for the woman.[12] Men impregnate; women are impregnated. From this phenomenology of sex, as it were, Daly begins to elaborate her metaphysics of abortion. If Beauvoir sees killing as the key, Mary Daly latches on to power as the key to understanding the abortion issue:

> "One hundred percent of the bishops who oppose the repeal of anti-abortion laws are men and one hundred per cent of the people who have abortions are women." I thought it clear and obvious—and outrageous—that men had appropriated the right to dictate to women in this matter. *I saw that the main issue was really power over women* (*Outercourse*, p. 142; my emphasis).

Angry at the way things stand between men and women, Mary Daly envisions a world for women without men. Her vision of a lesbian separatist world owes much to Beauvoir's ruminations on the institution of heterosexuality.[13] It is possible that Mary Daly's approach to the abortion situation was formulated with this very thought in mind. Why should women be in certain positions? Why should women be in positions of unwanted pregnancies at all? Precisely because of the humiliating nature of the procedure, Daly as we have seen comes to regard abortion as the microcosm of female oppression.

There is a secular and a religious way of translating Daly's abortion vision. Secular feminists who follow her lead take the same approach as Daly does: the sexual situation is itself humiliating. Especially prominent in this regard are two American feminists, Andrea Dworkin and Catherine MacKinnon.[14]

---

[12]In *The Second Sex*, p. 19, Beauvoir is talking of the male: "His domination is expressed in the very position of copulation—in almost all animals the male is *on* the female."

[13]In the culturalist credo which marks the thought of Simone de Beauvoir in *The Second Sex*, there is nothing natural; everything is cultural. This, of course, would include sexual relations. They have no inherent natural meaning, only the meaning human beings attach to them.

[14]Cf. Andrea Dworkin, *Intercourse* (New York: Free Press, 1987), and Catherine MacKinnon, *Feminism Unmodified: Discourses on Life and Law*. We note *en passant* that the title of Daly's *Outercourse* seems to be styled after Dworkin's volume.

A religious sort of explanation is also possible: abortion is sad and tragic but a necessity because of our low human state after the Fall; in a sense, abortion is an index of our fallen humanity. Judith Wilt is a colleague of Mary Daly at Boston College:

> As a feminist and a Catholic, I believe a woman's freedom to abort a fetus is a monstrous, a tyrannous, but a necessary freedom in a fallen world.[15]

Pursuing the same general line of thought is Catholic feminist Madonna Kolbenschlag: "Perhaps more than any other human phenomenon, abortion is indicative of our 'fallen' state. Whichever way we choose, there is some evil."[16]

Beauvoir's epistemology of abortion gives rise to Daly's metaphysics of abortion. Writing of the woman who seeks an abortion, Andrea Dworkin makes the correlation between the visions of Simone de Beauvoir and Mary Daly:

> She has learned (*learned* is a poor word for what has happened to her) that every life is more valuable than her own; her life gets value through motherhood, a kind of benign contamination.[17]

Put in this way, the knowledge of humiliation that abortion has taught Simone de Beauvoir and Mary Daly is a deeply pessimistic vision of human nature: most men are hypocrites and most women sheep in Simone de Beauvoir's view, while in Daly half the human race is

---

[15]Judith Wilt, *Abortion, Choice and Contemporary Fiction: The Armageddon of the Maternal Instinct* (Chicago: University of Chicago Press, 1990), p. xiii.

[16]Madonna Kolbenschlag, *Kiss Sleeping Beauty Good-Bye: Breaking the Spell of Feminine Myths and Models*, p. 158. Do we detect Mary Daly's presence in Kolbenschlag's text? In *Beyond God the Father*, Daly says: "As Mrs. Robinson of the once popular hit song knew: 'Every way you look at it, you lose'" (p. 109).

[17]Andrea Dworkin, *Right-Wing Women* (New York: Perigee Books, 1983), p. 74. Dworkin goes on to explain the humiliation endemic to abortion: "Women are humiliated because they hated themselves, their sex, their female bodies, they hated being female" (p. 75).

necrophilic and beyond redemption.[18] The feminist theoreticians of abortion needed an injection of optimism, and Carol Gilligan attempted to provide it.

Carol Gilligan: Psychology and Choice

The killing of Beauvoir's abortion analysis and the power perspective of Daly's give way to the choice paradigm of Gilligan: "The essence of moral decision is the exercise of choice and the willingness to accept responsibility for that choice" (*In a Different Voice*, p. 67).

The Harvard psychologist is very influential in her ability to translate the ponderous philosophical and theological language of Simone de Beauvoir and Mary Daly into a language more easily understandable and more readily accessible to the men and women of her day.[19] In her work on the psychological aspects of abortion and moral development, Carol Gilligan is saying that abortion, if done for the right reasons, can be an occasion for moral maturity and psychological growth.[20] Gilligan has spawned a cottage industry of sorts

---

[18]*The Second Sex* of Simone de Beauvoir is open to widely disparate interpretations. While one of her critics, Terry Keefe, *Simone de Beauvoir: A Study of Her Writings* (Totowa: Barnes and Noble, 1983), finds the optimism in *Le deuxième sexe* unwarranted, Jean Leighton, *Simone de Beauvoir on Woman*, finds Beauvoir's book unrelentingly pessimistic in its views on human nature. On occasion, Beauvoir sounds like Mary Daly in regarding half the human race as perfidious. See for example her remarks in Diana E. H. Russell and Nicole Van de Ven (eds.), *Crimes Against Women: Proceedings of the International Tribunal* (Brussels, March 4–8, 1976) (Milbrae, CA: Les Femmes, 1976), pp. xiii–xiv.

[19]Jean Bethke Elshtain, *Public Man, Private Woman*, constantly upbraids feminists such as Daly and Beauvoir for using arcane language that practically assures their message will be understood only by a few. Gilligan is free of this charge; in fact, Elshtain has good things to say about the way the Harvard psychologist utilizes her language of moral discourse (pp. 335–336).

[20]In her treatment of the psychological sequelae of abortion, Gilligan is following the lead of Hélène Deutsch, *The Psychology of Women: A Psychoanalytic Interpretation* (2 vols.) (New York: Grune and Stratten, 1945; Bantam reprint edition 1973). Writes Deutsch: "As a whole, the trauma of induced abortion is not irremediable unless it has caused an organic injury.
. . . Induced abortion is a more or less voluntary act, often a good adjustment to reality" (II, pp. 196–198). Beauvoir also depends heavily upon Deutsch for the chapter

in regard to the psychological aspects of the abortion question.[21]

At times, it is true, some authors will speak of abortion as an opportunity for growth, presenting the abortion experience as one without much ambivalence. On occasion, they can be quite explicit, going so far as to say, in effect, that "abortion makes you grow." Writes Marjory Skowronski: "For me, abortion has been a personal symbol of my awakening to the challenge of realizing my individual potential."[22] Such positive evaluations of abortion are by no means the norm.[23] Hence the importance of Gilligan's investigations; the growth that comes from the abortion experience often exacts a heavy price.[24]

Sue Nathanson is a psychologist who writes about her struggle to pick up the pieces of her own emotional life after an abortion. In a book replete with personal touches, Nathanson describes all the anguish and guilt she went through as she wrestled with her own abortion decision.[25] At the end, Nathanson gives a positive evaluation of her abortion experience.

---

on motherhood in *The Second Sex*.

[21]Two representatives of this literature: Angela Bonavoglia (ed.), *The Choices We Made: Twenty-Five Women and Men Speak Out About Abortion* (New York: Random House, 1991), and Sumi Hoshiko, *Our Choices: Women's Personal Decisions About Abortion* (New York: Harrington Park Press, 1993).

[22]Marjory Skowronski, *Abortion and Alternatives* (Milbrae CA: Les Femmes, 1977), p. 123. For some examples of this abortion as a positive growth experience, see Patricia Lunneborg, *Abortion: A Positive Decision* (New York: Bergin and Garvey, 1992), and Lynn Leight, "When Abortion Is a Blessing," in Ellen Cole and Esther D. Rothblum (eds.), *Women and Sex Therapy: Closing the Circle of Sexual Knowledge* (New York: Harrington Park Press, 1988), pp. 145–147. See also Kathleen McDonnell, *Not an Easy Choice: A Feminist Re-examines Abortion*, especially p. 38.

[23]Several comments made by Gloria Steinem, "Foreword," to Angela Bonavoglia (ed.), *The Choices We Made*, help explain: "My own abortion was pivotal in my life; the worst and the best of it; a symbol of fear, but also the first time I stopped passively accepting whatever happened to me and took responsibility" (p. x). And again: "I, too, had had an abortion, shortly after I got out of college. I had gone through it totally alone, out of both humiliation and pride" (p. xii).

[24]Judith Wilt, *Abortion, Choice and Contemporary Fiction*, p. 17, basing herself in part on Gilligan's "Sarah," concludes that there is a serious loss in the gain of abortion.

[25]Cf. Sue Nathanson, *Soul Crisis: One Woman's Journey Through Abortion to Renewal* (New York: Signet Books, 1989).

Simone de Beauvoir constantly emphasizes the hostility of each consciousness to every other consciousness; Mary Daly's is a world in which half the human race is unworthy of trust. In Sue Nathanson's vision, a non-judgmental community setting is a *sine qua non* of coming to the view adumbrated by Carol Gilligan, namely, that abortion—"if done for the right reasons"—can be a source of psychological growth. One passage gives the gist of Nathanson's position on her own "soul-crisis," the abortion experience:

> Soul-crises such as mine, if experienced within an empathic and compassionate human relationship, within a culture that makes room for them without judgment and condemnation, have the possibility of becoming opportunities for personal growth and transformation rather than dreadful experiences simply to be endured and survived.[26]

Elements of Beauvoir's epistemology of abortion, Daly's metaphysics of abortion, and Gilligan's choice or autonomy are woven together in the following text which comes from a ecofeminist theological perspective:

> Women who have not had abortions, and/or do not approve of abortion, can only be asked to consider cultivating an ontological trust of their sisters who do undergo abortion—we must begin believing, or rebelieving, that the female being, of its original nature, *knows* what it has to do, when it must be done, and why. If we reclaim this trust in ourselves, and in other women, we are reclaiming female autonomy—and this reclamation can help create a world in which much of the pain and ugliness of abortion no longer exists.[27]

---

[26]Sue Nathanson, *Soul Crisis*, p. 228. In chapter ten, "The Woman as Murderer," Nathanson blends together elements of Beauvoir's killing, Daly's power, and Gilligan's choice perspectives.

[27]Monica Sjöö and Barbara Mor, *The Great Cosmic Mother: Rediscovering the Religion of the Earth* (San Francisco: Harper and Row, 1987), p. 388. See also Deborah Mara, *Self-Ritual for Invoking Release of Spirit-life in the Womb: A Personal Treatise on Ritual Herbal Abortion* (Great Barrington, MA: Mother Spirit Publications, 1989), and

The theology of the authors of the above citation is that of a "religion of the earth," paganism. But Christian theology can also be pressed into the service of the abortion liberty. To the killing, the power, and the choice, Christian theologian Beverly Harrison adds the element of right.

Beverly Harrison: Theology and Right

Beverly Harrison sides with Gilligan in taking what amounts to an optimistic approach to the abortion question, attempting to accomplish on the theological level what the Harvard professor endeavors to do on the psychological plane.[28] If women can be helped to view abortion in the context of the total fabric of a woman's life, Harrison is telling women in effect that what she calls "our right to choose" is indeed the key to a new world for women.[29] Her emphasis on rights completes the pro-choice feminist picture:

> I will argue that once the material historical conditions exist to make procreative choice possible, there are excellent moral reasons for viewing it as a right all women should possess. No society is morally adequate which does not organize its life to encourage the existence and extension of procreative choice (*Our Right to Choose*, p. 4).

This notwithstanding, Beverly Harrison is aware of the difficulties of the abortion view she espouses. Indeed, the question that many feminists would like to avoid, the status of the fetus, is treated by the Protestant feminist ethician in the lengthiest chapter of *Our Right to Choose*. By the time she finishes her treatment of the fetus, noting as she does the moral ambiguity surrounding abortion, Harrison is contending,

---

Zsuzsanna E. Budapest, *The Grandmother of Time: A Woman's Book of Celebrations, Spells, and Sacred Objects for Every Month of the Year* (San Francisco: Harper and Row, 1989).

[28] Sondra Farganis, *The Social Reconstruction of the Feminine Character* (Totowa: Rowman and Littlefield, 1986), while dealing mainly with Gilligan, does note Harrison's attempt to frame the abortion question in a theological perspective.

[29] The phrase, "abortion must be the key to a new world for women," belongs to Stella Browne. See *Supra*, p. 11.

in effect, that she has raised enough doubts regarding the status of the fetus to enable women to choose abortion, at least until the time of fetal viability, with a relatively clear conscience.

In the eyes of many feminists, abortion has come to be seen as absolutely central to contemporary feminism. Full humanity for women has come to be linked with the right to abortion. Simone de Beauvoir is an atheist. Beverly Harrison is a Christian. Both believe in abortion as an essential part of the feminist message. How is this possible? The logic of ideas is at work.

Abortion and Christian Feminism

Compare, for example, how two Catholic women define "feminism" and "feminist":

> Feminism, in a generic sense, is a worldview or stance that affirms the dignity of women as fully human persons in their own right, critiques systems of patriarchy for their violation of this dignity, and advocates social and intellectual changes to bring about freeing relationships among human beings and between human beings and the earth.[30]

A "feminist," on the other hand, is defined as

> Anyone who is dedicated to the ideal that men and women, although possessed of different sexual natures (and thus, as we shall see, of differing way of relating to reality,) have equally valuable and valid contributions to make to the world, and therefore ought to have equality of opportunity. Furthermore, to be a feminist is to be wholly committed to making this world into one wherein both women and men are equally valued

---

[30]Elizabeth A. Johnson, CSJ, *Feminism and Sharing the Faith: A Catholic Dilemma* (Warren Lecture Series in Catholic Studies, No. 29. Tulsa: University of Tulsa, 1994), p. 2.

and respected.[31]

At the outset of our study, we noted that there are many feminisms and set as one of our two major tasks to show how abortion went from its atheistic roots in the existentialist philosophy of Jean-Paul Sartre and Simone de Beauvoir to the classrooms of Christians. How is it possible that the Christian Harrison and the atheist Beauvoir can both profess belief in "our right to choose" as "the essential feminist message"? I believe we are now in a position to answer the question. The answer must be found in the link we have seen being made that full humanity for women depends on abortion as "linchpin of modern culture."

In a book published in 1983, the same year as Harrison's *Our Right to Choose*, feminist theologian Rosemary Radford Ruether writes:

> The critical principle of feminist theology is the promotion of the full humanity of women. Whatever denies, diminishes, or distorts the full humanity of women is, therefore, appraised as not redemptive. Theologically speaking, whatever diminishes or denies the full humanity of women must be presumed not to reflect the divine or an authentic relation to the divine, or to reflect the authentic nature of things, or to be the message or work of an authentic redeemer or a community of redemption.[32]

In a book published in 1986, the year Simone de Beauvoir died, we see that the pro-choice legacy extends not only to mainstream Protestantism.[33] It is worth observing that when Evangelical Protestant

---

[31]Anne M. Maloney, "Cassandra's Fate: Why Feminists Ought to be Pro-Life," in Stephen Heaney (ed.), *Abortion: A New Generation of Catholic Responses* (Braintree, MA: The Pope John Center, 1992), p. 210.

[32]Rosemary Radford Ruether, *Sexism and God-Talk: Toward a Feminist Theology* (Boston: Beacon Press, 1983), pp. 18–19. See the comments made on Ruether's text by Lisa Sowle Cahill, *Women and Sexuality* (New York: Paulist Press, 1992), pp. 45–46, and by Catherine Mowry LaCugna, "Catholic Women as Ministers and Theologians," *America* 167 no. 10 (October 10, 1992), pp. 238–248.

[33]Cf. Letha Dawson Scanzoni and Nancy A. Hardesty, *All We're Meant to Be: Biblical Feminism for Today* (Nashville: Abingdon Press, 1986), pp. 163–169. The influence of Beverly Harrison's *Our Right to Choose* is clearly in evidence.

authors Scanzoni and Hardesty conclude their discussion of abortion, they bring in several key Beauvoirian themes. Indeed, our study of theologians Daly and Harrison, who follow in the wake of Beauvoir has prepared us for the move:

> Men have enjoyed procreative freedom and the ability to plan and control their lives in a way that women could not until comparatively recent times—a way made possible through improved contraceptive technology and, in certain necessary or emergency situations, through the availability of abortion. *To tell a woman that under no circumstances could she ever have an abortion is to place a burden on women that men have never had to bear.*[34]

In examining the writings of Beauvoir, Daly, Gilligan, and Harrison, we witness the consequences of the abortion idea. We see how the right to abortion has gone from being the bailiwick of atheistic adherents to becoming the centerpiece of certain theological theorists. Feminist theology—at least in part—has gone along with the move. For example, when Catholic nuns Barbara Ferraro and Patricia Hussey attempt to justify their pro-choice stance in the face of their Church's clear teaching on the matter, they acknowledge their debt to Beverly Harrison's work on abortion.[35]

---

[34]Letha Dawson Scanzoni and Nancy A. Hardesty, *All We're Meant to Be: Biblical Feminism for Today*, p. 169, my emphasis. See also the pro-choice collection of essays edited by Anne Eggebrooten, *Abortion: My Choice, God's Grace—Christian Women Tell Their Stories* (Pasadena: New Paradigm Books, 1994.)

[35]Cf. Barbara Ferraro and Patricia Hussey with Jane O'Reilly, *No Turning Back: Two Nuns' Battle With the Vatican Over Women's Right to Choose* (New York: Poseidon Press, 1990). The authors profess their indebtedness to Harrison's work on behalf of abortion on p. 259. (We note in passing that the expression "women's right to choose"—in the subtitle of the book—is the chief way the right to abortion is presented in its theological formulations.) Harrison reviews their book briefly in "Good Reading," *Christianity and Crisis* 50 nos. 4 & 5 (October 22, 1990), p. 315. The shift towards the regnant secular feminist view of abortion taken by certain American Catholic nuns has been chronicled by Rosalind Pollack Petchesky, *Abortion and Woman's Choice: The State, Sexuality, and Reproductive Freedom* (revised edition) (The Northeastern Series in Feminist Theory) (Boston: Northeastern University Press, 1990), p. 380. What is known as feminist theology is largely the preserve of Roman

This present study has shown that the Christian Harrison herself is heavily in debt to the atheist Beauvoir. Both secular and religious feminists have bought into the bodyright argument as the chief reason why women need the right to abortion. A man's body never becomes pregnant. It serves as the model. Be it in the atheist Beauvoir, the mainstream Protestant Harrison or in Evangelicals Scanzoni and Hardesty, the male as model and paradigm for women's emancipation is clearly in evidence. Men have never had to labor under a pregnancy; why should women? The right to choose is the rhetoric, the power to kill is the reality. Pro-choice feminism, be it secular or Christian—is it not saying in the final analysis: "There sits no higher court/Than man's red heart"?

Abortion as the Linchpin of Contemporary Feminism

The absolute right to abortion espoused for the first time by arch-atheist Marquis de Sade[36] has come to be seen as absolutely essential to the aims of much of contemporary feminism.[37] Indeed, the practice of human abortion has gone from unspeakable crime to a proud symbol of woman's full personhood: "The right to choose is crucial to the personhood of woman."[38] And again: "Reproductive self-determination is a basic condition for sexual equality and for women to assume full

---

Catholic women. On this, see Catherine Mowry LaCugna, "Catholic Women as Ministers and Theologians," pp. 238–248.

[36]Sade's hatred of God is by no means the least important element of his abortion vision. See Luigi Lombardi Vallauri, "Abortismo libertario e sadismo," in various authors, *Sul problema dell'aborto: Aspetti medico-giuridici* (Milan: Vita e pensiero, 1976), pp. 279–326: Pro-abortionism has its roots in the soil of hedonism, social masculinism, and atheism; in addition, the author contends that anti-Catholicism is common to all pro-abortion ideologies.

[37]Is it a coincidence that Sade may also be considered a feminist? See, for example, Constance Rover, *Love, Morals, and the Feminists*, esp. p. 9, where she cites a text from Sade's *La philosophie dans le boudoir* as proof of Sade's feminism. Beauvoir, we recall, has a fascination with her countryman and his work.

[38]Betty Friedan, *The Second Stage* (New York: Summit Books, 1981), p. 86. We note in passing the use of language: "the right of abortion" is expressed as "the right to choose." Seconding Friedan's sentiments is Letty Cottin Pogrebin, *Family Politics: Love and Power on an Intimate Frontier*, esp. p. 191.

membership in all other human groups."[39] Christian ethicist Beverly
Harrison nuances the matter in this way:

> The right in question is body-right, or freedom from
> coercion in childbearing. It is careless to say that the
> right in question is the right to an abortion. *Morally, the
> right is bodily self-determination, a fundamental condition
> for personhood and a foundational moral right.*[40]

Betty Friedan links the case for full humanity for women with
access to safe and legal abortion:

> As an example of the new feminism in action, consider
> the matter of abortion law repeal. NOW (National
> Organization for Women) was the first organization to
> speak on the basic rights of women on the question of
> abortion. We said that it is *the inalienable human
> right of every woman to control her own reproductive
> process... This question can only really be confronted in
> terms of the basic personhood and dignity of woman,*
> which is violated if she does not have the right to
> control her own reproductive process.[41]

In testimony she gives before a Congressional Committee in 1976,
Friedan is quite explicit in linking full personhood for women with the
new "theology of abortion" and its linchpin, the bodyright argument:

> We then had to confront this unique thing, the
> question, the right of the woman to control her own
> body because without this right it is not possible for a
> woman to really use her other rights and equality. And

---

[39]Linda Gordon, *Woman's Body, Woman's Right: A History of Birth Control in
America*, p. 417. Pro-life feminists, of course, would disagree.

[40]Beverly Wildung Harrison, *Making the Connections*, p. 288, note 2: my emphasis.

[41]Betty Friedan, "Our Revolution Is Unique," pp. 34–35: my emphasis. Cf. also Betty
Friedan, *It Changed My Life: Writings on the Women's Movement* (Random House,
New York 1977), p. 126.

we did, I believe, establish this, this new assumption of
our full personhood.

It is being accepted now in law, in new morality, new
theology, this assumption of new personhood.[42]

The same yoking together of the ideas of abortion and personhood is
made by Rosalind Pollack Petchesky:

Access to safe abortion is a fundamental need of women
as persons. . . . The compulsory pregnancy and
childbearing that the denial of abortion implies is
incompatible with the existence of women as moral
agents and social beings.[43]

Abortion—what nineteenth-century feminists regarded as an affront to
woman's dignity—has now become regarded by many in this latest
feminist wave as the "touchstone," "a central tenet" of contemporary
feminism.[44]

After a lengthy treatment of the abortion question in the

---

[42]"Statement of Betty Friedan," *Abortion—Part IV: Hearing before the Subcommittee
on Constitutional Amendments of the Committee on the Judiciary, Ninety-Fourth
Congress* (Washington, D.C: U. S. Government Printing Office, 1976), pp. 707–711.
The quote is from p. 708. Friedan goes on to recount her meeting with Pope Paul VI:
"I came in the hope that the church would confront in new theological terms the full
personhood of women."

[43]Rosalind Pollack Petchesky, *Abortion and Woman's Choice: The State, Sexuality, and
Reproductive Freedom* (Longman Series in Feminist Theory) (Boston: Northeastern
University Press, 1984), p. 388. The phrasing is gone in Petchesky's revised edition
of 1990, though the thought would seem to be the same. The joining together of
abortion with women's liberation is also made by Angela Y. Davis, *Women, Race and
Class* (New York: Vintage/Random House, 1981).

[44]Cf. Barbara Katz Rothman, *Recreating Motherhood: Ideology and Technology in a
Patriarchal Society*, p. 113: "Abortion today, like contraception in 1920, is the
touchstone for understanding motherhood, and womanhood." According to Sheryl
Ruzek, "Feminist Visions of Health: An International Perspective," in Juliet Mitchell
and Ann Oakley (eds.), *What Is Feminism? A Re-Examination* (New York: Pantheon,
1986), p. 186: "Abortion is not simply a neutral 'medical service,' but one which is
or is not available depending on historical circumstances. Therefore, ensuring every
woman's right to abortion (whether she chooses to have one or not) is a central tenet
of contemporary Western feminism."

context of contemporary feminist theory, Janet Radcliffe Richards concludes:

> In general the case which has been made out here does in theory fall short of the feminist claim for abortion and contraception free and on demand, but it comes as near to it as to make no practical difference.[45]

In the words of H. Tristram Engelhardt, Jr., an author sympathetic to the aims of feminism: "Abortion is becoming a linchpin of modern culture. It marks one of the elements of viewing women as free participants in society."[46] Under the title "Abortion" in her *Encyclopedia of Feminism*, Lisa Tuttle writes: "A basic feminist tenet of the latter half of the twentieth century is that every woman has the right to control her own reproductive life."

Andrea Dworkin sees abortion in this way:

> Abortion is also ideologically central to understanding women's condition. What abortion means to women is the absolute right to control the reproductive functions of our own bodies. . . But abortion is the symbol of a woman's life.[47]

While a host of other texts can be cited to make it clear that the right to abortion has become a practical absolute and a linchpin of the contemporary feminist movement,[48] this text from Mary Anne Warren

---

[45]Janet Radcliffe Richards, *The Sceptical Feminist*, p. 239.

[46]H. Tristram Engelhardt, Jr., "Concluding Remarks," to William Bondeson et al. (eds.), *Abortion and the Status of the Fetus* (Dordrecht: D. Reidel, 1983), p. 334. On the issue of abortion as a "symbolic linchpin," see Kristin Luker, *Abortion and the Politics of Motherhood*, p. 118. Interestingly, the same word "linchpin" is used by Beverly Wildung Harrison, Our Right to Choose, p. 237, to describe the regnant feminist view of procreative choice.

[47]Andrea Dworkin, *Letters From a War Zone: Writings 1976–1989*, pp. 144–145.

[48]A woman's absolute right to abortion without having to make any excuses for it is also the thought of Ninia Baehr, *Abortion Without Apology: A Radical History for the 1990s* (Boston: South End Press, 1990); the same view is expressed by Lynn Chancer, "Abortion Without Apology," in Marlene Gerber Fried (ed.), *From Abortion to Reproductive Freedom: Transforming a Movement* (Boston: South End Press, 1990), pp. 113–119. According to Monique Dumais, *Les droits des femmes*, p. 75, the right to

is representative:

> For women, the right to abort often seems a necessary
> condition for the free exercise of all other human
> rights, since there is not and never has been a fully
> reliable method of contraception (other than celibacy),
> and since bearing an unwanted child can be disastrous
> for a woman's health, happiness, personal life and
> career aspirations, and may even be fatal. No woman
> who constantly faces this threat can be fully free or
> equal.[49]

What Warren says in a paragraph, others put in a slogan: "A
woman's right to abortion is akin to her right to be."[50] Still others will
put it in a chant: "Our bodies, our lives, our right to decide."

Transition to the Final Chapter

As she writes in favor of abortion, secular feminist Gloria
Steinem speaks of it as an issue of "reproductive freedom—the right to
decide when and whether to have children." Reproductive freedom with
abortion as its linchpin is the central goal of women all over the world,
she avers; it is part of a democratic tidal wave:

> Make no mistake, these are not "little" stories. They are
> voices in a worldwide chorus that is adding the female
> half of humanity to the goal of global democracy. . .

---

abortion has become "the spearhead of the entire feminist battle." Cf. Eva R. Rubin,
Abortion, Politics and the Court: Roe v. Wade and its Aftermath, p. viii: "I think it
(abortion) is a necessary alternative at this time and should not be forbidden by law.
I also see reproductive control of some kind as a necessary part of the women's rights
movement."

[49]Mary Anne Warren, *The Nature of Woman: An Encyclopedia and Guide to the
Literature*, s. v. "Abortion," p. 2. Cf. Nadean Bishop, "Abortion: The Controversial
Choice," in Jo Freeman (ed.), *Women: A Feminist Perspective* (Third edition) (Palo
Alto, CA: Mayfield, 1984): Abortion is the core of reproductive freedom (p. 39).

[50]The slogan appears on p. 5 of a book put out by the Committee for Abortion
Rights and Against Sterilization Abuse, *Women Under Attack: Victories, Backlash and
the Fight for Reproductive Freedom* (Susan Davis, ed.) (Boston: South End Press, 1988).

And the point of democracy is not: *What* gets decided?
The point is: *Who* decides?[51]

Steinem is being true to the insights of Simone de Beauvoir's
project of existentialist ethics in its move away from the object and
toward the subject.[52] To those who would agree with Simone de
Beauvoir and Steinem, it is enough that the *woman* make the decision.
That women have "the right to choose" ends the abortion discussion. To
those who believe it important to ask *what* it is that is being chosen, we
must continue.[53]

While it may be true that abortion practically defines the
women's movement in the view of radical feminists, *pace* Catherine
MacKinnon and Beverly Wildung Harrison, radical feminism is not
feminism.[54] In our final chapter, we shall show that the link between
abortion and feminism is by no means inescapable. Unable to change the
nature of the abortion action, as it were, feminist ideology has to
attempt to change the attitudes of the subject undergoing the abortion.
Feminist labors notwithstanding, the nature of the abortion procedure
along with its attendant ambiguity and ambivalence will simply not go

---

[51]Gloria Steinem, "Foreword," to Angela Bonavoglia (ed.), *The Choices We Made:
Twenty-Five Women and Men Speak Out About Abortion*, p. xiii. See also Gloria
Steinem, "A Basic Human Right," *Ms.* 18 (July/August 1989), p. 39: "The most crucial
question of democracy, feminism, and simple self-respect is not: *What* get decided?
That comes second. The first question is: *Who* decides?"

[52]Cf. especially Simone de Beauvoir's "Introduction" to *The Second Sex*, pp. xii–xxix.

[53]A long-standing tradition in Catholic moral thought takes it as a given that there are
two poles of morality, the objective and the subjective. The latter is interested in *who*
does the deciding, the former deals with *what* is being decided. Together, they form
an integral ethical theory. Addressing as she does only one half of the moral equation,
Steinem, in my view, plunges into subjectivism.

[54]The expression, "Radical feminism *is* feminism," belongs to Catherine MacKinnon,
"Feminism, Marxism, Method and the State: Toward Feminist Jurisprudence," in
Katherine T. Bartlett and Rosanne Kennedy (eds.), *Feminist Legal Theory* (New
Perspectives on Law, Culture, and Society) (Boulder: Westview Press, 1991), p. 182.
Cf. Beverly Wildung Harrison, "Situating the Dilemma of Abortion Historically,"
Conscience 11 2 (March/April 1990), p. 16: "I was once a liberal feminist; I believe that
almost all of us began that way. My pilgrimage is the pilgrimage of so many women
during the last decades and, as Zillah Eisenstein has argued, liberal feminism, if it is
not to die, must become radical."

away for feminism. The stage is now set for pro-life feminism.

In a 1986 essay, Beverly Harrison discusses the pregnant woman, the child in the womb, and the moral imagination:

> It is morally wiser for a woman deliberating about abortion early in pregnancy to recognize that she has an *active* obligation to think of the embryo or fetus *not* as an existing human life, but as a powerfully potential soon-to-be human life that will require deep moral commitments and claim her obligations dramatically. The most conscientious decisions at this point in pregnancy can be made only if a woman or girl can free her imagination to ponder what it may mean to have a child. There is much to be gained morally from helping pregnant women to learn to think this way.[55]

If we free our moral imagination, is abortion the best we can do? Our concluding chapter will attempt to provide an answer.

---

[55]Beverly Wildung Harrison, "Feminist Realism," *Christianity and Crisis* 45 no. 10 (July 14, 1986), p. 235: author's emphasis.

CHAPTER SIX

PRO-LIFE FEMINISM

Pitting women against their own offspring is not only morally offensive, it is psychologically and politically destructive. Women will never climb to equality and social empowerment over mounds of dead fetuses, numbering now in the millions. As long as women choose to bear children, they stand to gain from the same constellation of attitudes and institutions that will also protect the fetus in the woman's womb—and they stand to lose from the cultural assumptions that support permissive abortion. Despite temporary conflicts of interest, feminine and fetal liberation are ultimately one and the same cause.[1]

In this chapter, our aim is to construct the outlines of a feminism without abortion as its linchpin. If 1949 witnessed the birth of *The Second Sex* and the pro-choice message of Simone de Beauvoir, it was also the year of Romano Guardini's *The Rights of the Unborn*.[2] If 1986 was the year of Simone de Beauvoir's death, it also saw the publication of one of the major criticisms of the abortion mentality, one which envisioned a "pro-life feminism."[3] Our previous chapter shows pro-choice feminism

---

[1]Sidney Callahan, "Abortion and the Sexual Agenda: A Case for Prolife Feminism," *Commonweal* 113 8 (1986), p. 236.

[2]Romano Guardini, *Das Recht des werdendes Menschenlebens. Zur Diskussion um den Paragraph 218 des Strafgesetzbuches* (Tübingen and Stuttgart: Wunderlich, 1949). It has been reprinted in Guardini's two-volume *Sorge un den Menschen* (Würzburg: Werkbund, 1962), I, pp. 162–185. References are to the 1962 edition.

[3]Cf. Sidney Callahan, "Abortion and the Sexual Agenda."

as unable to imagine a feminism without abortion as its linchpin; in this concluding chapter we discuss a feminism that can, namely, pro-life feminism.[4]

Ideas Have Consequences

In a book with the innocuous-sounding title, *Ideas Have*

---

[4]In addition to Guardini's 1949 essay and Sidney Callahan's 1986 article, other works of pro-life feminism include Janet E. Smith, "Abortion and Moral Development: Listening with Different Ears," *International Philosophical Quarterly* 28 (1988), pp. 311–51; Celia Wolf-Devine, "Abortion and the 'Feminine Voice,'" *Public Affairs Quarterly* 3 no. 3 (1989), pp. 81–97; and Stephen J. Heaney (ed.), *Abortion: A New Generation of Catholic Responses* (Braintree, MA: The Pope John Center, 1992), especially Part Three: "Feminist Issues." Elements of pro-life feminism are found in Janet E. Smith, "Abortion as a Feminist Concern," *Human Life Review* 4 no. 3 (1978), pp. 62–76; Edmée Mottini-Coulon, *De l'ontologie à l'éthique par la maternité* ("Problèmes et controverses") (Paris: Vrin, 1981); Mary R. Joyce, *Women and Choice: A New Beginning* (St. Cloud, MN: LifeCom, 1986); Ronda Chervin, *Feminine, Free and Faithful* (San Francisco: Ignatius Press, 1986); and Maggie Gallagher, *Enemies of Eros: How the Sexual Revolution Is Killing Family, Marriage, and Sex and What Can We Do About It* (Chicago: Bonus Books, 1989). There is also a collection of pro-life feminist articles in Gail Grenier Sweet, (ed.), *Pro-Life Feminism: Different Voices* (Toronto: Life Cycle Books). Several of the articles appearing in Sidney and Daniel Callahan (eds.), *Abortion: Understanding Differences* (New York: Plenum Press, 1984) can serve as examples of pro-life feminism; one of them is Sidney Callahan, "Value Choices in Abortion," pp. 285–301; another is Mary Meehan, "More Trouble Than They're Worth? Children and Abortion," pp. 145–170. See also the articles by Juli Loesch Wiley, "Solidarity and Shalom," pp. 39–50; and Sandra O. Smithson, O.S.F., "In Him Was Life, John 1:4," pp. 121–130, both found in Phyllis Tickle (general editor), *Confessing Conscience: Churched Women on Abortion* (Nashville: Abingdon Press, 1990). See also two writings by Denise Lardner Carmody, *The Double Cross: Ordination, Abortion and Catholic Feminism* (New York: Crossroad, 1986), and *Virtuous Woman: Reflections on Christian Feminist Ethics* (Maryknoll: Orbis Books, 1992). Several articles on the theme of a pro-life feminism are found in an unusual and uneven volume. See Jeannine Parvati Baker, Frederick Baker, and Tamara Slayton, *Conscious Conception: Elemental Journey Through the Labyrinth of Sexuality* (Berkeley: North Atlantic Books, 1986). See especially Juli Loesch, "Our Bodies, Their Lives," pp. 212–203, and two entries by Jeannine Parvati Baker, "Pro-life Feminism: A Spiritual Perspective," pp. 214–217, and "Pro Life/Choice," pp. 226–236. A similar listing of pro-life feminist writings is found in Elizabeth Mensch and Alan Freeman, *The Politics of Virtue: Is Abortion Debatable?* (Durham and London: Duke University Press, 1993), p. 165, note 18. There is also a journal called *Studies in Prolife Feminism*.

Consequences, Richard Weaver wrote in 1948—exactly one hundred years after the Seneca Falls Convention[5] and one year before the publication of *The Second Sex*—that "the social seduction of the female sex has occurred on a vast scale."[6] If proof were needed for Weaver's contention, the abortion problematic as we have seen it unfolding from Simone de Beauvoir to Beverly Wildung Harrison provides it.[7] Ideas indeed *do* have consequences.

In our examination of the writings of the four feminist theoreticians of abortion, two ideas have been especially prominent. The first we saw at the beginning, namely, the culturalist hypothesis of Simone de Beauvoir that "one is not born, but rather becomes, a woman." The second which we discover at the end of our journey is Beverly Harrison's espousal of the bodyright argument as the key to her theological enterprise of finding a high moral ground for a pro-choice position on the abortion question. As we reflect upon the birth of an abortion rights mentality in the evolution of these two ideas, we might well want to consider the possibility that we find the second in the Christian Harrison because we find the first in the atheist Beauvoir.

Beauvoir and Guardini on Abortion

Who really won World War II? In a *Festschrift* volume dedicated to one of her mentors and colleagues at Union Theological Seminary, Beverly Harrison observes that Roger Shinn came to see that World War

---

[5] Carol Gilligan begins the fifth chapter—"Women's Rights and Women's Judgment"—of *In a Different Voice* with a recounting of the 1848 Seneca Falls Convention. Marilyn French, *The War Against Women* (New York: Summit Books, 1992), regards the 1848 meeting as the start of feminism as a political movement. See also Riane Eisler, *The Chalice and the Blade: Our History and Our Future* (San Francisco: Harper and Row, 1987), p. 165.

[6] Richard Weaver, *Ideas Have Consequences* (Chicago: University of Chicago Press, 1948), p. 179.

[7] Weaver traces the decline of the West to the late medieval period's attack on universals and regards the notion of the equality of the sexes as a destructive notion. Both ideas are central to the existentialism of Sartre and Beauvoir.

II cost humanity dearly, not only in lives but also in ideals.[8] Harrison and Shinn are not alone in pondering the effects of the Second World War.[9]

Four years after the end of the bloodiest war in human history, the year 1949 saw the publication of Simone de Beauvoir's massive *The Second Sex* and Romano Guardini's brief *The Rights of the Unborn*. Both works were written with the horrors of the Second World War fresh in the minds of their authors. Both writers believed they had a plan for civilization to follow for the future and spelled this out: Beauvoir, as we have seen, in her analysis of woman's existential situation, concludes that killing is "the key to the whole mystery" of woman's subjugation. Guardini, on the other hand, insists that the defense of civilization requires the defense of the fetus;[10] any view which denigrates the dignity of the child in the womb injures the dignity of the mother and places humanity on the road to barbarism.[11]

The positions staked out by Beauvoir and Guardini bear the

---

[8]Cf. Beverly Wildung Harrison, "The Quest for Justice," in Beverly Wildung Harrison, Robert Stivers, and R. Stone (eds.), *The Public Vocation of Christian Ethics* (New York: Pilgrim Press, 1987), pp. 289–310, especially at pp. 297–298, where she cites a text of Shinn: "*For it seems sometimes that even the ideals of civilized men must be written among the casualties of war. . . .* The question is whether we can find any meaning in the confusion and conflict of this age—whether God is here" (emphasis found in Harrison's text).

[9]Who won the Second World War? Jesuit James Schall, *Welcome Number 4,000,000,000* (Canfield OH: Alba House, 1977), pp. 112–113, cites George Tavard to the effect that the brutality unleashed by the war gives evidence that it is by no means certain Hitler lost the war. Bernard Nathanson with Richard Ostling, *Aborting America*, p. 250, points out that the drive to legalize abortion came about only after Stalin, Hitler, the Holocaust and Hiroshima. Roger Rosenblatt, *Life Itself: Abortion in the American Mind* (New York: Random House, 1992), traces the rise of the abortion mentality to the shift from the humanistic to the social sciences; he dates the shift from World War II.

[10]Romano Guardini, *Das Recht des werdendes Menschenlebens*, pp. 169–171. Both the feminist philosopher and the Catholic theologian touch upon the question of the bodyright argument. See Beauvoir's comments in *Memoirs of a Dutiful Daughter* and compare them with those of Guardini, p. 172.

[11]Cf. Guardini, pp. 172–173: if the fetus is regarded as a part of the mother, why not say that human beings belong to the state? If parents can destroy their children, then how can the state be prevented from doing the same?

seeds of a pro-choice feminism and a pro-life feminism. The first five chapters of this work have endeavored to understand Beauvoir's 1949 claims regarding abortion as we examine the underpinnings of pro-choice feminism. This concluding chapter takes up Guardini's vision with its promise of a pro-life feminism.

"The Question That Will Not Go Away"

Has abortion proven to be what Lawrence Lader told Betty Friedan it was? Is abortion, as Lawrence Lader has contended, "the ultimate freedom"? Has this final freedom ushered in a golden age of an enduring sexual revolution, as Lader thought it would? While the atheist Simone de Beauvoir is able to regard the right to abortion as the "essential feminist message," and the Christian Beverly Harrison speaks of "our right to choose" as "a social good that all women require" (*Our Right to Choose*, p. 3), other feminists are not so sanguine regarding the abortion liberty. Andrea Dworkin sees the decriminalization of abortion to be little more than what she calls "the final fillip" to the sexual revolution, one that serves male lust more than female needs.[12] Mary Daly does not agree with Lader's contention. Neither should we.[13]

Ingrid Bengis, herself a child of the sexual revolution, tries to put her finger on it: "No matter what a pregnancy is an expression of, it is always an expression of a need more complicated than the needs that abortion can satisfy."[14] According to Bengis, our supposedly enlightened society has a way of packaging solutions to problems which glosses over some very important issues; it tells women "nothing about the fact that a general callousness in human relationships is what makes abortions necessary in the first place."[15]

---

[12]Cf. Andrea Dworkin, *Right-Wing Women*, p. 95.

[13]That the right to abortion and the sexual revolution are far from being woman's ultimate freedoms, cf. Mary Daly, *Beyond God the Father*, p. 112.

[14]Ingrid Bengis, *Combat in the Erogenous Zones* (New York: Alfred A. Knopf, 1972), pp. 78–79.

[15]*Ibid.* Edwin A. Schur, *The Awareness Trap: Self-Absorption Instead of Social Change* (New York: McGraw-Hill, 1976), p. 129, is critical of Bengis for personalizing the abortion issue so much that "we can never really tell where she stands." Bengis is praised, on the other hand, by John Gordon, *The Myth of the Monstrous Male, and*

Whatever it was that lurked behind Betty Friedan's famous "problem that had no name,"[16] the right to abortion is not the answer. Abortion remains, simply put, the question that will not go away.[17] In the words of Black American poet Gwendolyn Brooks, "Abortions will not let you forget."[18] As Adrienne Rich expresses the matter: "Abortion is violence: a deep desperate violence inflicted by a woman upon, first of all, herself."[19]

Abortion haunts the human landscape. Even staunch abortion advocates such as Laurence Tribe attest to this fact:

> Most of us are torn by the abortion question. . . For nearly everyone, the deepest truth is that the clash is an internal one. Few people who really permit themselves to feel all of what is at stake in the abortion issue can avoid a profound sense of internal division.[20]

The Haunting Violence

Abortion is a haunting experience, and this haunting character stalks the literature. Linda Bird Francke gives expression to it as she

---

Other Feminist Fables, for writing "an honest feminist memoir" (p. 148).

[16]Cf. chapter one of Betty Friedan, *The Feminine Mystique* (New York: Dell, 1963).

[17]Cf. the last two chapters of Rosalind Pollack Petchesky, *Abortion and Woman's Choice: The State, Sexuality, and Reproductive Freedom* (revised edition) (The Northeastern Series in Feminist Theory) (Boston: Northeastern University Press, 1990).

[18]Cf. Gwendolyn Brooks' poem, "The Mother."

[19]Adrienne Rich, *Of Woman Born: Motherhood as Experience and Institution*, pp. 268–269. The tortured cadence of the text captures, for me at least, some of the violence of which Rich is speaking.

[20]Laurence Tribe, *Abortion: The Clash of Absolutes*, pp. 229–230. The text continues: "A story told in a recent newspaper interview by Dr. Warren Hern, director of the Boulder Abortion Clinic in Colorado, demonstrates this well. Dr. Hern recounts calling one of his closest friends, a 'strongly pro-choice' physician who had 'done abortions himself.' When Dr. Hern told his friend that he was at work at his office, his friend asked, 'Still killing babies this late in the afternoon?' Dr. Hern recalls: 'It was like a knife in my gut. . . it really upset me. What it conveys is that no matter how supportive people may be, there is still a horror at what I do.'"

describes the time following her own abortion when she and her husband plan for the future:

> It certainly does make more sense not to be having a baby right now—we say that to each other all the time. But I have this ghost now. A very little ghost that only appears when I'm seeing something beautiful, like the full moon on the ocean last weekend. And the baby waves at me. And I wave at the baby. "Of course, we have room," I cry to the ghost. "Of course, we do."[21]

Simone de Beauvoir and Carol Gilligan attest to this haunting character of the abortion experience. Here is the author of *The Second Sex*:

> For if it is not true that abortion is murder, it still cannot be considered in the same light as a mere contraceptive technique; an event has taken place that is a definite beginning, the progress of which is to be stopped. . . . Some women will be haunted by the memory of this child which has not come into being (p. 462).

Speaking of the conflicting emotions felt by women as they contemplate how their abortion decisions will touch the others in their lives, Carol Gilligan speaks in her own voice:

> Conflict arises specifically over the issue of hurting. When no option exists that can be construed as being in the best interest of everybody, when responsibilities conflict and decision entails the sacrifice of somebody's needs, then the woman confronts the seemingly

---

[21]Linda Bird Francke, *The Ambivalence of Abortion*, pp. 16–17. The *New York Times* ran her article, "There Just Wasn't Room In Our Lives for Another Baby," on its op-ed page on May 14, 1976. The ghost haunted Francke for six months before it went away (p. 345). Cf. Mary Kenny, *Abortion: The Whole Story*, p. 24. She cites the ghost story and notes the fittingness of the word "ambivalence" as the one which best describes a woman's attitude towards the experience of abortion (p. 19).

impossible task of choosing the victim.[22]

We see the anguish of the haunting violence that is abortion in Gilligan's poignant expression, "the seemingly impossible task of choosing the victim."

Though Gilligan has her share of critics for the way she expresses herself on the matter of abortion, the language of the women who speak is real enough, with all the emotional complexities and rational tergiversations that accompany the haunting ambivalence that is abortion. At the very least, Gilligan perceives in the abortion experience some of the real paradoxes of our modern world, contradictions that Gilligan did not create; they go with the territory of abortion. Gilligan touches a responsive chord with her studies on the psychology of abortion.

Sallie Tisdale was a nurse who worked at an abortion clinic; she resorts to an oxymoron to explain what it is that she does: abortions are bad but in this real world of ours, someone has to do them, someone has to exercise what she calls this "merciful violence," this "sweet brutality" that is abortion.[23]

Describing herself as a "proabortionist with a bad secular conscience,"[24] Magda Denes touches the heart of the matter with a simple observation: if abortion does *not* trouble you, you are not normal.[25] While it is true that some feminists will latch on to the

---

[22] *In a Different Voice*, p. 80. Cf. Barbara Katz Rothman, *The Tentative Pregnancy: Prenatal Diagnosis and the Future of Motherhood*, p. 243. She comments on this passage from Gilligan in the context of women undergoing amniocentesis.

[23] Cf. Sallie Tisdale, "We Do Abortions Here," *Harper's Magazine* 275 no. 1649 (1987), pp. 66–70.

[24] Magda Denes, *In Necessity and Sorrow: Life and Death in an Abortion Hospital*, p. xv. In *Our Right to Choose*, pp. 183–184, Beverly Harrison believes that Denes' "powerful work" generally advances Harrison's version of the bodyright argument.

[25] Cf. *In Necessity and Sorrow*, p. 147. Denes is relating the words of a black physician who performs abortions: "I suppose that if you want to go below the surface, and thinking about it, I do feel you'd be an abnormal person if you could really honestly say that abortion didn't bother you at all. It goes against all things which are natural. It's a termination of life, however you look at it. It just goes against the grain. It must. . . . " See also David Plante, *Difficult Women: A Memoir of Three* (New York: E. P. Dutton, 1984), p. 153. In the course of an interview, Germaine Greer tells Plante

bodyright argument—adumbrated by Beauvoir and elaborated by Harrison—with all their might and claim abortion is justified for any and all reasons, "for whatever reasons," here too, we find that the question of abortion will not go away, and some are honest enough to say so.[26]

The same author who contends that one would be abnormal *not* to be troubled by abortion also wants abortion on demand at the mother's request to be legal throughout the whole world, and safe, and dignified, and free, and to be "supported with mercy by the church."[27] Magda Denes wants it all from a problematic notoriously disinclined to give it all. She is aware of this, of course: "Abortion is an abomination unless it is experienced as a human event of great sorrow and terrible necessity."[28]

If abortion is the ultimate freedom, the feminist revolution is over. The violence has won. If we can envision a world without abortion, the revolution has not yet begun. It is a world without abortion that would be the one to work for, not the world in which abortion already is a violent and surgical solution to a human relational problem. What Stella Browne imagined to be the key to a new world for women, what Lawrence Lader imagined to be women's final freedom has become something far different.

In their awareness of the ambiguity and ambivalence

---

that pro-lifers "are entirely right to make us aware of the horror of abortion because it is terrible."

[26]Though the right to abortion may appear to be so central and necessary to feminist ideology that there should be no restrictions, some feminists remain uneasy about the question that will not go away. One of them is Ruth Hubbard, *The Politics of Women's Biology* (New Brunswick: Rutgers University Press, 1990), p. 197: "A woman must have the right to abort a fetus, whatever her reasons, precisely because it is a decision about her body and about how she will live her life. But decisions about what kind of baby to bear are inevitably bedeviled by overt and unspoken judgments about which lives are 'worth living.'" Hubbard goes back to the same thought, adding a clarification that puts the question of abortion not in a solitary but in a communal, societal context: "Yes, a woman must have the right to terminate her pregnancy, whatever her reasons, but she must also feel empowered not to terminate it, confident that the society will do what it can to enable her and her child to live fulfilling lives."

[27]Cf. Magda Denes, *In Necessity and Sorrow*, p. xv.

[28]*Ibid*, p. 245.

surrounding the situation of an unwanted pregnancy, the women who speak of their abortion experiences give witness to the fact that the humanity of the fetus is not the real *punctum dolens* of the abortion controversy. In a sense, all of Beverly Harrison's labors in trying to raise enough questions regarding the status of the fetus to enable abortions in good conscience until viability end up stillborn.[29] Everybody really knows what goes on in an abortion, and no one is really doubting but that the fetus is human.

> Since the old ethic has not yet been fully displaced it has been necessary to separate the idea of abortion from the idea of killing, which continues to be socially abhorrent. The result has been a curious avoidance of the scientific fact, which everyone really knows, that human life begins at conception and is continuous whether intra- or extra-uterine until death.[30]

What I stated at the very beginning of this work, I feel must be repeated once again at the end: it is not the humanity of the fetus that is at issue. At stake is *ours*.[31]

The Pro-Life Worldview

What sort of world will we live in? The world of business as usual or the world that ought to be? We touch on the question of worldviews—one old, one new, one going out, one coming in, one

---

[29]Beverly Harrison, *Our Right to Choose*, p. 129, chides Susan Nicholson (and anyone else for that matter) for accepting without question John Noonan's claim about the value of fetal life in the Christian tradition. Harrison thinks the real question is female sexuality, not fetal humanity.

[30]The text comes from the editorial, "A New Ethic for Medicine and Society," *California Medicine: The Western Journal of Medicine* 113 no. 3 (1970), pp. 67–68.

[31]Cf. Stanley Hauerwas, "Abortion: The Agent's Perspective," *The American Ecclesiastical Review*, 167 no. 1 (January 1973), p. 105: "What is at stake in this question is whether we deny significant aspects of our own being by our failure to regard and treat the fetus as life." According to Robert Kress, *Whither Womankind? The Humanity of Women* (St. Meinrad, IN: Abbey Press, 1975), p. 210: "All of these attempts to denigrate the fetus end up, of course, denigrating all of human existence. 'In our beginning is our end' is, after all, much more than a pious platitude."

moving backward, one progressing.[32] Our age has to decide which is
which:

> The traditional Western ethics has always placed great
> emphasis on the intrinsic worth and equal value of
> every human life regardless of its age or condition. This
> ethic has had the blessing of the Judeo-Christian
> heritage and has been the basis for our laws and much
> of our moral policy. The reverence for each and every
> human life has also been a keystone of Western
> medicine and is the ethic which has caused physicians
> to try to preserve, protect, repair, prolong and enhance
> every human life which comes under their surveillance.
> The traditional ethics is still clearly dominant, but there
> is much to suggest that it is being eroded at its core and
> may eventually even be abandoned. This of course will
> produce profound changes in Western medicine and in
> Western society.[33]

A Question of Anthropology

In the four feminist authors whose thought we have examined,
we have detected a faulty anthropology. God created human beings
intelligent. God created human beings free. It is in their choice of
abortion as a way of exercising this intelligence and freedom that their
anthropology is fatally flawed. Simply stated, abortion is forgetting that

---

[32]The worldview approach is treated in some detail by Stephen M. Smith,
"Worldview, Language, and Radical Feminism: an Evangelical Appeal," in Alvin
Kimel, Jr., (ed.), *Speaking the Christian God: The Holy Trinity and the Challenge of
Feminism*. Grand Rapids: Eerdmans, 1992, pp. 258–275. Smith defines a worldview
as "a metaphysical vision that defines reality, identity, morality, and destiny" (p. 260).
Cf. Carl Horn, "'World Views' and Public Policy," in Carl Horn (ed.), *Whose Values?
The Battle for Morality in Pluralistic America* (Ann Arbor: Servant Books, 1985), pp.
167–186. For an instance of the worldview approach as it pertains to the abortion
question, see Gary Crum and Thelma McCormack, *Abortion: Pro-choice or Pro-life?*
(The American University Press Public Policy Series) (Washington, D.C.: The
American University Press, 1992).

[33]Editorial, "A New Ethic for Medicine and Society."

it is *God* who creates human beings. In a sense, they want it all from life. But it is in the nature of reality that human beings cannot have it all. Either the bodyright argument is correct: "Our bodies, our lives, our right to decide," or else the text from scripture has it right:

> Your body, you know, is the temple of the Holy Spirit, who is in you since you have received him from God. You are not your own property; you have been bought and paid for. That is why you should use your body for the glory of God (1 Cor 6:19-20).

Limitation is an integral part of who we are as male and female human beings. Here, for example, is Magda Denes, as she ends her third chapter, "Saline Floor: Patients and Parents":

> I am caught by the horror of helplessness and apathy that lies at the core of most of these lives. I am astonished at the meaning of being female. To be impregnable suddenly looks to me the heart of vulnerability, the very essence of dependence and limitation.[34]

In Simone de Beauvoir's atheist vision, human beings are alone in the universe. Women seek through abortion as much power and control as possible before passing from being into nothingness. Indeed, abortion is proof of this aloneness: faced with the existence of another, the choice is to say no. This, in fact, is what the atheist does. This is the atheistic origin of abortion: when confronted with the existence of the *other*, human beings can always say no.[35] At times they do, as Beverly Harrison attests:

> For a vital human life to be born, a woman must say

---

[34]Cf. Magda Denes, *In Necessity and Sorrow*, p. 126. Cf. also Martha C. Nussbaum, *The Fragility of Goodness: Luck and Ethics in Greek Tragedy and Philosophy* (New York: Cambridge University Press, 1986), who argues—on the basis of Greek philosophy and literature—that the good human life is *not* under total human control. It is especially the women who appear in Greek literature—Hecuba and Antigone among them—that are the special object of Nussbaum's study.

[35]We remember that the epigram of Simone de Beauvoir's first novel, *She Came to Stay*, is Hegel's "Each consciousness pursues the death of the other."

yes in a strong and active way and enter positively into
a life-bearing, demanding, and, at times, extremely
painful process. Freedom to say yes, which, of course,
also means the freedom to say no, is constitutive of the
sacred covenant of life itself (*Our Right to Choose*, p.
256).

The reason why the abortion situation is a question that will not
go away is that it poses to us the question of God's existence and human
aloneness. Women often feel alone in facing an unwanted pregnancy.
While their men may have left or threatened to leave, the fetus remains,
a tangible other. Disgusted at the way things are,[36] women are tempted
to regard abortion as a possible solution to a human problem. Abortion
is the choice to remain alone, birth is the choice to believe in the *other*.
The child in the womb is not only a symbol of divinity besieged by
modernity.[37] The child in the womb is a chance to transcend our
loneliness and reach the other. Where Simone de Beauvoir sees in
motherhood no chance to transcend and hence decides to emulate
masculine modes of transcendence, we find precisely the way of
breaking out and finding true transcendence. The existential loneliness
is overcome, not by women acting like men but by women loving like
women.

Try as Harrison might to inject a social component into the
abortion problematic, the logic of ideas dictates that the cornerstone of
her pro-choice edifice, the bodily integrity argument, in the final
analysis, brings her hoped-for socially conscious feminism back to
Beauvoir's isolated self as the touchstone of reality.[38] In a word, we are

---

[36]Cf. Harrison, *Our Right to Choose*, p. 184, who relates the comment she found in
Magda Denes, *In Necessity and Sorrow*: "My rage. . . is at the human predicament."

[37]Cf. Anne E. Patrick, "Virtue, Providence, and the Endangered Self: Some Religious
Dimensions of the Abortion Debate," in Patricia Beattie Jung and Thomas Shannon
(eds.), *Abortion and Catholicism: The American Debate*, p. 180 note 9.

[38]In *Memoirs of a Dutiful Daughter*, p. 188, Beauvoir is contemplating the changes in
her life and how they are reflected in her diary entries: "My diary gives very little
indication; I passed over many things in silence, and I couldn't see things in their
proper perspective. Yet on re-reading it, a few salient facts emerge. . . . 'I am alone.
One is always alone, I shall always be alone.'"

back to a world without God.[39]

A Pro-Life Feminism

    Talking about pro-life and pro-choice worldviews, Sidney and Daniel Callahan, parents of a large family, raise the question: who is the authentic realist and who the real idealist on the abortion question?[40] Daniel calls himself a "51% prochoice advocate."[41] Sidney elaborates a pro-life feminism. The world as it ought to be is Sidney's choice as she makes a choice for life, fully aware of all its attendant difficulties. She phrases her position in the context of a Christian worldview:

> Thus, in any debate over bringing life into the world, the believer in ultimate goodness will probably cast the question as one of "Why not?" rather than "Why?"[42]

In commenting on his wife's position, Daniel opts for the world as it is, that is, he opts for abortion, albeit with a heavy heart. After acknowledging that hers would be the healthier moral universe; he adds: "I cannot soar but can only muddle through at a more pedestrian level."

    There are many feminisms. While on some issues there will be differences of opinion among pro-life feminists as well, those who embrace this vision are united in their conviction that "no matter what a pregnancy is an expression of, it is always an expression of a need more complicated than the needs that abortion can satisfy."[43] Abortion

---

[39]We remember Beauvoir's observation in *The Ethics of Ambiguity*, p. 16: "A god can pardon, efface, and compensate. But if God does not exist, man's faults are inexpiable." Another way of expressing this: "Without God, all things are possible."

[40]See the volume they co-edited, *Abortion: Understanding Differences*. Each has written an article upon which the other has commented and both make telling points.

[41]Cf. Daniel Callahan, "The Abortion Debate: Is Progress Possible?" in Sidney and Daniel Callahan (eds.), *Abortion: Understanding Differences*, pp. 320–321.

[42]Sidney Callahan, "Value Choices in Abortion," in *Abortion: Understanding Differences*, p. 294.

[43]Cf. Ingrid Bengis, *Combat in the Erogenous Zones*, pp. 78–79. Bengis herself is not a pro-life feminist.

offends against justice; its "terrible finality" is haunting.[44] Pro-life feminists take such insights as their starting point.

Some Elements of a Pro-Life Feminism

1. Pro-life feminism looks upon the practice of human abortion as a violent, unacceptable, solution—*masculine*, if you will—to a human relational problem.[45] *Pace* feminist arguments, abortion exploits women. Faye Ginsburg quotes the words of a leader in the pro-life movement:

> Pro-abortion feminists open themselves to charges of crass hypocrisy by indulging in the very same behavior for which they condemn men: the unethical use of power to usurp the rights of the less powerful.[46]

2. Pro-life feminism seeks a more inclusive ideal of justice than the standard feminist bodyright argument. All things considered, pro-life feminism regards the bodyright argument to be more in line with an atomistic, individualistic view of the human person than it is with the social consciousness of authentic feminism.

> The same legal tradition which in our society guarantees the right to control one's own body firmly recognizes the wrongfulness of harming other bodies, however immature, dependent, different looking, or powerless. The handicapped, the retarded, and newborns are legally protected from deliberate harm. *Pro-life feminists reject the suppositions that would except*

---

[44]Mary Meehan, "More Trouble Than They're Worth? Children and Abortion," in Sidney and Daniel Callahan (eds.), *Abortion: Understanding Differences*, p. 147, speaks of the violent nature and the "terrible finality" of abortion.

[45]See the pertinent remarks on the patriarchal character of pro-choice feminism made by Anne M. Maloney, "Cassandra's Fate: Why Feminists Ought to Be Pro-life," pp. 209–217. What I call "pro-choice feminism" is referred to by Maloney as "mainline feminism." She explains that her use of the term is occasioned "by the simple fact that the great majority of feminists *are* pro-abortion" (p. 210).

[46]Faye Ginsburg, "The 'Word-Made' Flesh: The Disembodiment of Gender in the Abortion Debate," p. 72.

the unborn from this protection.[47]

3. Pro-life feminism seeks to transform the autonomy and choice arguments of feminist ideology and rhetoric into an expanded sense of responsibility. In a word, pro-life feminism is against instrumentality in human relationships. Pro-choicers, in defining abortion into feminism, define the unborn out of personal, relational existence. As Sidney Callahan has it, pro-life feminism goes "from the moral claim of the contingent value of fetal life to the moral claim for the intrinsic value of human life."[48]

4. Pro-life feminism aspires to an inclusive, expanded sense of membership in the human community. While the pro-choice feminism we have seen finds it well-nigh impossible to think of the abortion issue in the sense of preserving both the mother and the unborn child, pro-life feminism is animated by a both/and approach: *both* the woman *and* the child.[49]

Guardini in *The Rights of the Unborn* has this social concern uppermost in his thoughts as he envisions a world in which both mother

---

[47]Sidney Callahan, "Abortion and the Sexual Agenda," p. 234: my emphasis.

[48]For this and other of the points, see the strategy of Sidney Callahan, "Abortion and the Sexual Agenda," pp. 232–238. Rosalind Pollack Petchesky, "A Framework for Choice," *Christianity and Crisis* 46 no. 10 (July 14, 1986), pp. 247–250, is probably right when she observes that "most feminists will hardly give a sisterly embrace to such 'pro-life feminists' as Sidney Callahan" (p. 247). By *most* feminists, of course, Petchesky refers to "pro-choice," "mainline" feminists such as Catherine MacKinnon for whom "radical feminism *is* feminism." By defining abortion *into* feminism, Petchesky is able to dismiss pro-life feminists. The pluralist "mainstream" feminist tent is not *that* big. Callahan, of course, must be aware she is swimming against the current feminists. If I may paraphrase her view, she is saying in effect, "pro-life feminism *is* feminism."

[49]Whatever moral theory is utilized by pro-life feminism, *inclusivism* would seem to be one of its distinguishing features. In *L'existentialisme et la sagesse des nations* (Paris: Les éditions Nagel, 1948), Simone de Beauvoir reflects: "All the faults and even all the crimes by means of which individuals assert themselves against society can be forgiven. But when someone deliberately attempts to degrade a human being into a mere thing—this is an affront and a scandal which is inexpiable. This is the one sin against humanity which cries out for vengeance. When such a sin has been brought to light, leniency is out of the question; humanity demands that the offender be punished" (pp. 135–136: my translation).

and child have a place. He is not alone.[50] For pro-choice feminists, when the fetus wins, the woman loses. For pro-life feminists, when the fetus wins, the woman wins too.

5. Pro-life feminism endeavors to safeguard the moral right of women to full social equality, not by patterning themselves on a male model of sexuality but by respecting their own female sexuality.

> To say that in order to be equal with men it must be possible for a pregnant woman to become unpregnant at will is to say that being a woman precludes her from being a fully functioning person. . . . Of all the things which are done to women to fit them into a society dominated by men, abortion is the most violent invasion of their physical and psychic integrity.[51]

Pro-life feminism, in this view, refuses to regard male irresponsibility as a viable sexual paradigm for women to follow.

The "male as model" is an especially hazardous game for women to play. To buy into the abortion model is to fall into the masculine trap. Sidney Callahan gives this thought expression in her observation that "abortion helps a woman's body be more like a man's."[52] The abortion mentality of much of contemporary feminist ideology—is it not another way of saying: "There sits no higher court/ Than man's red heart"?

6. Pro-life feminism attempts to elaborate a more just social order, beginning with the sociological insight that *men and women*

---

[50]See also Mary Ann Glendon, *Rights Talk: The Impoverishment of Political Discourse* (New York: The Free Press, 1991). Of our four authors, Beverly Harrison and Carol Gilligan are certainly aware of this public dimension of the abortion decision; even Simone de Beauvoir is not unaware of it. How this awareness is translated is, of course, another matter.

[51]Daphne de Jong, "The Feminist Sell-Out," *New Zealand Listener* (January 14, 1976). It is reprinted with the title, "Legal Abortion Exploits Women," in Charles P. Cozic and Stacey L. Tipp (eds.), *Abortion: Opposing Viewpoints* (Opposing Viewpoints Series) (San Diego: Greenhaven Press, 1991), pp. 183–186.

[52]"Abortion and the Sexual Agenda," p. 238. For women to buy into the male as model theory of human sexuality is another way of saying, in the words of Edna O'Brien, "Oh God, who does not exist, you hate women, otherwise you'd have made them different."

become pregnant,[53] and that no abortion is ever a private matter. While it is true that some feminists, Gilligan and Harrison among them, are certainly aware of the societal dimensions of the abortion decision, their devotion to the bodyright argument prevents them from seeing the deep truth undergirding the sociological insight. Pro-life feminism labors under no such misconception. A woman does not conceive a child alone and male irresponsibility must not be followed as the model here.

Challenges Facing a Christian Pro-Life Feminism

Several tasks remain to be accomplished for a truly viable pro-life feminism, especially one to be elaborated from a Christian perspective. Among them:

1. The notion of human agency has to be expanded into something more like the vision of Simone Weil and less like that of Simone de Beauvoir. What is needed is a process of re-envisioning the notions of *activity* and *active receptivity*. While some recent feminist theological writing on this point shows promise,[54] when the discussion gets around to the issue of abortion, the promise ends.

2. There is needed an elaboration of the teaching of the Church in the matter of motherhood along the general lines of showing the great dignity and responsibility and love which motherhood entails. Far from denigrating the moral agency of women, Roman Catholic teaching on the immorality of abortion must be seen as one of truly ennobling features of women's moral progress. Catholic teaching on respect for human life places great trust in women to make the choice for life.[55]

3. The role of *sacrifice* in an authentic vision of the human person, male and female, must be highlighted, especially in light of what

---

[53]Cf. Kristin Luker, *Taking Chances*, p. 136. What follows in Luker's text is not quite as discerning, taking as it does an individualistic, atomistic approach to the male-female sexual scenario.

[54]Margaret Farley, for one, comes to mind.

[55]If the Church is to be blamed for anything in the way the abortion question is treated, it is *not* the charge of hypocrisy that comes to mind. Given the *Zeitgeist*, to believe that women are immune to the temptations to emulate masculine modes of action—Killing (Beauvoir), Power (Daly), Rights (Gilligan), and Control (Harrison)—seems to come close to presumption.

we have adverted to as the antisacrificial current of third-wave feminism.[56] "Sacrifice," in the etymological sense of "making holy," must be lived as a Christian response to the current trend towards *desacralization* (in effect, a "making unholy"). Whatever else the Christian faith may be, the notion of sacrifice, of making holy, remains an absolutely ineradicable part of its message.[57] If there is agreement on this point, the possiblity of dialogue on other points can begin. Without sacrifice, we are not talking about Christianity.

Abortion and the Male as Model

We have been arguing that the right to choose is the rhetoric, the power to kill is the reality. I believe we can make a further conclusion: If pro-abortion feminism is the practice, the "Male as Model" is the theory.

While favoring abortion herself, Faye Ginsburg's insight into the way pro-life women consider women who are pro-choice is particularly perspicacious: "A woman who endorses abortion denies the links between female reproduction and nurturant character and thus becomes *culturally male*."[58] The expression "culturally male" evokes memories of Beauvoir's culturalist hypothesis, the view that lies at the heart of much contemporary feminist ideology.

Far from being a new and better way of doing ethics, a feminism with abortion as its linchpin continues "The Male as Model" theory. Case in point: Carol Gilligan:

> The blind willingness to sacrifice people to truth, however, has always been the danger of an ethics

---

[56]Note the narration in Alice Walker's short story, "The Abortion": "Somewhere her child—she never dodged into the language of 'fetuses' and 'amorphous growths'—was being flushed down a sewer. Gone all her or his chances to see the sunlight, savor a fig. . . . 'Well,' she said to the child, 'it was you or me, Kiddo, and I chose me." Text in *You Can't Keep a Good Woman Down* (New York: Harcourt, Brace, Jovanovich, 1983), p. 70.

[57]On the need for the Cross as "the price to be paid," see Carolyn Osiek, R.S.C.J., *Beyond Anger: On Being a Feminist in the Church* (New York: Paulist, 1986).

[58]Faye Ginsburg, "The 'Word-Made' Flesh: The Disembodiment of Gender in the Abortion Debate," p. 72: my emphasis.

abstacted [sic] from life. This willingness links Gandhi to the biblical Abraham, who prepared to sacrifice the life of his son in order to demonstrate the integrity and supremacy of his faith. Both men, in the limitations of their fatherhood, stand in implicit contrast to the woman who comes before Solomon and verifies her motherhood by relinquishing truth in order to save the life of her child.[59]

These words appear at the end of chapter 3 of *In a Different Voice*, the chapter in which Gilligan elaborates a position which comes close to saying that abortion, if done for the right reasons, can be an occasion for psychological growth. The unnamed woman in the Biblical narrative who chooses life for her child does so "by relinquishing truth," in the view of Carol Gilligan. It is the view of pro-life feminism that the woman confronted with a difficult pregnancy who chooses life for her child is relinquishing falsehood.

One author who believes that abortion is a particularly violent way of solving human relational problems wonders if Gilligan is being faithful to the voice of care she has tried to present:

Quite simply, abortion is a failure to care for one living being who exists in a particularly intimate relationship to oneself. If empathy, nurturance, and taking responsibility for caring for others are characteristic of the feminine voice, then abortion does not appear to be a feminine response to an unwanted pregnancy. If, as Gilligan says, "an ethic of care rests on the premise of non-violence—that no one should be hurt" [*In a Different Voice*, p. 174], then surely the feminine response to an unwanted pregnancy would be to try to find a solution which does not involve injury to anyone, including the unborn.[60]

Commenting on the apparent incongruity of Gilligan endorsing

---

[59]The text is found in *In a Different Voice*, pp. 104–105. The biblical reference is to the "Judgment of Solomon" episode in 1 Kings 3:16–28.

[60]Cf. Celia Wolf-Devine, "Abortion and the 'Feminine Voice,'" p. 87.

abortion in what she styles an ethic of care, Celia Wolf-Devine
entertains for a moment the possibility that abortion *is* an expression of
legitimate concern and care, especially at the highest level of moral
development. She answers:

> This is an implausible view of the actual feelings of
> women who undergo abortions. They may believe
> "they are doing something for themselves" in the sense
> of doing what they must do to safeguard their
> legitimate interests. But the operation is more naturally
> regarded as a violation of oneself than as a nurturing of
> oneself. This has been noted, even by feminists who
> support permissive abortion laws. For example,
> Carolyn Whitbeck speaks of "the unappealing prospect
> of having someone scraping away at one's core."[61]

If Gilligan is being inconsistent on the abortion issue, she is surely not
alone.[62] Yet as Wolf-Devine presses her argument, other factors emerge
that cause us to ponder her central point:

> It is rather striking that feminists defending abortion
> lapse so quickly into speaking in the masculine voice. Is
> it because they feel they must do so in order to be
> heard in our male dominated society, or is it because no
> persuasive defense of abortion can be constructed from
> within the ethics of care tradition?[63]

One of Wolf-Devine's contentions goes to the heart of the
feminist enterprise as we have seen it unfolding. Contemporary
feminism prides itself on its ability to discover connections; indeed, the
stressing of connections is central to contemporary feminism.
Wolf-Devine touches on this and several other issues:

> Abortion is a separation—a severing of a life-preserving
> connection between the woman and the fetus. It thus

---

[61]"Abortion and the 'Feminine Voice,'" p. 89.

[62]For another example, see René Frydman, *L'irrésistible désir de naissance* (Paris:
Presses universitaires de France, 1986), pp. 35–36.

[63]Celia Wolf-Devine, "Abortion and the 'Feminine Voice,'" p. 88.

fails to respect the interconnectedness of all life. . . . It shows a willingness to use violence in order to maintain control. . . . If masculine thought is naturally hierarchical and oriented toward power and control, then the interests of the fetus (who has no power) would naturally be suppressed in favor of the interests of the mother. But to the extent that feminist social thought is egalitarian, the question must be raised of why the mother's interests should prevail over the child's (pp. 86–87).

Like their pro-choice counterparts, pro-life feminists also look for connectedness, but they happen to believe that the haunting, violent abortion procedure is a particularly poor paradigm for showing the links that unite human beings one to another. It is in this sense, then, that abortion continues to foster the "Male as Model Theory."

The Two Worldviews and the Moral Imagination

Following the logic of her world without God, Simone de Beauvoir comes to see killing as the key to the whole mystery of woman's second sex status. If we follow Beauvoir's logic, killing is the index of our humanity. Ideas have consequences, after all. Is Beauvoir right or is she rationalizing?

The human capacity to give "good" reasons for being able to ignore the existence of the other, even to killing him, should never be underestimated.[64]

Beauvoir's lifelong friend and companion, Jean-Paul Sartre, had once written: "Hell is other people." Beauvoir's classmate and quondam gadfly Simone Weil had a vastly different view of the matter: "Belief in the existence of other human beings as such is *love*."[65]

These are two possible approaches to the question of abortion.

---

[64]Stanley Hauerwas, "Abortion: The Agent's Perspective," *The American Ecclesiastical Review*, 167 no. 1 (January 1973), p. 108.

[65]Simone Weil, *Gravity and Grace* (translated by Emma Crawford) (London and New York: Ark Paperbacks, 1987; original French edition of 1947), p. 56: author's emphasis.

Both are prevalent. Only one, I maintain, is a viable Christian position. Only one is worthy of the woman and the child as the creatures of a loving God. Only one is worthy of the Christian community. That is the one that impels the Christian community to work for the construction of a world in which killing is not regarded as the index of our humanity.

Beverly Harrison once observed:

> We are at our best, morally, when we find new ways to act, explore previously untried social strategies to meet our moral dilemmas, or discover fresh approaches to old problems (*Our Right to Choose*, pp. 103–104.)

What will happen if we take these words to heart? When we are "morally at our best," will we find a feminism with abortion as its linchpin? I do not think so. If I may be allowed to sound like a Catherine MacKinnon for a moment: "Pro-choice feminism is a dead-end; pro-life feminism *is* feminism."

Defining abortion *into* feminism as certain feminist theorists have done is a relatively recent and a totally unimaginative way of resolving real human difficulties. Defining abortion *out* of feminism will bring with it the challenge of creating social structures for women and men, born and unborn, that will allow for the free range of the moral imagination. Anything less is unworthy of the woman and the man and the child as all creatures of a loving God.

Pro-life feminism is nothing if not a plea for bringing out the absolute best in our moral imagination.

> Let us not forget that our lack of imagination always depopulates the future (*The Second Sex*, p. 687).

BIBLIOGRAPHY

Aaron, Scott. "The Choice in 'Choose Life': American Judaism and Abortion," in *Bioethics*, 61-68.

Abortion Action Coalition. *More Than a Choice: Women Talk About Abortion.* Somerville, MA: New England Free Press, n.d.

Advisory Council on Church and Society. *Christian Reflection on the Issue of Abortion: a Collection of Articles for Study.* New York: Advisory Council on Church and Society, 1983.

Albrecht, Gloria H. "Myself and Other Characters: A Feminist Liberationist Critique of Hauerwas's Ethics of Christian Character," *The Annual: Society of Christian Ethics* (1992), 97-114.

Alcorn, Randy. *Pro Life Answers to Pro Choice Arguments.* Foreword by Thomas A. Glessner. Sisters, OR: Multnomah, 1992.

Allen, Sr. Prudence. "Rationality, Gender, and History," *Proceedings of the American Catholic Philosophical Association* 68 (1994) 271-288.

Alpern, Kenneth D., ed. *The Ethics of Reproductive Technology.* New York: Oxford University Press, 1992.

Alvaré, Helen. "The Cultural Impact of Abortion and Its Implications for a Future Society (Part Two)," in *Post-Abortion Aftermath*, 100-105.

Andrews, Lori B. "Feminism Revisited: Fallacies and Policies in the Surrogacy Debate." *Logos: Philosophic Issues in Christian Perspective*, 9 (1988) 81-96.

Andrusko, Dave, ed. *To Rescue the Future: the Pro-life Movement in the 1980s.* Toronto: Life Cycle Books, 1983.

Antony, Louise M. and Charlotte Witt, eds. A *Mind of One's Own: Feminist Essays on Reason and Objectivity.* Feminist Theory and Politics Series. Boulder, CO: Westview Press, 1993.

Arcana, Judith. "Abortion Is a Motherhood Issue," in *Mother Journeys*, 159-163.

Aronson, Ronald and Adrien ven der Hoven, eds. *Sartre Alive.* Detroit: Wayne State University Press, 1991.

Barry, Fr. Robert, O.P. "Thomson and Abortion," in *Abortion: A New Generation of Catholic Responses*, 163-176.

Beckwith, Francis J. *Politically Correct Death: Answering Arguments for*

Abortion Rights. Grand Rapids: Baker Books, 1993.

Benjamin, Jessica. *The Bonds of Love: Psychoanalysis, Feminism, and the Problem of Domination*. New York: Pantheon Books, 1988.

Bergoffen, Debra B. "The Look as Bad Faith." *Philosophy Today*, 36 3/4 (1992) 221-227.

Bologh, Roslyn W. *Love or Greatness: Max Weber and Masculine Thinking--A Feminist Inquiry*. London: Unwin Hyman, 1990.

Boss, Judith A. *The Birth Lottery: Prenatal Diagnosis and Selective Abortion*. Chicago: Loyola University Press, 1993.

Brennan, Teresa. *The Interpretation of the Flesh: Freud and Femininity*. London: Routledge, 1992.

Brody, Baruch A. *Abortion and the Sanctity of Life: a Philosophical View*. Cambridge, MA: MIT Press, 1975.

Caldwell, Lesley. "Feminism and Abortion Politics in Italy," in *The New Politics of Abortion*, 105-123.

Carter, Stephen L. *The Culture of Disbelief: How American Law and Politics Trivialize Religious Devotion*. New York: Basic Books, 1993.

Chandrasekhar, S. *Abortion in a Crowded World: The Problem of Abortion with Special Reference to India*. The John Danz Lectures. Seattle: University of Washington Press, 1974.

Cole, Eve Browning and Susan Coultrap-McQuin, eds. *Explorations in Feminist Ethics: Theory and Practice*. Bloomington: Indiana University Press, 1992.

Conn, Joann Wolski and Walter E. Conn, eds. *Horizons on Catholic Feminist Theology*. Washington, D.C: Georgetown University Press, 1992.

Conn, Joann Wolski. "New Vitality: the Challenge from Feminist Theology." *America* 165 9 (1991) 217-219.

Conn, Joann Wolski. "A Discipleship of Equals: Past, Present, Future," In *Horizons on Catholic Feminist Theology*. 3-36.

Connell, George. "Pierre Klossowski's 'Sade my Neighbor' and the Hermeneutics of Suspicion," *Faith and Philosophy*, 104 (1993) 553-566.

Copelon, Rhonda and Kathryn Kolbert. "Imperfect Justice." *Ms.* 18 nos. 1 & 2 (July/August 1989) 42-44.

Cornell, Drucilla. *Beyond Accommodation: Ethical Feminism,*

Deconstruction, and the Law. Thinking Gender Series. New York: Routledge, 1991.

Craig, Barbara Hinkson and David M. O'Brien. *Abortion and American Politics.* Chatham, NJ: Chatham House Publishers, 1993.

Crysdale, Cynthia S. W. "Gilligan and the Ethics of Care: An Update." *Religious Studies Review*, 20 1 (1994) 21-28.

Daniels, Cynthia R. *At Women's Expense: State Power and the Politics of Fetal Rights.* Cambridge, MA: Harvard University Press, 1993.

Derr, Mary Krane, M. S. W. "Feminism, Self-Estrangement, and the 'Disease' of Pregnancy." *Studies in Prolife Feminism* 1 1 (1995) 1-10.

Dietz, Mary G. "Introduction: Debating Simone de Beauvoir." *Signs*, 18 (1992) 74-87.

Donovan, Josephine. *Feminist Theory: The Intellectual Traditions of American Feminism.* New York: Continuum/ F. Ungar Book, 1990.

Eisenstein, Hester. *Gender Shock: Practicing Feminism on Two Continents.* Boston: Beacon Press, 1991.

Ellin, Joseph. "Reproductive Technology, Catholicism, Feminism, and the Thesis of Bootstrap Pessimism," *Logos: Philosophic Issues in Christian Perspective* 9 (1988) 37-49.

Elshtain, Jean Bethke. "The New Eugenics and Feminist Quandaries: Philosophical and Political Reflections," in *Guaranteeing the Good Life*, 68-88.

English, Deirdre. "The Fear that Feminism Will Free Men First," in *Powers of Desire*, 477-483.

Fauser, Patricia. "Authentic Existence in Simone de Beauvoir's 'She Came to Stay,'" *Proceedings of the American Catholic Philosophical Association* 68 (1993) 203-217.

Fisk, Milton. "Ethics, Feminism, and Abortion," in *Moral Controversies*, 10-20.

Flax, Jane. *Thinking Fragments: Psychoanalysis, Feminism, and Postmodernism in the Contemporary West*, Berkeley: University of California Press, 1990.

Ford, Norman F., S.D.B. *When Did I Begin? Conception of the Human Individual in History, Philosophy and Science.* Cambridge: Cambridge University Press, 1988.

Forelle, Helen. *Conversations in a Clinic*. 2d ed. Harrisburg, SD: Private Printing, 1981.

Fox-Genovese, Elizabeth. "Rethinking Abortion in Terms of Human Interconnectedness." *Studies in Prolife Feminism* 1 2 (1995) 91-104.

Friedman, Leon, ed. *The Supreme Court Confronts Abortion: The Briefs, Argument, and Decision in 'Planned Parenthood v. Casey'*. New York: The Noonday Press, 1993.

Frug, Mary Joe. *Postmodern Legal Feminism*. New York: Routledge, 1992.

Fullbrook, Kate and Edward. *Simone de Beauvoir and Jean-Paul Sartre: The Remaking of a Twentieth-Century Legend*. New York: Basic Books, 1994.

Gardiner, Judith Kegan, ed. *Provoking Agents: Gender and Agency in Theory and Practice*. Urbana: University of Illinois Press, 1995.

Garrow, David J. *Liberty and Sexuality: The Right to Privacy and the Making of 'Roe v. Wade'*. New York: Macmillan, 1994.

Gass, Michael. "Abortion and Moral Character: a Reply to Smith." *International Philosophical Quarterly* 33 no. 1 (# 129) (March 1993) 101-108.

Gentles, Anne, ed. *A Time to Choose Life: Women, Abortion, and Human Rights*. Toronto: Stoddart Press, 1990.

Gold, Steven Jay. *Moral Controversies: Race, Class, and Gender in Applied Ethics*. Belmont, CA: Wadsworth, 1993.

Green, Garrett. "The Gender of God and the Theology of Metaphor." In *Speaking the Christian God: the Holy Trinity and the Challenge of Feminism*, 44-64.

Gudorf, Christine E. *Body, Sex, and Pleasure: Reconstructing Christian Sexual Ethics*. Cleveland: The Pilgrim Press, 1994.

Harris, James F. *Against Relativism: A Philosophical Defense of Method*. LaSalle, IL: Open Court, 1992.

Harrison, Beverly Wildung. "Abortion: Protestant Perspectives." in *Encyclopedia of Bioethics*, 34-38.

Hartmann, Betsy. *Reproductive Rights and Wrongs*. Revised ed. Boston: South End Press, 1995.

Harvey, Brett. *The Fifties: A Women's Oral History*. New York: HarperCollins, 1993.

Hayden, Mary. "The 'Feminism' of Aquinas' Natural Law: Relationships, Love and New Life," in *Abortion: A New Generation of Catholic Responses*, 237-242.

Heaney, Stephen J., ed. *Abortion: a New Generation of Catholic Responses*. Braintree, MA: The Pope John Center, 1992.

Held, Virginia. *Feminist Morality: Transforming Culture, Society, and Politics*. With a Foreword by Catharine R. Stimpson. Chicago: University of Chicago Press, 1993.

Hitchcock, Helen Hull, ed. *The Politics of Prayer: Feminist Language and the Worship of God*. San Francisco: Ignatius Press, 1992.

Hitchcock, James. "American Culture and Reverence for Human Life," in *Linking the Human Life Issues*, 22-55.

Hittinger, Russell, ed. *Linking the Human Life Issues*. Chicago: Regnery, 1986.

Holmes, Helen Bequaert and Laura M. Purdy, eds. *Feminist Perspectives in Medical Ethics*. Bloomington: Indiana University Press, 1992.

Holmes, Helen Bequaert, ed. *Issues in Reproductive Technology*. New York: New York University Press, 1992.

Hubbard, Ruth. *Profitable Promises: Essays on Women, Science, and Health*. The Politics of Science Series. Monroe, ME: Common Courage Press, 1995.

Hunt, Mary E. "Shifting Spiritual Authorities for Feminist Ethics," *The Annual: Society of Christian Ethics*, (1994) 267-273.

Hynes, H. Patricia, ed. *Reconstructing Babylon: Essays on Women and Technology*. Bloomington: Indiana University Press, 1991.

Jaggar, Alison, ed. *Living With Contradictions: Controversies in Feminist Social Ethics*. Boulder, CO: Westview Press, 1994.

Jantzen, Grace M. "Connection or Competition: Identity and Personhood in Feminist Ethics," *Studies in Christian Ethics* 5 1 (1992) 1-20.

John Paul II, Pope. *The Gospel of Life*.

Kaplan, Gisela. *Contemporary Western European Feminism*. Washington Square, NY: New York University Press, 1992.

Kaufmann, Linda S, ed. *American Feminist Thought at Century's End: a Reader*. Cambridge, MA: Blackwell, 1993.

King, Ursula, ed. *Women in the World's Religions: Past and Present*. God, the Contemporary Discussion Series. New York: Paragon

House/ New Era Book, 1987.

Klinkenborg, Verlyn. "Violent Certainties," *Harper's*, 289 1736 (1995) 37-52.

Koterski, Joseph, S.J., ed. *Life and Learning: Proceedings of the Second University Faculty for Life Conference*, Washington, D.C: University Faculty for Life, 1993.

Kreeft, Peter. "Gender and the Will of God," *Crisis*, September (1993) 20-28.

Kruks, Sonia. "Beauvoir, Gender and Subjectivity," *Signs*, 18 (1992) 89-109.

Kruks, Sonia. "Simone de Beauvoir: Teaching Sartre About Freedom," in *Sartre Alive*, 285-300.

LaFleur, William R. *Liquid Life: Abortion and Buddhism in Japan*. Princeton: Princeton University Press, 1992.

Lovenduski, Joni and Joyce Outshoorn, eds. *The New Politics of Abortion*. London: Sage Publications, 1986.

MacKinnon, Catherine. "A Feminist Perspective on the Right to Abortion," in *Morality in Practice*, 163-172.

Maggio, Rosalie, compiler. *The Beacon Book of Quotes by Women*. Boston: Beacon Press, 1992.

Mahowald, Mary Briody. *Women and Children in Health Care: An Unequal Majority*. New York: Oxford University Press, 1993.

Mannion, Michael T., ed. *Post-Abortion Aftermath: A Comprehensive Consideration*. Kansas City: Sheed & Ward, 1994.

Martin, Francis. *The Feminist Question: Feminist Theology in the Light of Christian Tradition*. Grand Rapids: Eerdmans, 1994.

Mathewes-Green, Frederica. *Real Choices: Offering Practical Life-Affirming Alternatives to Abortion*. Sisters, OR: Multnomah Books, 1994.

Mathewes-Green, Frederica. "Feminist for Life," *Crisis*, March (1990) 47-48.

McCorvey, Norma with Andy Meisler. *I Am Roe: My Life, Roe v. Wade, and Freedom of Choice*. New York: HarperCollins Publishers, 1994.

Meehl, Joanne H. *The Recovering Catholic: Personal Journeys of Women Who Left the Church*. Amherst, NY: Prometheus Books, 1995.

Mercadante, Linda A. *Gender, Doctrine and God: The Shakers and*

Contemporary Theology. Nashville: Abingdon Press, 1990.

Miller, Amy T., Esq. *Against the Tide: Pro-Lifer as Feminist.* Washington, D.C: NCCB Secretariat for Pro-life Activities, n.d.

Minas, Anne, ed. *Gender Basics: Feminist Perspectives on Women and Men.* Belmont, CA: Wadsworth, 1993.

Moi, Toril. *Simone de Beauvoir: The Making of an Intellectual Woman.* Cambridge, MA: Blackwell, 1994.

Morowitz, Harold J. and James S. Trefil. *The Facts of Life: Science and the Abortion Controversy.* New York: Oxford University Press, 1992.

Mulligan, Rev. Msgr. James J. *Choose Life.* Braintree: Pope John Center, 1991.

Nelson, Lynn Hankinson. *Who Knows: From Quine to Feminist Empiricism.* Philadelphia: Temple University Press, 1990.

Neuhaus, Richard John, ed. *Guaranteeing the Good Life: Medicine and the Return of Eugenics.* Encounter Series # 13. Grand Rapids: Eerdmans, 1990.

Olasky, Marvin. *Abortion Rites: a Social History of Abortion in America.* Wheaton, IL: Crossway Books, a Division of Good News Publishers, 1992.

Oppenheimer, Helen. "Abortion: A Sketch of a Christian View," *Studies in Christian Ethics,* 5 2 (1992) 46-60.

Overall, Christine, ed. *The Future of Human Reproduction.* Toronto: The Women's Press, 1989.

Overall, Christine. *Human Reproduction: Principles, Practices, Policies.* Toronto: Oxford University Press, 1993.

Patai, Daphne and Noretta Koertge. *Professing Feminism: Cautionary Tales from the Strange World of Women's Studies.* New York: New Republic Book, 1994.

Pearsall, Marilyn, ed. *Women and Values: Readings in Recent Feminist Philosophy.* 2d ed. Belmont, CA: Wadsworth, 1993.

Pilardi, Jo-Ann. "Philosophy Become Autobiography: The Development of the Self in the Writings of Simone de Beauvoir," in *Writing the Politics of Difference,* 155-161.

Piontelli, Alessandra. *From Fetus to Child: an Observational and Psychoanalytic Study.* The New Library of Psychoanalysis, no. 15. New York: Routledge, 1992.

Pollitt, Katha. *Reasonable Creatures: Essays on Women and Feminism.* New York: Alfred A. Knopf, 1995.

Quay, Paul M., S.J. "The Philosophical Underpinnings of the Prolife Movement," in *Life and Learning,* (1993) 215-228.

Quebedeaux, Richard. "We're On Our Way, Lord!: The Rise of 'Evangelical Feminism' in Modern American Christianity," in *Women in the World's Religions,* 129-144.

Raymond, Janice. "Fetalists and Feminists: They Are Not the Same," in *Made to Order,* 58-66.

Raymond, Janice. *Women as Wombs: Reproductive Technologies and the Battle Over Women's Freedom.* San Francisco: Harper, 1993.

Reddy, Maureen T., Martha Roth, and Amy Sheldon, eds. *Mother Journeys: Feminists Write about Mothers.* Minneapolis: Spinsters Ink, 1994.

Reich, Warren Thomas, Editor in Chief. *Encyclopedia of Bioethics,* Revised edition. In 5 volumes. New York: Macmillan, 1995.

Reti, Irene, ed. *Childless by Choice: A Feminist Anthology.* Santa Cruz, CA: Herbooks, 1992.

Rice, Charles. *Fifty Questions on the Natural Law: What It Is and Why We Need It.* San Francisco: Ignatius Press, 1993.

Richardson, Laurel and Verta Taylor, eds. *Feminist Frontiers: Rethinking Sex, Gender and Society.* New York: Random House, 1983.

Rohrlich, Ruby and Elaine Hoffman Baruch, eds. *Women in Search of Utopia: Mavericks and Mythmakers.* New York: Schocken Books, 1984.

Rohrlich, Ruby. "Introduction: The Quest and the Questions," in *Women in Search of Utopia,* xv-xxvii.

Roiphe, Katie. *The Morning After: Sex, Fear, and Feminism.* Boston: Back Bay Books, 1994.

Rowland, Robyn. "Of Women Born, But for How Long? The Relationship of Women to the New Reproductive Technologies and the Issue of Choice," in *Made to Order,* 67-83.

Ryan, Maura A., Ph.D. "The Argument for Unlimited Procreative Liberty: A Feminist Critique," in *Bioethics,* 81-96.

Sartre, Jean-Paul. *Notebooks for an Ethics.* Tr. David Pellauer. Chicago: University of Chicago Press, 1992.

Scheffler, Samuel. *Human Morality,* New York: Oxford University

Press, 1992.

Schneir, Miriam, ed. *Feminism in Our Time: The Essential Writings, World War II to the Present.* New York: Vintage Books, 1994.

Schwarz, Stephen D. *The Moral Question of Abortion.* Chicago: Loyola University Press, 1990.

Seidman, Steven. *Embattled Eros: Sexual Politics and Ethics in Contemporary America.* Thinking Gender Series. New York: Routledge, 1992.

Shannon, Thomas A., ed. *Bioethics.* 4th ed. Mahwah, NJ: Paulist, 1993.

Sherwin, Susan. *No Longer Patient: Feminist Ethics and Health Care,* Philadelphia: Temple University Press, 1992.

Shrage, Laurie. *Moral Dilemmas: Prostitution, Adultery, and Abortion.* Thinking Gender Series. New York: Routledge, 1994.

Sichtermann, Barbara. *Femininity: The Politics of the Personal.* Tr. John Whitlam. Ed. Helga Geyer-Ryan. Minneapolis: University of Minnesota Press, 1984.

Silverman, Hugh J., ed. *Writing the Politics of Difference.* Albany: SUNY Press, 1991.

Simons, Margaret. "Beauvoir's Lesbian Connections," *Signs,* 18 (1992) 136-161.

Simons, Margaret. "Sexism and the Philosophical Canon: On Reading Beauvoir's 'The Second Sex'," *Journal of the History of Ideas,* 51 (1990) 487-504.

Singer, Peter, ed. *Ethics,* New York: Oxford University Press, 1994.

Sloan, Don, M.D. with Paula Hartz. *Abortion: a Doctor's Perspective, a Woman's Dilemma.* New York: Donald I. Fine, Inc., 1991.

Smith, Janet E. "Moral Character and Abortion," in *Abortion: A New Generation of Catholic Responses,* 189-208.

Snitow, Ann, Christine Stansell, and Sharon Thompson, eds. *Powers of Desire: The Politics of Sexuality.* New Feminist Library. New York: Monthly Review Press, 1983.

Solinger, Rickie. *The Abortionist: A Woman Against the Law,* New York: The Free Press, 1994.

Spallone, Patricia and Deborah Lynn Steinberg, eds. *Made to Order: The Myth of Reproductive and Genetic Progress.* The Athene Series. Oxford: Pergamon Press, 1987.

Spretnak, Charlene, ed. *The Politics of Women's Spirituality: Essays on the*

Rise of Spiritual Power Within the Feminist Movement. Garden City: Anchor Books, 1982.

Steinbock, Bonnie. *Life Before Birth: The Moral and Legal Status of Embryos and Fetuses.* New York: Oxford University Press, 1992.

Sterba, James P., ed. *Morality in Practice.* 4th ed. Belmont, CA: Wadsworth, 1994.

Strossen, Nadine. *Defending Pornography: Free Speech, Sex, and the Fight for Women's Rights.* New York: Scribner, 1994.

Taylor, Verta. "The Future of Feminism in the 1980s: A Social Movement Analysis," in *Feminist Frontiers*, 434-451.

Tooley, Michael. *Abortion and Infanticide.* New York: Clarendon Press/ Oxford, 1983.

Torre, Christine Smith, et al. "Amicus Brief in 'Bray v. Alexandria'," *Studies in Prolife Feminism,* 1 1 (1995) 59-85.

Townsend, Rita and Ann Perkins. *Bitter Fruit: Women's Experiences of Unplanned Pregnancy, Abortion, and Adoption,* Alameda, CA: Hunter House, 1992.

Trask, Haunani-Kay. *Eros and Power: The Promise of Feminist Theory.* Philadelphia: University of Pennsylvania Press, 1986.

Tronto, Joan. *Moral Boundaries: A Political Argument for an Ethic of Care.* New York: Routledge, 1993.

Tuana, Nancy and Rosemarie Tong, eds. *Feminism and Philosophy: Essential Readings in Theory, Reinterpretation, and Application.* Boulder, CO: Westview Press, 1995.

VandeVeer, Donald and Tom Regan, eds. *Health Care Ethics: An Introduction.* Philadelphia: Temple University Press, 1987.

Vertefeuille, John. *Sexual Chaos: the Personal and Social Consequences of the Sexual Revolution.* Westchester, IL: Crossway Books, 1988.

Visser, Susan Ostrov and Jennifer Fleischner, eds. *Feminist Nightmares: Feminism and the Problem of Sisterhood.* New York: New York University Press, 1994.

Walker, Margaret U. "What Does the Different Voice Say? Gilligan's Women and Moral Philosophy," *Journal of Value Inquiry* 23 (1989) 123-134.

Warren, Mary Anne. "The Abortion Issue," in *Health Care Ethics: An Introduction*, 184-214.

Weddington, Sarah. *A Question of Choice.* New York: G. P. Putnam's

Sons. A Grosset/Putnam Book, 1992.

Wilcox, John T. "Nature as Demonic in Thomson's Defense of Abortion." *The New Scholasticism* 43 4 (1989), pp. 463-484.

Wilt, Judith. "Catholic, Feminist, Ubiquitous," *Boston College Magazine* 52 1 (1993) 26-31.

Wilt, Judith. "Ubiquitous, Lost, Found: A Study of Catholic Identities," *Initiatives: Journal of the National Association for Women in Education* 54 4 (1992) 1-7.

Wolf, Naomi. *Fire with Fire: The New Female Power and How to Use It.* New York: Fawcett Columbine, 1994.

Yanay, Niza. "Authenticity of Self-Expression: Reinterpretation of Female Independence Through the Writing of Simone de Beauvoir," *Women's Studies*, 17 (1990) 219-233.

Zerilli, Linda. "A Process Without a Subject: Simone de Beauvoir and Julia Kristeva on Maternity," *Signs*, 18 (1992) 111-135.

Zimmerman, Jan. "Utopia in Question: Programming Women's Needs into the Technology of Tomorrow," in *Women in Search of Utopia*, 168-176.

Zweig, Connie, ed. *To Be a Woman: The Birth of the Conscious Feminine.* Los Angeles: Jeremy P. Tarcher, Inc., 1990.

INDEX

Abraham: 222.
Absolutes: 26, n. 27; 110-112; 125.
Adam and Eve: 121, n. 48.
Alzon, Claude: 51, n. 102; 84, n. 65.
American Humanist Association: 158, n. 64.
Andolsen, Barbara Hilkert: 52, n. 103; 137, n.2; 153, n. 51; 156, n. 57; 182, n. 3.
Androgyny: 74, n. 44; 120, n. 45.
Andrusko, Dave: 118, n. 40.
Appignanesi, Lisa: 20, n. 5.
Ascher, Carol: 33 n. 52; 51, n. 99; 58, n. 116.
Atheism: xxii; 1; 11; 16-17; 21, n. 9; 23; 25-27; 48, n. 92; 58; 68, n. 21; 69; 92-3; 180; 195; 214-6; 224-5.
Atkinson, Ti-Grace: 45, n. 87,
Attarian, John: 48, n. 92.
Auerbach, Judy: 107, n. 12.
Augustine, St.: 64; 96, n. 89.
Autonomy: 72, n. 36; 97, n. 93; 116, n. 33; 125; 134, n. 77; 138; 170, n. 90; 182-5; 190.
Badinter, Elizabeth: 38, n. 69; 58; 120, n. 45.
Baehr, Ninia: 199, n. 48.
Bair, Deirdre: 19, n. 3; 58, n. 117.
Baker, Jeannine Parvati: 204, n. 4.
Barth, Karl: 152, n. 46; 154, n. 53.
Baruch, Elaine Hoffman: 88, n. 70.
Battaglia, Anthony: 162, n. 71.
Baum, Gregory: 168, n. 87.
Bayles, Martha: 130, n. 65.

Beauvoir, Simone de: *Passim*.
Bellenzier, Maria Teresa: 140, n. 17.
Bengis, Ingrid: 207; 216, n. 43.
Berger, Brigitte and Peter: 143, n. 23.
Birth: 41-2; 77, n. 51; 97, n. 93; 109, n. 20; 164; 174, n. 98.
Bishop, Nadean: 199, n. 49.
Bleier, Ruth: 38, n. 68.
Bloch, Dr. Iwan: 48, n. 92.
Blum, Lawrence: 108, n. 17.
Body: 34-37; 68; 187, n. 17.
Bodyright Argument: 11; 54; 70; 83; 91; 142, n. 21; 147; 153, n. 50; 161-2; 166; 206, n. 10; 210, n. 24; 211; 217; 214.
Bok, Sissela: 126, n. 57.
Bonavoglia, Angela: 189, n. 21; 200, n. 51.
Bonhoeffer, Dietrich: 165, n. 79.
Bottcher, Rosemary: 118, n. 40.
Bowers, Marilyn: 66, n. 13.
Bray, Louise Hardin: 182, n. 3.
Brooks, Gwendolyn: 208.
Brosman, Catherine Savage: 30, n. 41.
Browne, Stella: 7; 10-11; 54, n. 105; 191, n. 29; 211.
Budapest, Zsuzsanna E.: 191, n. 27.
Butler, Judith: 59, n. 119.
Byrn, Robert: 83.
Cahill, Lisa Sowle: 80, n. 55; 154, n. 51; 193, n. 32.
Calabresi, Guido: 12; 166, n. 83.
California Medicine Editorial: 13-

14; 212-3.

Callahan, Daniel: 81; 178. n. 106; 216.

Callahan, Joan C.: 164, n. 76.

Callahan, Sidney: xv; 14, n. 42; 64, n. 8; 138, n. 4; 203-4; 216-218.

Carmody, Denise Lardner: 82, n. 58; 204, n. 4.

Casey, Juliana: 135, n. 80.

Castro, Ginette: 38, n. 68; 79, n. 41.

Catholicism, Roman: xv; 2-3; 5-8; 26-7; 46-8; 70; 73; 86; 90; 93-97; 122-6; 128, n. 63; 140; 146, n. 30 and n. 31; 156, n. 58; 172; 172; 172-175; 182; 194; 200, n. 53; 220-1.

Cervantes, Lucius, S.J.: 39, n. 68.

Chancer, Lynn: 199, n. 48.

Chervin, Rhonda: 204, n. 4.

Chodorow, Nancy: 103, n. 5; 114, n. 30.

Christ, Carol: 63, n. 5.

Christen, Yves: 115, n. 32.

Churchill, Larry: 153, n. 49.

Cisler, Lucinda: 98, n. 96; 166, n. 81.

Cobb, John: 63.

Code, Lorraine: 116, n. 34.

Colker, Ruth: 26, n. 29.

Complementarity: 107; 112-3; 128; 132-3; 138, n. 6.

Condit, Celeste Michelle: 55, n. 109.

Connery, John, S.J.: 157; 164, n. 76.

Cooke, Terence Cardinal: 14, n. 44.

Crossland, Margaret: 20, n. 3.

Crum, Gary: 213, n. 32.

Culturalism: xix; xx, n. 3; 2; 15; 38; 68; 80; 82; 89; 115; 135, n. 80; 150; 144; 162; 186, n. 13; 221.

Curran, Charles: 13, n. 40.

Cushing, Richard Cardinal: 80, n. 54.

Daly, Mary: *Passim.* esp. chapter two.

Davaney, Sheila Greeve: 63, n. 5; 120, n. 45; 155, n. 54.

Davion, Victoria: 131, n. 68.

Davis, Angela: 197, n. 43.

De Jong, Daphne: 219, n. 51.

Delphy, Christine: 9; 115.

Demarco, Donald: 38, n. 66; 179, n. 107.

Demeter: 121, n. 47.

Denes, Magda: 9, n. 26; 210, n. 24; 210-11; 214.

Derrick, Christopher: 179, n. 107.

Descartes, René: 23; 34; 109, n. 18.

Desimone, Diane: 179, n. 108.

Deutsch, Hélène: 63; 188, n. 20.

Dewart, Leslie: 63.

Difference: 113-115; 128.

Dinnerstein, Dorothy: 103, n. 5; 114, n. 30.

Dostoevsky, Fyodor: 58.

Drinan, Robert, S.J.: 80, n. 54.

Dualism: 34; 74; 91; 98; 110, n. 21; 115; 138, n. 8; 148, n. 35.

Dumais, Monique: 182, n. 3; 199, n. 48.

Durden-Smith, Jo: 179, n. 108.

Dworkin, Andrea: 37, n. 63; 47, n. 92; 52, n. 104; 84; 186, n. 14; 187, n. 17; 198;

207, n. 12.

Dworkin, Ronald: 166, n. 82.

Echols, Alice: 85-86, n. 67.

Eggebrooten, Anne: 6, n. 20; 194, n. 34.

Ehrmann, Jacques: 38, n. 68.

Eisenstein, Zillah: 201, n. 54.

Eisler, Riane: 205, n. 5.

Elitism: 41.

Elliott, Patricia: 123, n. 53.

Ellis, Havelock: 10; 54, n. 105.

Ellis, Msgr. John Tracy: 175, n. 99.

Elshtain, Jean Bethke: 3; 34, n. 58; 66, n. 17; 128, n. 62; 188, n. 19.

Engelhardt, H. Tristram, Jr.: 15, n. 45; 153, n. 51; 198.

Epstein, Lee: xxii, n. 9.

Eucharist: 86.

Falik, Marilyn: 5, n. 17; 139, n. 12.

Fall, The: 71, n. 35; 187.

Fallaize, Elizabeth: 28, n. 34; 29, n. 39.

Faludi, Susan: 102, n. 4; 114, n. 29; 116, n. 34.

Farganis, Sondra: 191, n. 28.

Farley, Margaret: 37, n. 65; 156, n. 57; 220, n. 54.

Feinberg, Joel: 183, n. 4.

Female Superiority Ethic: 107-108; 130, n. 65; 148.

Feminism, Definition of: 4; 192.

Feminism: *Passim*.

Feminist, Definition of: 192.

Ferraro, Barbara: 194.

Ferree, Myra Marx: 3.

Fetus: 36; 42, n. 76; 46-7; 50, n. 98; 57; 72, n. 36; 76; 8, n. 55; 83-5; 91; 97; 119, n. 41 and n. 45; 126, n. 57; 150;

157; 160-5; 175, n. 100; 191-2; 203; 206; 212; 218; 221, n. 56; 224.

Finnis, John: 13, n. 40.

Fiorenza, Elizabeth Schüssler: 78, n. 52; 114, n. 28.

Firestone, Shulamith: 9; 45, n. 88.

Flanagan, Owen: 107, n. 14.

Flax, Jane: 114, n. 30.

Foh, Susan: 183, n. 5.

Foot, Philippa: 126, n. 57.

Fox-Genovese, Elizabeth: 153, n. 50.

Francke, Linda Bird: 41, n. 76; 208; 209.

Frankfurt, Ellen: 83.

Franz, Wanda: 118, n. 40.

Freeman, Alan: 167, n. 83; 184, n. 6.

Freeman, Jo: 70; 199, n. 49.

French, Marilyn: 205, n. 5.

Freud, Sigmund: 2; 52, n. 103; 63, n. 7; 103-5; 111; 145, n. 29.

Friedan, Betty: xix; xxii-iv; 7; 40; 52, n. 104; 58, n. 118; 63; 195, n. 38; 196-7; 207-8.

Frydman, René: 223, n. 62.

Gage, Matilda Joslyn: 84, n. 62.

Gallagher, Maggie: 40, n. 72; 42, n. 77; 119, n. 43; 179, n. 108; 204, n. 4.

Gandhi, Mahatma: 84, n. 63; 222.

Gardella, Peter: 151, n. 44.

Gatens, Moira: 68, n. 23; 85, n. 67.

Gender: 1-2.

Gensler, Harry J.: 170, n. 90.

Gilligan, Carol: *Passim*, esp. chapter three.

Ginsburg, Faye: 94, n. 84; 217, n.

46; 221.

Ginsburg, Ruth Bader: xxiv.

Glen, Kristen Booth: 166, n. 81.

Glendon, Mary Ann: 132, n. 71; 152, n. 47; 219, n. 50.

Goldenberg, Naomi: 103, n. 6.

Gordon, John: 83, n. 59; 89, n. 71; 207, n. 15.

Gordon, Linda: 52, n. 104; 196, n. 39.

Gordon, Mary: xx.

Graef, Hilda: 27, n. 31.

Greer, Germaine: 8; 152, n. 45; 210, n. 25.

Grisez, Germain: 152; 157; 162, n. 71; 178.

Gross, Elizabeth: 182, n. 3.

Guardini, Romano: 95, 203, 205-7; 218.

Gudorf, Christine: 147, n. 34.

Gustafson, James: 81, n. 57.

Hammarskjöld, Dag: 84, n. 63.

Hardesty, Nancy: 193, n. 33.

Hardwig, John: 152, n. 47.

Häring, Bernard, C.SS.R.: 154, n. 53.

Harrison, Beverly Wildung: Passim, esp. chapter four.

Hartshorne, Charles: 163, n. 72; 169.

Hartsock, Nancy: 51, n. 102; 114, n. 30.

Harvard University: 101-102.

Hatcher, Donald: 33, n. 51.

Hauerwas, Stanley: 142; 162, n. 70; 212, n. 31; 224-5, n. 64.

Hegel, Georg Wilhelm Friedrich: 33; 97; 214, n. 35.

Heidegger, Martin: 113,, n. 25.

Heinzelmann, Gertrud: 64, n. 9.

Held, Virginia: 41, n. 73 and 75.

Henry, A. M., O.P.: 27, n. 31.

Herman, Ellen: 134, n. 76.

Hern, Warren: 208, n. 20.

Hess, Beth B.: 3.

Heyward, Isabel Carter: 137, n. 2; 158, n. 61.

Hildebrand, Alice Von: xix.

Hill, Thomas E.: 182, n. 2

Hines, Mary: 65, n. 13.

Historical Consciousness: 13, n. 40; 154-5.

Hoagland, Sarah Lucia: 72, n. 36.

Homosexuality: 44; 82; 154, n. 53.

Horn, Carl: 213, n. 32.

Hoshiko, Sumi: 189, n. 21.

Houston, Barbara: 104, n. 8.

Hubbard, Ruth: 211, n. 26.

Hughes, Judith: 5, n. 18; 33, n. 51; 126, n. 57.

Humm, Maggie: 45, n. 87; 70, n. 30; 106, n. 10; 141, n. 18.

Hunt, Mary: 66, n. 15.

Hussey, Patricia: 194.

Hypocrisy: 50; 72; 75; 93-5; 99; 122, n. 49; 145; 174; 187; 217; 221, n. 55.

Ice, Martha Long: 120, n. 45.

Incarnation: 42; 86, n. 68.

Irigaray, Luce: 113,, n. 25.

Is Nature Misogynist? 9; 12; 44, n. 83; 57, n. 113; 72, n. 37; 96-7; 141; 144; 177, n. 103.

Jacklin, Carol Nagy: 113, n. 25; 114, n. 29.

Jackson, Jeremy: 6, n. 20.

Jackson, Kathryn: 107, n. 14.

Jaggar, Alison: 3.

Janssen-Jurreit, Marielouise: 102,

n. 3.

Javits, Senator Jacob: 71, n. 32.

Jeanson, Francis: 22, n. 11; 26.

John Paul II, Pope: 114; 179, n. 107.

Johnson, Elizabeth, C.S.J.: 192, n. 30.

Joyce, Mary: 204, n. 4.

Judaeo-Christianity: 110; 118; 121; 213.

Jung, Carl: 63, n. 7; 103, n. 6.

Jung, Patricia Beattie: 98, n. 97.

Kaufmann, Dorothy: 20, n. 5.

Kaveny, M. Cathleen: 179, n. 109.

Keefe, Terry: 188, n. 18.

Kelleher, Anne: 126, n. 57.

Keller, Catherine: 52, n. 103; 132, n. 70.

Kelly, James R.: 146, n. 31.

Kenny, Mary: 6-7; 126, n. 57; 209, n. 21.

Kerber, Linda K.: 106, n. 11.

Killing: xxi; 14; 46, n. 89; 50, n. 98; 51-3; 58-9; 91; 98; 133-135; 160; 183-5; 190, n. 26; 190-1; 208, n. 20; 224-5.

Kilpatrick, William Kirk: 109, n. 19.

Kimel, Alvin F., Jr.: 83, n. 60; 213, n. 32.

Kirkendall, Lester: 158, n. 64.

Kittay, Eva Feder: 108, n. 16; 128, n. 64; 182, n. 3.

Klein, J. Theodore: 131, n. 67.

Kobylka, Joseph F.: xxii, n. 9.

Kohlberg, Lawrence: See "Gilligan," chapter three.

Kolbenschlag, Madonna: 116, n. 33; 121, n. 47; 133, n. 72;

170, n. 92; 187.

Koster, Nancy: 118, n. 40.

Kress, Robert: 212, n. 31.

Kristeva, Julia: 123, n. 53.

Kurtz, Paul: 24, n. 23.

Lacugna, Catherine Mowry: 113, n. 25; 193, n. 32.

Lader, Lawrence: xxiii-iv; 39; 81; 207; 211.

Laeuchli, Samuel: 158.

Lake, Randall: 71, n. 35.

Lamb, Rosemary Wittman: 118, n. 39.

Langer, Monika: 23-24.

Language: xix-xxii; 55; 62, n. 5; 66, n. 17; 76; 102; 145-7; 188.

Larrabee, Mary Jeanne: 108, n. 16.

Lauer, Rosemary: 63.

Lawrence, T. E.: 84, n. 63.

Leclerc, Annie: 84, n. 65.

Leighton, Jean: 29, n. 38; 35, n. 59; 188, n. 18.

Lesbianism: 45; 69, n. 27; 70, n. 30; 71; 72, n. 36; 86-7; 158, n. 61.

Levin, Michael: 2, n. 6; 108, n. 15.

Lewis, Neil: xxiv.

Lilar, Suzanne: 32, n. 47.

Lloyd, Genevieve: 88, n. 70.

Loades, Ann: 7.

Loesch, Juli: 147, n. 33; 204, n. 4.

Lombardi Vallauri, Luigi: 48, n. 92; 195, n. 36.

Lonergan, Bernard, S.J.: 13, n. 40; 155, n. 55.

Lorde, Audre: 136, n. 84.

Lotstra, Hans: 94, n. 85.

Lowinsky, Naomi Ruth: 185, n. 9.

Luker, Kristin: 7, n. 23; 13, n. 39; 117; 198, n. 46; 220, n. 53.

Lunneborg, Patricia: 189, n. 22.

Maccoby, Eleanor Emmons: 113, n. 25; 114, n. 29.

Mackenzie, Catriona: 35, n. 59; 41, n. 74.

Mackinnon, Catherine: 3; 4; 12, n. 37; 37, n. 63; 75, n. 45; 113, n. 27; 166, n. 81; 186, n. 14; 200; 218, n. 48; 225.

Macrae, Jean: 77.

Maguire, Daniel: 162, n. 71.

Male as Model Theory: xxi; 2, n. 5; 10; 12-13; 184; 195; 219-222.

Mall, David: 117, n. 38.

Malone, Mary: 113, n. 25.

Maloney, Anne M.: 192-3; 217, n. 45.

Mangan, Joseph, S.J.: 162, n. 71.

Manifesto of the 343: 20, n. 3; 70

Manning, Rita: 108, n. 16; 131, n. 67.

Mannion, M. Francis: 89.

Mara, Deborah: 190, n. 27.

Maradona, Diego: xxi.

Marcel, Gabriel: 89.

Marchocki, Kathryn: 65, n. 12; 91, n. 76.

Marcuse, Herbert: 1; 63, n. 6; 90; 96, n. 91.

Maritain, Jacques: 63.

Marks, Elaine: 21, n. 9.

Mary, Mother of Jesus: 156, n. 57.

Masculinism: 41, n. 74; 88; 90; 92; 136; 168, n. 88; 195, n. 36; 223-4.

Mathieu, Vittorio: 94, n. 84.

McCall, Dorothy Kaufmann: 20, n. 5; 51, n. 102.

McCormack, Thelma: 213, n. 32.

McCormick, Richard A., S.J.: 162, n. 70; 175-6.

McDonnell, Kathleen: 181, n. 1; 189, n. 22.

McEnroy, M. Carmel: 65, n. 13.

McLouth, Gary: 117, n. 35.

McMahon, Joseph: 22, n. 14.

McMahon, Kevin: 179, n. 107.

McMillan, Carol: 9; 50, n. 98; 68, n. 22; 126, n. 57; 136, n. 83; 179, n. 108.

Mead, Margaret: 71, n. 32.

Meehan, Mary: 204, n. 4; 217, n. 44.

Mensch, Elizabeth: 167, n. 83; 184, n. 6.

Meyers, Diana T.: 108, n. 16; 128, n. 64; 182, n. 3.

Midgely, Mary: 5, n. 18; 33, n. 51; 126, n. 57.

Milbauer, Barbara: 134, n. 78.

Miller, Jean Baker: 110; 114, n. 30.

Millett, Kate: 1-2.

Misogyny: 140-2; 162, n. 71; 176-8.

Mitchell, Juliet: 9, n. 26; 103, n. 5; 197, n. 44.

Mohr, James: 83, n. 62.

Moi, Toril: 21, n. 9.

Moody-Adams, Michèle: 116, n. 34.

Mor, Barbara: 190, n. 27.

Moran, Gabriel: 63.

Morgan, Robin: 47, n. 91; 85, n. 67.

Motherhood: 37-42; 59, n. 119; 80, n, 54; 88; 131, n. 69; 151, n. 43; 169-70; 187; 197, n. 44; 220-2.

Mottini-Coulon, Edmée: 135, n. 80; 204, n. 4.

Nails, Debra: 108, n. 17.

Nathanson, Bernard: 47, n. 90; 143, n. 23; 164, n. 76; 165, n. 78; 172,, n. 95; 206, n. 9.

Nathanson, Sue, Ph.d.: 189-90.

Natural Law: 8, n. 25; 88, n. 71; 138, n. 6; 162, n. 71; 178.

Neal, Sr. Marie Augusta: 155.

Nicholson, Susan Teft: 157; 212, n. 29.

Nietzsche, Friedrich: 33, n. 51; 63; 66; 75; 109, n. 19.

Noonan, John T., Jr.: 16-17; 47, n. 92; 59; 77; 152, n. 46; 157; 175-6; 180, n. 110; 212, n. 29.

Nussbaum, Martha: 214, n. 34.

O'Brien, Edna: 10, 219, n. 552.

O'Brien, Mary: 84, n. 64; 159, n. 65.

O'Connor, John Cardinal: 65, n. 12.

O'Loughlin, Mary Ann: 117, n. 37.

O'Neill, Onora: 126, n. 57.

Okin, Susan Moller: 12, n. 38; 114, n. 30; 115-6;

Oppenheimer, Robert: 84, n. 63.

Ortner, Sherry: xx, n. 3.

Osiek, Carolyn, R.S.C.J.: 221, n. 57.

Paglia, Camille: 19, n. 2.

Paracelsus: 63.

Parasite: 36; 84; 93.

Paris, Ginette: 130, n. 66; 185, n. 10.

Pateman, Carole: 35, n. 59; 182, n. 3.

Patriarchy: 9; 43; 48-50; 62; 70; 72; 75-76; 79-80; 87-8; 91-3;

103; 217, n. 45.

Patrick, Anne E., S.N.J.M.: 215, n. 37.

Patterson, Yolanda Astarita: 20, n. 4; 22, n. 16; 29, n. 37; 39, n. 70; 40, n. 71; 51, n. 99.

Paul VI, Pope: 197, n. 42.

Perry, William: 111.

Pétain, Marshall: 93.

Petchesky, Rosalind Pollack: 5, n. 16; 138, n. 4; 171, n. 94; 194, n. 55; 197; 218, n. 48.

Piaget, Jean: 104; 111.

Piercy, Marge: 133, n. 75.

Plante, David: 210, n. 25.

Plaskow, Judith: 63, n. 5.

Plath, Sylvia: xxi; xxiii-iv; 136.

Pogrebin, Letty Cottin: 131, n. 69; 195, n. 38.

Potter, Ralph: 77, n. 49.

Pride, Mary: 179, n. 108.

Pro-life Feminism: chapter six.

Problem That Has No Name: xxii-xxiii.

Process Thought: 62-3; 155; 162-3;

Protagoras: 92.

Protestantism: 5; 75; 81; 140; 154-5; 193-4.

Quere-Jaulmes, Frances: 178, n. 104.

Rader, Rosemary, O.S.B.: 65, n. 13.

Ramsey, Paul: 81, n. 57.

Ranke-Heinemann, Uta: 158, n. 62.

Rape: 79.

Reardon, David: 134, n. 78.

Reed, James: 4, n. 14.

Relativism: 24, n. 22; 110-112; 118; 119; 125; 155.

Reproductive Rights: 43-46; 69; 73; 82; 106, n. 10; 139; 145.

Ribes, Bruno, S.J.: 80, n. 54.

Rich, Adrienne: 34, n. 56; 74; 106, n. 10; 126, n. 58; 141, n. 18; 208.

Richards, David: 147, n. 34.

Richards, Janet Radcliffe: 4; 126, n. 57; 166, n. 83; 198.

Roach, Archbishop John R.: 14, n. 44.

Robb, Carol: 138.

Roe V. Wade: xxiii; 119; 71, n. 32; 144; 166-7; 173.

Rossi, Alice: 44, n. 84; 71, n. 32.

Rossi, Philip J., S.J.: 152, n. 49.

Rothman, Barbara Katz: 95, n. 87; 127, n. 61; 197, n. 44; 210, n. 22.

Rousselle, Aline: 158, n. 62.

Rover, Constance: 4; 195, n. 37.

Rubin, Eva: 166, n. 80; 199, n. 48.

Ruddick, Sara: 38, n. 68; 114, n. 30.

Ruether, Rosemary Radford: 37, n. 64; 63; 193.

Russell, Letty: 68, n. 24; 83, n. 60.

Ruzek, Sheryl: 197, n. 44.

Sacrifice: 110; 122, n. 49; 123; 131, n. 67; 156; 220.

Sade, Marquis de: 33, n. 51; 46, n. 92; 51, n. 99; 195.

Sadism: 47; 93; 95-6; 99.

Saiving, Valerie: 120, n. 45.

Sanday, Peggy Reeves: 51, n. 102.

Sartre, Jean-Paul: See Beauvoir; 64; 83; 115, n. 31; 224.

Scanzoni, Letha Dawson: 193, n. 33.

Schall, James, S.J.: 179, n. 107; 206, n. 9.

Schlafly, Phyllis: 86-7.

Schlesinger, Arthur: 175, n. 99.

Schneiders, Sandra: 65, n. 13.

Schur, Edwin: 207, n. 15.

Schwarzer, Alice: 21, n. 10; 31, n. 44; 32, nn. 47 & 49; 181, n. 1;

Scruton, Roger: 179, n. 108.

Secular Humanism: 24.

Segers, Mary C.: 79, n. 53; 119, n. 41; 168, n. 88.

Serrano, Lucienne J.: 88, n. 70.

Sexual Revolution: 43-45; 86, n. 67; 89.

Shannon, Thomas: 98, n. 97.

Shapiro-Libai, Nitza: 171, n. 74.

Shinn, Roger: 206.

Shostak, Arthur B.: 117, n. 35.

Simons, Margaret: 32, n. 46.

Singer, Linda: 32, n. 46.

Singles, Donna: 114, n. 28.

Sjöö, Monica: 190, n. 27.

Skowronski, Marjory: 189.

Slama, Beatrice: 38, n. 68.

Smart, Ninian: 13, n. 39.

Smetana, Judith: 125, n. 55.

Smith, Janet E.: 117, n. 37; 125, n. 55; 127, n. 60; 204, n. 4.

Smith, Stephen M.: 213, n. 32.

Smithson, Sandra, O.S.F.: 204, n. 4.

Solomon: 222.

Sommers, Christina Hoff: xxi; 1; 15, n. 46; 113, n. 27.

Sophie's Choice: 127, n. 61.

Stannard, Una: 51, n. 103.

Stanton, Elizabeth Cady: 4; 107.

Starhawk: 156, n. 56.

Steichen, Donna: 66, n. 13.

Steinem, Gloria: xix; 6, n. 19; 31,

n. 43; 54, n. 105; 189, n. 23; 199-200.

Stenger, Mary Ann: 62, n. 4.

Stith, Richard: 164, n. 76.

Stoltenberg, John: 117, n. 35.

Stout, Jeffrey: 182, n. 2.

Strebeigh, Fred: 113, n. 27.

Subjectivism: 155-6; 200, n. 53.

Sullerot, Evelyne: 38, n. 67 and 68.

Sumner, L. W.: 32, n. 45; 43, n. 80; 173-4.

Suspicion, Hermeneutics of: 78.

Tavard, George: 206, n. 9.

Technology: 7-10; 43; 48; 56-7; 65; 69; 85; 89; 92; 109; 120; 145; 159.

Teilhard de Chardin: 63.

Teresa, Mother: xv; 86-7; 131, n. 67.

Thelma and Louise: 90.

Thibault, Odette: 38, n. 68.

Thielicke, Helmut: 152, n. 16.

Thomas Aquinas, St.: 62-4.

Thompson, Mary Lou: 52, n. 104.

Thomson, Judith Jarvis: 5, n. 16; 14, n. 41.

Thorez, Maurice: 3.

Tillich, Hannah: 62, n. 4.

Tillich, Paul: 62.

Tisdale, Sally: 210.

Tong, Rosemarie: 3; 34, n. 58; 66.

Toulat, Jean: 3; 49, n. 95; 131, n. 66.

Tribe, Laurence: 9, n. 27; 12; 166, n. 82; 183; 208.

Tuttle, Lisa: xxiii; 2; 3; 10, n. 28; 92, n. 80; 198.

Vanzan, Piersandro, S.J.: 38, n. 68.

Violence: 52; 91; 125f; 208-212;

217.

Walker, Alice: 221, n. 56.

War: 79; 81, n. 57.

Warnock, Mary: 126, n. 57.

Warren, Mary Anne: 4; 5, n. 16; 96, n. 89; 95, n. 89; 97, n. 93; 164, n. 76; 199.

Weaver, Mary Jo: 66. n. 15; 67, n. 18.

Weaver, Richard: 206.

Weightman, John: 20, n. 6.

Weil, Simone: xx; 102; 220; 224.

Weill-Halle, Lagroua: 46, n. 90; 55; 56.

Welch, Sharon: 78, n. 52.

Wertheimer, Roger: 94, n. 85.

Whitbeck, Caroline: 223.

Whitehead, Alfred North: 63; 120, 45.

Whitmarsh, Anne: 38, n. 68.

Williams, George Huntston: 76, n. 47.

Willis, Ellen: 160; 184-5.

Wilt, Judith: 39, n. 69; 187; 189, n. 24.

Winegarten, Renée: 26, n. 27.

Wolf-Devine, Celia: 132, n. 70; 204, n. 4; 222-4.

Worldviews: 13; 33, n. 53; 65; 112; 113; 155, nn. 54 and 55; 168, n. 87; 192; 213-6; 224-6.

Young, Iris Marion: 34, n. 58; 120, n. 46.

Zaza (Elizabeth Mabille): 27; 42.

Zephir, Jacques: 32, n. 48.